B-SIDES, UNDERCURRENTS AND OVERTONES: PERIPHERIES TO POPULAR IN MUSIC, 1960 TO THE PRESENT

for
Julie, Anaïs, and Rivers,
heArt and soul

B-Sides, Undercurrents and Overtones: Peripheries to Popular in Music, 1960 to the Present

GEORGE PLASKETES
Auburn University, USA

LONDON AND NEW YORK

First published 2009 by Ashgate Publishing

Published 2016 by Routledge
2 Park Square, Milton Park, Abingdon, Oxon OX14 4RN
711 Third Avenue, New York, NY 10017, USA

Routledge is an imprint of the Taylor & Francis Group, an informa business

Copyright © George Plasketes 2009

All rights reserved. No part of this book may be reprinted or reproduced
or utilised in any form or by any electronic, mechanical, or other means,
now known or hereafter invented, including photocopying and
recording, or in any information storage or retrieval system, without
permission in writing from the publishers.

Notice:
Product or corporate names may be trademarks or registered trademarks,
and are used only for identification and explanation without intent to
infringe.

George Plasketes has asserted his moral right under the Copyright, Designs and Patents Act,
1988, to be identified as the author of this work.

British Library Cataloguing in Publication Data
Plasketes, George
    B-sides, undercurrents and overtones : peripheries to popular in music, 1960 to the
    present. – (Ashgate popular and folk music series)
    1. Popular music – United States – History and criticism
    I. Title
    781.6'4'0973

Library of Congress Cataloging-in-Publication Data
Plasketes, George.
    B-sides, undercurrents and overtones : peripheries to popular in music, 1960 to the
    present / George Plasketes.
        p. cm.—(Ashgate popular and folk music series)
    ISBN 978-0-7546-6561-8 (hardcover : alk. paper)
   1. Popular music—United States—History and criticism. I. Title.

    ML3477.P63 2009
    781.640973'09045–dc22

                                                     2008046196

ISBN 9780754665618 (hbk)

Contents

General Editor's Preface	vii
Preface: My Back Pages	ix
Acknowledgements	xi
Introduction: The Flip Side: Let It B	1
1 Get Your 45s On: Terry Melcher, Lost in the Surf and Sun of the 1960s Sound Waves	13
2 How the Midwest Was Won: The Chicago Suburbs Seven, a Mid-1960s Regional Rotation	25
3 Covering Outside the Lines: Hans Fenger and the Langley Schools Music Project	35
4 Geffen Records v. Neil Young: The Battle of the Brands	51
5 Music and Movie Mutuality: Ry Cooder, the Involved Bystander	69
6 World Music Missionaries: Cross Cultural Convergences	85
7 The Vital Visual Voice of the Videotape Editor: Seamlessly Sculpting *Graceland: The African Concert*	101
8 Rock Around the Cop: Bochco's Broadway Blue Print as Television Musical Muse and Martyr	119
9 Must Sing TV: Pop Rock Sitcom Cameo Obscuras	135
10 Umbilical Musical Chords: Lineage, Legacy and Mom and Pop Pedigree	153
11 Die Another Day: Warren Zevon's Desperado "Deteriorata"	173
Bibliography	195
Index	203

General Editor's Preface

The upheaval that occurred in musicology during the last two decades of the twentieth century has created a new urgency for the study of popular music alongside the development of new critical and theoretical models. A relativistic outlook has replaced the universal perspective of modernism (the international ambitions of the 12-note style); the grand narrative of the evolution and dissolution of tonality has been challenged, and emphasis has shifted to cultural context, reception and subject position. Together, these have conspired to eat away at the status of canonical composers and categories of high and low in music. A need has arisen, also, to recognize and address the emergence of crossovers, mixed and new genres, to engage in debates concerning the vexed problem of what constitutes authenticity in music and to offer a critique of musical practice as the product of free, individual expression.

Popular musicology is now a vital and exciting area of scholarship, and the *Ashgate Popular and Folk Music Series* presents some of the best research in the field. Authors are concerned with locating musical practices, values and meanings in cultural context, and may draw upon methodologies and theories developed in cultural studies, semiotics, poststructuralism, psychology and sociology. The series focuses on popular musics of the twentieth and twenty-first centuries. It is designed to embrace the world's popular musics from Acid Jazz to Zydeco, whether high tech or low tech, commercial or non-commercial, contemporary or traditional.

Derek B. Scott
Professor of Critical Musicology
University of Leeds, UK

Preface
My Back Pages

B-Side Baptism: The Bee (Geez), Busted and Bail

The backbeat and spirit between the lines on these pages is rooted in and inspired by my 45 r.p.m. experience beginning in the 1960s. Mid decade. On the first "eve of destruction," on the verge of the Wonder Years, in the midst of the ongoing British Invasion. The world seemed to be spinning at 45 revolutions per minute. Something in the air, and on the air. At the time, AM radio. In the Chicago vicinity and well beyond, the source was the legendary station, WLS, 890 on the dial. An audio umbilical chord, a simultaneous soundtrack and wish list. My g-g-generations' version of the contemporary *Now!* and *Totally Hits* single compilations in the good old daze, before Napster Nation, iPod people, and burn, baby, burn.

The hit single sounds emanating from the airwaves translated into artifact and ritual, baptizing a passionate record relationship and vinylogical time line. The little black discs began to accumulate, a complementary collection to baseball cards. Prized possessions. And they cost less than a dollar. One lawn mowed in the summer, a yard of leaves raked in the fall, and a driveway or sidewalk of shoveled snow in the winter each were worth about six stackable singles for the turn, turn turntable. A decent B-side made the black 7-inch cylinder a two-for-one bonus.

Though a bargain, I nonetheless attempted to exit a store without paying for a 45 record (a.k.a. "shoplifting") one sunny Saturday afternoon at E.J. Korvette's department store, on the suburb border between North Riverside and Berwyn, fifteen minutes west of the city. The record was the Bee Gees, "New York Mining Disaster, 1941," a decade before they went disco. Of all the great music circulating at the time, my choice of a song to be a part of my permanent record rather than my record collection was a bit conspicuous. Getting busted for under a buck was bad enough. But having the brothers Gibb as partners in crime rather than Lennon-McCartney, Jagger-Richards, local colors such as the Ides of March or New Colony Six, or any number of one hit wonders of the era, softened the edge-worthiness of the transgression, and compounded the embarrassment. My indiscretion left a dumb as(s)terisk on my juvenile rap sheet, as well as a secretly stupid scar on the soul of my soundtrack. Over the years, I affectionately refer my adolescent act and attraction to the Bee Gees song as a "miner offense," one that was subconsciously and cosmically connected to my Father's family's West Virginia coal mining roots.

The happening proved to be a moment of B-side affirmation within my formative 45 experience. When the store detective asked "why?"—that is, why I lifted the record, not why I chose a Bee Gees single—I managed to mutter an octave, each word slightly climbing the sentence scale to a concluding question: "Well, the song sounds like a Beatles B-side?" My record review reply may have sounded insecurely sarcastic, but I was serious; my seventh grade, hit single savvy in full display. Having flipped enough singles in my youthful record ritual to uncover the beauty of a bonus on its backside, I had experienced a B-side baptism. Perhaps confounded by my peculiar, yet remorseful rationale, the store detective granted me a "Get out of jail" card, letting me slide with a warning. B-side bail. (With a Hail Mary marathon the penance prescribed by the parish priest one week later.) As I stood to leave, resisting the urge to ask if I could buy the 45 on the way out, the song's lyric about "knowing what it's like on the outside" cued and played in my head like closing credits, providing soft, mocking accompaniment for my exit from the solitary security space.

The scene of the crime, E.J. Korvette's, is long gone from its Harlem and Cermak corner, but its landmark will always remain within. The escalator to the second floor was a stairway to heaven ascending to a sacred soundtrack site of my earliest record store ritual, beginnings with 45s and B-sides, and growing into the album age and the larger, more difficult to smuggle, long play $33\frac{1}{3}$ album format. Some of my fondest, most vivid youth years memories, in monaural and stereo, are those Sundays in the record department, "The Fabulous All Label Sale!," shopping with my Father, who never did find out about my felonious 45 Bee Gees blunder, as far as I know. It was my Father, Charles Plasketes, who instilled the virtues of vinyl and fostered my music appreciation, from 45s to LPs, listen-up lessons that have been passed on to our daughter, Anaïs, and son, Rivers, and their downloads and iPods. The permanence of records, the affection for and appreciation of the B-side.

george plasketes
Sweet Home Alabama

Acknowledgements

B-Sides might have lingered in Proposal Purgatory, between a rock and marketplace outside Publication Paradise, were it not for Commissioning Editor, Heidi Bishop, and Music Series Editor, Professor Derek Scott. From the beginning, Heidi and Derek were very in tune with my "peripheral vision" of *B-Sides.* They never flinched at the concept and my somewhat unconventional approach, nor did my writing style deter them. Both remained steadfast in their commitment to my B-cause, and insisted that I not compromise my voice and vision. Their response was immensely gratifying. I was at the time, and always will be, profoundly moved and indebted to Heidi and Derek for their heroic advocacy of my project, and for allowing me to remain true to myself writing *B-Sides.* Endless thanks for embracing B-Side possibility and for having a little faith in me. I am truly honored to be a part of Ashgate's *Popular and Folk Music Series*, and humbled to be in the company of its exceptional editors, authors and works.

In addition to Heidi and Derek, the Ashgate staff has been thorough, efficient, highly professional, very patient, and pleasant at every stage of this project, from contents to cover, from proposal to proofs and print: Anne Keirby, Contracts; Ann Allen, Editorial Manager; Nicole Norman in marketing; and Sarah Charters, Senior Editor, Humanities. Thank you all so much. And praise and appreciation to Albert Stewart for his meticulous proof reading of the text, for tidying up my messy manuscript, and for his editorial open-mindedness toward my writing quirks. I am also grateful to Heidi and the Ashgaters for the opportunity to have input in the cover design. The image of the boy with the buzz cut lost in his 45's, courtesy of the Alamy Photography archive, is picture perfect. More than a nostalgic glimpse of preoccupations back in The Day , B.C. (before cable), without iPods, Play Station, Wii, cell phones, lap tops, Blackberries, twitter, text and other tech toys, the simple snapshot is a kindred spirit that wonderfully captures *B-Sides* essence.

There are many others who contributed behind the scenes and between the lines of these pages. Several songwriters graciously provided lyric permissions for epigraphs which are important to me as prefixes and accents. I am grateful to Mose Allison, Jim Peterik and the Ides of March, particularly Chuck Soumar for his down-to-earthness, assistance, and Riverside reminisces; and John Hiatt via Catherine Walker at Music Sales Limited, for the privilege of their words which frame my chapters so nicely.

I owe so much to Gary Edgerton as a friend and Master Mentor. Always available, upbeat, perceptive and pragmatic, Gary continues to hearten and guide. My gratitude runs deep to Gary for his wisdom, calm, generosity and overall great-guyness.

A nod and a wink to the Usual Suspects, longtime friends and contemporaries Berwyn Bill Kolar, the best; John Fortenberry; my Lindley legionnaire/Cooder cohorts in Oxford Town, Ron Shapiro and Jim Dees; Pacific Coast correspondent George Lewis; Gary Burns and *Popular Music and Society*, Lee Cooper, Greg Metcalf, and the security guard at E.J. Korvette's, wherever you may be.

At Auburn University, I am among the many Liberal Arteries who have benefited from a leadership trio that has cultivated a resourceful research and writing environment that fosters faculty productivity: Mary Helen Brown, Chair Deluxe of the Department of Communication & Journalism; Anne-Katrin Gramberg, Dean of the College of Liberal Arts; and Associate Dean of Research, Paula Bobrowski. Thanks for the ways and means, especially for the gift of time.

A meaningful mention of my departmental colleagues, particularly the Radio-Television-Filmsters Ric Smith, Hollie Lavenstein, and, above all, loyalists Emmett Winn and Susan Brinson, for their kindness, chemistry and remarkable professional standards. Shannon Solomon was indispensable with manuscript preparation, Microsoft Word wizardry and answering my questions, no matter how laughable or lame. Josh Hillyer was a relentless research assistant. Josh's diligent digging and conscientious efforts were vital to the depth of several chapters.

Distant, but genuine, thanks to the artists, creators, songwriters, musicians and bands who I have chronicled here. I hope these chapters convey, to some degree, my lifelong admiration and appreciation of their meaningful words, music and productions.

I must acknowledge, Lulu, my faithful, fluffy canine companion, and best birthday present ever. Always by my side, she makes writing a little less lonely.

Gratitude always to my family for their love and support in ways great and small, from the Plasketes and Piekarskis in Chicago to the Ryan and Rewis foursomes in The ATL, to the entire cast of Williams, from Mississippi to Mobile, especially Mom and Dad —Joan and Rodger—whose extraordinary Oneness has been a wellspring of inspiration. And spirited thanks to my Father, who in many ways wrote the first words of this book a long time ago. I wish he were here to read the rest.

And finally, first, foremost and forever, there is the A-Side of my B-eing: my loving wife and best friend, Julie; daughter Anaïs, and son Rivers. They are my garden, my daily grace and gravity. A sweet source that surrounds me with countless colours and qualities that are beyond my comprehension—courage and compassion, creativity and cool; boundless beauty and beats, radiance and rhythms; art and music, song and dance, drama, both on stage and off, for better or worse, whistling and laughter, intelligence and conversation, wonder and joy, hopes and dreams, purpose, perseverance and passion. On and on... I cannot express how down-on my-knees thankful I am for the particles of Julie's, Anaïs's and Rivers's wondrous presence that grace these pages, and the ones we write together every day as Family. The old Timbuk 3 lyric still rings true: "we're happy living on the B-side of Life."

Introduction
The Flip Side: Let It B

I wonder what is happening on the flip side of the world,
...The side you never like to play...
I know you say you need the A-side all the time
But the B-side, I just wonder what you say.

"Flip Side" J.M. Peterik (Ides of March), 1972
© Jim Peterik Music 2008

The B-side's job is to complement the A-side.

(Dawson and Propes 2003:72)

According to popular adages, there are "two sides to every story" and "two sides to every coin." There are also two sides to every record. The "A-side" and the "B-side." These designations originated in popular music with 78 r.p.m. shellac records and became more significant as formats evolved to 7-inch vinyl. Initially, "taking sides" was not an issue. Radio stations had little preference and played songs on either face of the record.

In the early 1950s with the advent of the 45 r.p.m., "singles" became the standard. Unlike the previous era when there was often more than one song to a side, the conventional record release contained two songs, one on each side of a record. Initially, most record labels randomly assigned which song was the A-side and which was the B-side. As a result, several artists had "double-sided hits" where both songs made the national sales charts. Among them were Elvis Presley's "Don't Be Cruel/"Hound Dog" and Ritchie Valens' "Donna"/"LaBamba."

By the 1960s, perhaps one of the most prolific periods for hit singles in popular music, the terms "A-side" and "B-side" became more common vinyl vernacular, and their differentiation more defined. The A-side was synonymous with "air play." It was the song the record company wanted radio stations to play; the hopeful hit, the catchy tune that would also help promote the artist's 33⅓ long play album. The record's reverse side, the B-side, for the most part, became the disc deposit for a comparably "inferior" recording. Materials commonly found on the B-side included non-album tracks, "throwaway" songs that may have been considered stylistically unsuitable for an album, experimental or instrumental songs, acoustic or *a capella* versions and alternate renditions of the A-side. Symbolically, and perhaps idealistically, the B-side offered a metaphor for musicians, a place of possibility. The "flip side" was an outlet for conceiving and dividing their work, a line of demarcation, a detachment or diversion from the commercially viable art, airplay and industry expectations that accompanied the A-side. There was little to lose and much to gain from the grooves of least resistance that were the B-side.

Not all B-sides were rejects or remixes. Some would occasionally catch the attention of a radio station music or program director or a maverick disc jockey and receive airplay, though not as routinely in the rotation as the designated single side. At Chicago's legendary station, WLS-890 AM, such record releases were billed as "TSWs"—two-sided winners. For a generation of listeners, record consumers and collectors, these 45s represented a "two for one" bargain. Discovering a three-minute gem or curiosity on a B-side was an iconic era experience analogous with artifactal expeditions—digging for the cool prize in a box of Cracker Jack or opening a nickel pack of baseball cards to find a favorite player and get a powdery stick of pink bubblegum.

Popular B-sides frequently originated from bands that produced strings of chartable songs in assembly line fashion in the 1960s hit factory, among them the Byrds' ("All I Really Want to Do"/"I'll Feel A Whole Lot Better" and "Turn, Turn Turn"/"She Don't Care About Time") and Creedence Clearwater Revival's ("Down on the Corner"/"Fortunate Son"). And there was the Beatles remarkable record run, twenty seven number one songs during an eight year period, from "Love Me Do" to "The Long and Winding Road" in 1970. At one point in the mid-1960s, the Fab Four held the first five spots on the U.S. Hot 100 singles charts. Just as their melodic A-sides were abundant and automatic hits, their B-sides were bountiful bonuses that underscore the breadth and enduring magnificence of the Lennon/McCartney songbook.

The accumulation of B-sides that appeared on the U.S. and U.K. versions of the Beatles' singles remains a pop treasure trove: "P.S. I Love You," "Thank You Girl," "She's A Woman," "This Boy," "I Saw Her Standing There" "Things We Said Today," "I Should Have Known Better," "I'm A Loser," "Baby's in Black," "I Don't Want to Spoil the Party," "Rock and Roll Music," "Act Naturally," "I'm Down," "Yes It Is," "You Can't Do That," "Rain," "Day Tripper." During the second half of the decade, song symmetry between the sides of Beatles singles was standard: "Yellow Submarine"/"Eleanor Rigby," "Penny Lane"/"Strawberry Fields Forever," "Hey Jude"/"Revolution," "Get Back"/"Don't Let Me Down," "Come Together"/"Something." Even songs that the Beatles wrote but did not record had a B-side knack. "Bad to Me," recorded by Billy J. Kramer, reached number nine as the flip side of his hit "Little Children," which charted at number seven in 1964.

Beyond the Beatles, the list of B-sides that eclipsed their A-sides during the 45 era is significant. "Earth Angel" (The Penguins), "The Twist" (Hank Ballard and the Midnighters), "Louie Louie" (Richard Berry), "You Send Me" (Sam Cooke), "Rockin' Robin" (Bobby Day), "Hushabye" (The Mystics), "The Wanderer" (Dion), "The Lion Sleeps Tonight" (The Tokens), "Save the Last Dance for Me" (the Drifters), "Surfin' Safari" (the Beach Boys), "To Sir With Love" (Lulu), "Incense and Peppermints" (Strawberry Alarm Clock), "Signs" (Five Man Electrical Band), and "Na Na Hey Hey Kiss Him Good Bye" (Steam) are among hit songs that were originally slated to be B-sides. Likewise, in 1971, Rod Stewart's signature song, "Maggie May," began as the flip side to "Reason to Believe," the first single from his album *Every Picture Tells A Story*. "Maggie May" transformed the single from minor hit to sustaining chart topper, as it reached and remained at number one in the U.S. and UK for five weeks. Whether due to record executives' inability to recognize hits or savvy, bored, curious or influential disc jockeys turning an A-side over determined to design their own play lists, these B-sides were converted from backside tag-along tunes to chart climbers. To counter the side swiping, producer Phil Spector routinely put instrumental jams with obscure titles on the B-sides of singles to assure that disc jockeys would play only the intended hit sides. (Dawson and Propes 2003: 157)

The Fading Flip Side

The rock and roll B-side began to recede as early as the late 1970s, with KISS's "Beth" among the last "surprise" flip side hits in 1976. The B-side, or "flip," became widely viewed as an inconvenience to record companies due to additional royalty fees and as potential competition to the hit side. As music formats continued to downsize and digitalize, the A-side/B-side dichotomy gradually diminished. The advent of the cassette and compact disc singles in the 1980s foreshadowed the imminent obsolescence of the B-side. Cassettes briefly matched the vinyl arrangement of a song per side, but maxi singles with more than two songs became the music marketplace preference.

By the early 1980s, the B-side was used primarily as a marketing ploy geared to the predominantly album-oriented audience. Record companies employed the same strategy they used in the 1960s with the Beatles, The Who and Bob Dylan, placing songs on B-sides that were unavailable anywhere else. A few major artists such as John Mellencamp and Bruce Springsteen remained faithful to the B-side tradition by routinely including "previously unavailable" songs on the flip sides of their numerous hit singles during the decade. The Springsteen B-sides were original compositions. For example, "Shut Out the Light" on the flip side of "Born in the U.S.A." and "Pink Cadillac" from "Dancing in the Dark" were non-album tracks. Mellencamp's B-sides were predominantly cover versions ("Pretty Ballerina," "Shama Lama Ding Dong," "Under the Boardwalk") and acoustic renditions of his own songs ("Small Town," "Little Pink Houses," "Jackie Brown"). The appeal of these vinyl 45s was further enhanced by the attractive picture sleeve packaging. The songs eventually resurfaced in other convenient collector configurations such as the box set (Springsteen's *Tracks* (1998)) and the compilation (Mellencamp's *Rough Harvest* (1999). In 1984, seventeen of *Billboard*'s top 40 singles, including songs by Madonna, R.E.M. and the Bangles, had non-album B-sides, ranging from remixes to instrumentals, often of the A-side. Warner Brothers employed the strategy so extensively with its releases that it was able to compile non-LP sides by artists such as Prince, the Pretenders, and the Talking Heads into two albums, *Attack of the Killer B's* (1983) and *Revenge of the Killer B's* (1985).

Branding and Duality: Hit Me Baby One More Time

Into the 1990s, with the vinylogical time clock ticking as the compact disc replacing vinyl and cassette as the dominant music medium and digital downloading rapidly developing, the physical flip side distinction of the B-side was virtually extinct, a casualty of progress, both technological and economic. However, the term "B-side" persists, its meaning and application slightly modified in the music marketplace as a brand. Not only has "B-side" been adapted into a common referent to "bonus" tracks on CD singles and EPs, it continues to be a familiar catchphrase loosely linked with "previously unreleased materials" such as demos, rarities, out takes, alternate versions and other non-album tracks. The rare recordings are commonly compiled for collections and multi-disc anthologies that attract curious consumers and have profit potential that appeals to record labels. For artists, the projects provide an opportunity to re-visit their vaults and versions of their songs. "B-sides and Rarities" has become a music market standard and distinct record sub genre. Nick Cave, Moby, Cake, Smashing Pumpkins, Pixies, Cure, Cowboy Junkies, Sonic Youth, Deftones, Steve Earle, Tori Amos, Prince and Sarah McLachlan are among the countless artists who have released the requisite record of B-side material.

As the digital mode continues to develop, deepen and dominate, the B-side's parallel progression accumulates a hint of irony. The non-commercial nature of the material that was a defining characteristic of the B-side became a primary marketing tool and a commercially viable selling point. The music industry engaged in a constant cycle of customizing, expanding and upgrading records. Following the involuntary vinyl replacement revolution, fans were more easily swayed to buy recordings for a second, if not third time, if their reward was a visit to an artist's music vault. Early Elvis Costello albums—*My Aim is True, This Year's Model, Blood and Chocolate*—are representative of an artist's catalog being remastered and reissued, often by archival label Rhino Records, with standard repackaging that includes a (B)onus disc of demos, rarities, live and alternative takes transformed from their original neglected status on the B-side. The B-side staple—cover versions—were also common content of the enhanced packaging.

The B-side concept has been adapted into anniversary editions commemorating debuts such as Counting Crowe's *August and Everything After*, classics like *Born to Run* and *Thriller*; Lucinda Willams's masterpiece *Car Wheels on a Gravel Road* and the long awaited completion of Brian Wilson's *Smile*. Artist's discographies expanded with multiple greatest hits and essential collections. Like soundtrack snowflakes, no two were alike, as each contained "previously unavailable" songs.

Even box sets suggested that "definitive" is fleeting. In 2001, Columbia released *18 Tracks*, "highlights" from Springsteen's B-side box *Tracks*. The condensed album contained three songs bearing the B-side badge and bait— "previously unavailable." The trio of tunes were conspicuously absent from *Tracks* comprehensive four discs. *18 Tracks* suggested a new niche, "the B-side of B-sides," and foreshadowed a maximum marketing strategy and B-side branding. The Byrds *There is A Season* (2006) reprised its box set from 1990, and a number of their greatest hits compilations in between, including *20 Essential Tracks from the Boxed Set*. The only distinguishable difference between the Byrds boxes was an impressive deal breaker, a hard core collector appealing DVD of the group's early television performances. The Band's epic *A Musical History* (2005) provides a five-disc encore to its previous three disc box *Across the Great Divide* (1994), suggesting that Robbie Robertson and Levon Helm located more tapes in the basement. Artists themselves fostered the B-side revival and brand via music and video downloads available exclusively at their web sites.

"Deluxe," "limited," "exclusive," "special," "expanded," and "legacy" were among the labels affixed to editions of records. The B-side brand and packaging became a confounding constant and seductive siren song for music consumers, particularly when bonus materials commonly showed up in special editions months after the initial release, or when retailers such as Target, Wal Mart and Best Buy each had exclusive editions of a record. Music consumers were confronted with a deluxe dilemma.[1]

By 2004, in the midst of the one-sided compact disc and digital downloads of the iPod age, the technological advances that contributed to the gradual fading of the B-side in its purest form, further reconfigured the flip side concept into a visual variation—the Dual Disc. Designed to provide multi media music consumers with an alternative to the conventional CD, the Dual Disc was a slightly higher priced ($1.50-$2.50), enhanced package that basically converted the B-Side into a DVD. This technological twin contained the familiar B-side "bonus" trait incentives for music consumers. Common content on the DVD included the entire album in higher quality stereophonic and/or surround sound, documentaries, interviews, music videos, footage from live performances, studio recording sessions, artist discography and website links. Record companies hoped that the Dual Disc format would eventually replace the CD as the preferred medium in the music marketplace. By the end of 2005, there were approximately 200 Dual Disc titles with sales reaching over 2,000,000 units. Some major titles, such as Bruce Springsteen's *Devils and Dust* (2005), have been released exclusively in the Dual Disc format.

The pervasiveness of remastered reissues, special, deluxe and limited editions, multiple versions of greatest hits, "essential" collections and box sets were

---

1 For a cantankerous, in depth discussion of this issue, please check out my Forum piece, "Pimp My Records: The Deluxe Dilemma and Edition Condition: Bonus, Betrayal, or Download Backlash?" *Popular Music and Society,* Vol. 31, No 3, July 2008, pp. 389-393.

6   *B-SIDES, UNDERCURRENTS AND OVERTONES*

innately "dual discs." The B-side—whether viewed as a brand, bonus, betrayal or downloading backlash—was alive and well in the music marketplace; reinvented, reconfigured and repackaged from its spinning 45-r.p.m. roots.

Both Sides Now: The B-Side of Popular Music and Media

The "B-side" endures as a flip-side phenomenon, a cultural catchphrase and sub-icon of an icon of the 45 r.p.m. record era. "B's" multiple meanings and modifiers range from backside, balance and bonus to bastard and low budget (a common designation for the B-side's secondary sibling in film). True to its artifact origins in vinyl as a complementary companion to its more prominent, popular and parental-side single, the B-side is both orphan and outsider, inherently unsung, unassuming and sometimes unusual. As "the under side," it is an under dog, under the radar and underappreciated, though not underground nor subculture. The B-side is situated in a cultural crevice that straddles or lies somewhere between the mainstream and the underground; the blanks and blind spots; the backsides, borders and in betweens. Suzanne Vega's litany of "Left of Center" locales provides a fitting composite: in the outskirts, fringes, edges, off the avenues and strips, in the corner, against the grain, out of the grip.[2]

The B-side's character is relatively anonymous and occasionally obscure; easily or unintentionally overlooked, unnoticed or sometimes dismissed, a designated fringe dweller, designed and destined for tags such as cult classic or critical favorite, a curiosity or collectable. In short, the B-side embodies the peripheries, those under-appreciated artists, productions, genres, rituals, artifacts and events that are situated on the flip side, slightly outside, buried beneath, a turn over from the A-side plane.

"The B-side" does not have to be limited to records, but can be reconfigured and recontextualized for broader application in popular music and culture. Considering the polysemic nature of cultural texts, the duality represented in the iconic A-side/B-side dichotomy can be adapted as a unique and useful conceptual framework for categorizing, contrasting, chronicling, and critically interpreting peripheries in popular music and media. As a text, B-sides can be located in, and marked by trends, transitions and turning points, genres and generation, artist and artifact, record and ritual, productions, patterns and processes, successes and even failures.

The A-side/B-Side is a cultural dichotomy, one that may not be as contradictory as it is complementary and connected. The predominant taste tendency echoes the title of the band Sloan's singles collection: *A-Sides Win*; whereas B-sides may be characterized by the label describing the contents inside Rhino Records attractive (hat) box set, *One Kiss Can Lead to Another: Girl Groups, Lost and Found—*

---

2   "Left of Center." Lyrics by Suzanne Vega. WB Music Corp/Waifersongs Ltd (ASCAP) 1986.

"unjustly overlooked and criminally ignored." While the broad commercial, critical and convenient preference may be to place more value and emphasis on culture's A-sides—the visible, popular and successful—making the effort to turn the hit side over and consider the viability and value of its less familiar and often neglected B-side often uncovers gems, cultural curiosities and context that is connected to the A-side.

The B-sides' approach may work as an "A-side antidote" that provides counter views and counterbalance to commercialism, yet they reveal important meanings about the A-side. B-sides furnish valuable cases, context and clues about cultural continuity and the complex convergences between the creative and commercial processes. Many B-side subjects serve as historical hinges, pivotal points and precursors that foreshadow and outline trends and shifting values in the production of culture. They also offer perspective on the evolving roles and interrelationships between the artist, industry, technology and economics. Collectively, this cross section of B-sides unfolds into an unconventional connect-the-dots complementary chronicle—an alternative history and parallel place—of music and media undercurrents that generate overtones which significantly shape and define, ripple and resonate through the mainstream popular culture on many meaningful levels.

Peripheral Vision: An Offbeat Ode to Blanks and Blind Spots

In *Everything That Rises: A Book of Convergences* (2006), art historian/journalist Lawrence Weschler explores correspondences and continuity between seemingly disparate subjects, uncanny moments and unusual associations from the art world. *B-Sides: Undercurrents and Overtones, Peripheries to Popular in Music, 1960 to the Present* pursues a similar path of peculiarity, possibility and parallel perspective between the peripheries and the popular, tracing fringe footprints across music, media and popular culture during the past 40 years.

B-Sides blends the common anthology approach with the less prevalent "unsung" case study, emphasizing the unusual, rather than the usual subjects. The B-side as a metaphorical method is accented by a B-side "letter for," an alliterative list of linkages that intrinsically buoys and threads the themes of each chapter. Among the "B" letter fors are Baby Boomer, biography, barriers, bridges, borders, backsides, branding, building blocks and burial. The central topics of the eleven chapters are subjectively selected. They are an essential set, but by no means a complete or definitive collection. Every music fan, critic, scholar and observer carries with them a set of unsung subjects which reflect personal preference, taste, experience, time and place. E Street Band guitarist Steven Van Zandt's syndicated radio series, *Little Steven's Underground Garage*, provides steady documentation of the abundant B-side archive. Among other "unsung" approaches is Roni Sarig's *The Secret History of Rock* (1998), which makes a case for underappreciated influential bands.

The array of B-sides flipped to familiarity in these chapters form a diverse and quietly curious collection with a blatant Baby Boom bend. They begin with the B-side base—the 45 r.p.m. The first two chapters recognize undercurrents within the prolific pop and rock hit singles soundscape of the the mid- to late-1960s charts. Songwriter, recording artist, and producer Terry Melcher's career was bracketed by "B's." Melcher's low profile music biography provides an engaging portrayal of Southern California's thriving 1960s scene, sound, spirit and setting, from "Mr. Tambourine Man" to "Kokomo." As Brian Wilson's B-side, Melcher and his contributions were overshadowed and blurred by the Beach Boys, Beatles, and British Invasion. Melcher was a key figure at the forefront of the early wave of pop rock producers during the music industry's commercial infancy and hit single explosion. The son of actress Doris Day and an alleged target of the Charles Manson Family, Melcher's imprint is on numerous genres and blends, surf, country, blues, garage pop and perhaps most significantly, folk rock, pioneered by the sound and music of another "B"—the Byrds.

The Midwest had its own regional rotation that was modestly, but markedly represented in the 1960s pop pantheon. Chapter 2 portrays the "'burbs" as a B-side through the "Chicago Suburbs Seven." Between 1966 and 1971, seven bands from the outskirts of Chicago—The Buckinghams, New Colony Six, Ides of March, Cryan' Shames, Shadows of Knight, Mauds, and The American Breed—produced nearly 40 singles that reached the national charts. Thirty of those hits were concentrated between 1966 and 1968. Within Chicago's rich musical heritage of jazz, blues, rock, Chess studio, and the brassy sound of the band Chicago, the "Chicago Suburbs Seven" represents a unique cluster, distinctive regional rotation and musical marker of an era and area.

"Outsider" is a prevalent B-side trait, just as the cover song is a B-side convention. Both are central to Chapter 3's account of Hans Fenger and the Langley Schools Music Project. In the mid 1970s, guitar strumming hippie turned teacher, Hans Fenger, assembled a children's chorus in a school gymnasium in rural Western Canada for an organic sing along of 1960s and 1970s pop songs by the Beatles, Beach Boys, David Bowie, the Eagles, Neil Diamond and others. Fenger blended the borrowed tunes with instrumentation from German behaviorist Carl Orff and inspiration from Phil Spector, Philip Glass and Brian Wilson. The resulting "untrained" children's cover choir, with its off key melodies and off beat primitive percussions, was a musical variation of "outsider art." In B-side flip fashion, the recordings were accidentally discovered and released twenty years later as *Innocence and Despair: The Langley Schools Music Project* (2001). The "Orff pop" project and its arc from peripheral to popular represents one of the more unusual cover compilations to appear in a music market saturated with tributes and cover variations.

Branding, B-side material and bizarre legal briefs converge in Chapter 4. In 1984, entertainment mogul David Geffen and his record label sued his friend and rock legend Neil Young for "not being Neil Young." Following his critical and commercial success in the 1970s, Young frustrated many of his fans as well as Geffen, by swerving sharply into a seemingly random artistic course. Collectively,

Young's 1980s recordings might be viewed as B-side of a prolific career. The series of stylistic extremes included power chording guitar, computers, synthesizers, rockabilly, country and brassy blues. A frustrated Geffen responded by suing Young for producing "uncharacteristic Neil Young records." The case remained a B-side brief rather than a legal landmark case in the rock annals. However, the conflict provides context for issues such as artistic freedom, commercial imperatives and the complex relationship between creators and organizations in the popular arts during the postmodern period. The conflict also foreshadowed the increasing emphasis on branding, whether artist, genre, or record company.

The counter commercial undercurrent continues in Chapter 5 with Ry Cooder, who is a significant thread through several *B-Side* chapters. A multiple Grammy winner who is reverently regarded as a "musician's musician" and "ethnomusicologist," Cooder prefers to wear unassuming background badges of brilliance—"involved outsider" and "interested innocent bystander." The epitome of anonymity and anti-fame, Cooder is averse to self-promotion. He appears to be most comfortable in self-exile on the fringes. "I could almost disappear from the street and no one would ever know," says Cooder, delivering a quintessential B-side proclamation. (Hoskyns 2005:67) Cooder's rich forty year musical career has been marked by several distinct, yet interconnected stages, including extensive session work, a solo career that yielded 11 albums, extensive World Music collaborations and most recently a conceptual "California Trilogy." One of the peripheral preferences for the versatile guitarist has been behind the scenes exploring "mutuality" in music and movies. Cooder's characteristic ethnographic compositions have appeared in songs, scores and soundtracks of more than 20 films during a 30 year period between 1968 and 1998. This chapter traces Cooder's musicological quest from session and solo work to soundtrack specialization.

Cooder continues as a thread in the "obscuriences," geomusical borders, barriers and bridges of Chapter 6. World Music can be considered B-side genre in the American music marketplace. During the past several decades, many of the roots and rhythms of these exotic strands of music have been imported by way of the discoverer spirit and cultural curiosity of several American musicians. The most familiar may be Paul Simon's *Graceland* (1986), the A-side of American world music projects. Yet, there are a number of artists who represent the B-Side of Simon's critical and commercial success with *Graceland*. One of the initial music mergers in the pop music realm predates Simon's venture by 20 years. In 1970, an unlikely source—Neil Diamond—integrated African sounds into pop music on his album *Tap Root Manuscript*. Post-*Graceland*, there was more interest and activity, an undercurrent that included artists such as Peter Gabriel, David Byrne, Keith Richards with Wingless Angels, Jules Shear with "mento" and the Jolly Boys, David Lindley and Henry Kaiser's excellent adventures in Madagascar and Norway, and Ry Cooder in India, West Africa and Cuba with Buena Vista Social Club. As continental drifters, these musicians have been important world music missionaries who have explored and exposed a vast number of B-sides in international artists and their indigenous musical forms in the global and American music marketplaces.

A visual version of Simon's *Graceland* provides a concert construction context in Chapter 7. This post-production case study not only magnifies the conventions of the concert film, but provides a detailed account of the construction stages, processes and creative and technical contributions of Broadway Video editor John Fortenberry in shaping and "sculpting" the music and images of Simon's award-winning *Graceland: The African Concert* (1987), a Showtime cable network special. While the directorial efforts of notable rockumentarians such as D.A. Pennebaker, Michael Wadleigh, the Maysles brothers, Martin Scorsese and Jonathan Demme are easily recognized, there are many voices contributing to the collaborative chorus of any music-film-video performance presentation. Fortenberry's virtually anonymous, yet vital role in the *Graceland* concert production is typical of the numerous individuals who work behind the scenes, particularly during the equally underappreciated B-side stage of post production.

The next two chapters are also television texts, from singing cops to pop rock cameos. Chapter 8 is rich in "'B' letters for" encompassing blue, bomb, building block, bastard and Steven Bochco, one of contemporary television's most successful and important creators. In the 1980s, Bochco brought the large ensemble, hand held camera, and cluttered, gritty realism to network dramas such as *Hill Street Blues* and *L.A. Law*. Perhaps his most interesting, innovative and unusual production was *Cop Rock* (1990), a *Hill Street Blues* B-side which merged conventions of the stage musical with the television cop drama into the "soap copera." Despite its spectacular failure, the production was both muse and martyr that foreshadowed the further exploration and integration of music into dramatic and comic narratives in television and film beyond *Miami Vice*'s mid-1980s soundtrack touchstone. *Cop Rock* was also a hinge that linked Dennis Potter's BBC production *The Singing Detective* (1986) with cross-genre aesthetic advancement through the BBC series, *Viva Blackpool*, and its short-lived Americanized televersion, *Viva Laughlin* (2007), a karaoke musical murder mystery with sex, drugs and gambling.

Chapter 9 highlights baby boomer bit players in television comedies. Pop and rock performers have always been a presence in television programming, a span extending from Ricky Nelson in *Ozzie and Harriet* in the 1950s to *The Osbournes* (sur)reality series in the 1990s. One of the more unusual undercurrents during television's reality show dominated era has been the number of baby boomer rockers who have strangely, surprisingly surfaced in broadcast and cable situation comedy episodes. Bob Dylan, Tom Petty, Elvis Costello, Los Lobos, Yoko Ono and John Hiatt have been among the singer songwriters cast in comedy cameos. In addition, shows such as the animated *The Simpsons* and Nickelodeon network's *The Adventures of Pete and Pete* have been showcases for cartoon and alternative rock cameos. This chapter backtracks, tracing the little trend of pop and rock star cameo obscuras from the 1960s to contemporary television presentations.

The blessings and burdens of biology and biography as they relate to baby boomer baby bands are presented in Chapter 10. One of the mini-trends in 1990s popular music was the emergence of a wave of children of folk, pop and rock singer songwriters pursuing their own musical careers. These offspring might be viewed as the "B-sides" of their A-side parents. This chapter traces the branches of family trees and pop music progeny from the 1960s to the most recent wave that includes Sean Lennon, Jakob Dylan, Rufus Wainwright, and Lisa Marie Presley.

The collection concludes with burial rites and the great beyond. A number of familiar figures, including Rick Danko of the Band, George Harrison, Mama and Papa John Phillips, June Carter Cash and Johnny Cash, marked music's mere mortal march during the first few years of the new millennium. During the same period, singer-songwriter Warren Zevon was diagnosed with terminal lung cancer. The initial three month prognosis prolonged past one year, allowing Zevon, whose songwriting career was marked by a preoccupation with death, to decompose his own "Deteriorata." During that time, Zevon wrote, arranged and recorded his own black swan song while marching in his own funeral procession, which included an entire hour on the *Late Show with David Letterman*, a farewell record *The Wind*, and accompanying VH-1 *(Inside)Out* documentary of the recording session with musician friends and family. The experience was analogous to "disincorporating," a concept presented in the science fiction novel *Stranger in A Strange Land* in which an artist dies in the middle of a project on Mars. This chapter chronicles Zevon's unprecedented rock "dieography," from diagnosis through posthumous tributes, record reissues and a published oral history. Zevon's funereal small scale spectacle illustrates death's ironic, yet typical artist ascension from the B-side to the A-side, while simultaneously passing from life (the A-side) to the afterlife (the B-Side). In addition, the "dieography" reconfigures the stereotypical rock death ritual from recklessness, overdose, shot gun blast and plane crash to a living wake and reality show.

Just as the "dieography" provides a time line for Zevon's deteriorata, several other chapters feature similar reference resources such as artist and genre discographies, chart information, and episode guides which complement the critical narrative.

The outskirt observations, bystander profiles and fringe fascination within these chapters translate into a series of stanzas that echo Pat MacDonald's "B-Side of Life" The Timbuk 3 tune is a modest anthem to an anonymous way of life, an acknowledgment of the unknowns and the no names who "tear the tickets at the Hall of Fame."[3] *B-Sides, Undercurrents and Overtones* is a kindred spirit; an offbeat ode to obscurity that endeavors to fill in blanks, illuminate blind spots and frame the unfamiliar with affection and appreciation. In the simplest sense, *B-Sides* is about peripheral vision; looking over the overlooked and listening to the back beat, wondering about the "flip side," what the B-side has to say.

---

3   "B-Side of Life." Words and music by Pat MacDonald. Mambadaddi Music/I.R.S. Music, Inc. BMI. 1989 (current spelling preference pat mAcdonald).

Chapter 1

Get Your 45s On:
Terry Melcher, Lost in the Surf and Sun
of the 1960s Sound Waves

A curious California chronicle ended on November 19, 2004, when songwriter, artist, and record producer Terry Melcher died at age 62, following a lengthy struggle with melanoma.[1] If the name Terry Melcher sounds familiar, it may be because his name is about familiar sounds. To paraphrase from Sheryl Crow's "Soak Up the Sun," Melcher, unfortunately, may not have had his 45 (sunblock) on, but he certainly left his mark on a lot of 45 (singles) "so we could all rock on."[2] Melcher was at the forefront of the emerging cluster of 1960s era pop rock producers, a secondary, yet significant set of studio supervisors whose signatures shaped a steady stream of hit singles in between early 1960s surf and Spectorian spectacle, the seminal *Pet Sounds* in 1966, and *Sgt. Pepper* and the Summer of Love. Just as Melcher established an identity with the Byrds and Paul Revere and the Raiders, other "one man band" producers of the era included Lou Adler (Mamas and Papas), P.F. Sloan and Steve Barri (Grass Roots), Snuff Garrett (Gary Lewis and the Playboys) and Gary Usher (Byrds).

Melcher's low key career provides an engaging B-Side portrayal of the mid- to late 1960s Southern California setting and its shifting sounds and spirit. From "Que Sera, Sera" to "Kokomo," Melcher's time line contains some colorful character contrasts, from the clean cut of his mother, singer-actress Doris Day to cult leader Charles Manson. Melcher's musical markers span the obscure Rip Chords, Rising Sons and Gentle Soul to the Raiders, Byrds and Beach Boys.

Something in the Air(waves): 45 Revolutions per Minute

In the mid-1960s, between the British Invasion and the "Eve of Destruction," the name "Terry Melcher" was a familiar footnote in the fine print of the compacted credits on the colored label logo inner circle space of the black 45 records that

---

1 This chapter evolved out of a eulogy "In Memoriam: Terry Melcher (1947-2004) Lost in the Mid-1960s Sun?," *Popular Music & Society* Vol. 30, No. 2, May 2007: 267-273.

2 "Soak Up the Sun." Sheryl Crow/Jeff Trott. Warner-Tamerlane Publishing/Old Crow Music BMI/ASCAP (2002).

were hit single vessels. The Melcher mantra, whether "Arranged by," "Produced by," or co-writer credits, repeated routinely in the early 1960s, and nearly a dozen different times in the prolific parenthesis that was 1965-66. Melcher's name was particularly prevalent on the red Columbia label of singles by the Byrds and the Paul Revere and the Raiders.

Melcher migrated west from New York where he began his own recording career as Terry Day, releasing his first 45 r.p.m., "That's All I Want" in June 1962.[3] In California, Melcher teamed with future Beach Boy Bruce Johnston. The duo, along with Brian Wilson, Jan and Dean and Gary Usher, caught the crest of a similar surf and drag stylistic wave, managing a few fun in the sun, hot rod hits with the genre bending Rogues, Rip Chords ("Hey Little Cobra") and Bruce and Terry ("Summer Means Fun").[4] Melcher's songwriting and production credits steadily accumulated into an impressive forty two chart singles, most in the new California genre, during a two year period. Among his collaborators were Bobby Darin, Glenn Campbell, Wayne Newton, Pat Boone, Randy Newman, and many of the Brill Building songwriters.

At age 22, Melcher became an in-house producer for the Columbia label. Melcher's biggest influence was his musical mentor Jack Nitzsche, who at age 25, was a prodigious studio veteran on his way to becoming a legendary arranger and composer.[5] He credits Nitzsche with being the first to recognize Melcher's musical abilities, nurture his instincts, and make him feel comfortable working with renowned West Coast session players. "Prod. by Terry Melcher Arr. & Cond. by Jack Nitzsche" became a familiar stamp of studio alchemy on 45s of the era, from the Rip Chords to Al Hazan, Eddie Hodges and Frankie Laine.[6] Melcher continually displayed instincts for choosing material, and his approach favored a sound from car radio speaker more than a studio control room, mixing multiple tracks of hand claps, extra vocals and drums to create a "dynamic squashing" and "dense mid range-y wash of music" (Quaglieri 1998).

---

3   There are several insightful, though occasionally contradictory sources chronicling Melcher's early career, among them Stephen J. McParland's interview-oriented volumes published by CMusic Books (2001, 2002) and Al Quaglieri's liner notes in the compilation *Best of Bruce and Terry* (Sundazed 1993).

4   The relationship casts an intriguingly ironic shadow on Johnston's characterization of suddenly stigmatized Beach Boys as "surfing Doris Days" following the collapsed *Smile* project in 1967.

5   The Melcher/Nitzsche relationship is well documented in an excellent eight part series, "Prod. By Terry Melcher Arr. & Cond. Jack Nitzsche" posted at http://spectrropop. com/TerryMelcher.

6   During a Frankie Laine recording session, singer Jackie DeShannon, who was Melcher's girlfriend at the time, was part of the chorus for "Go Away Little Girl." A jealous Phil Spector, wearing dark glasses, sat opposite Melcher, glaring at him for six hours. Spector warned Nitzsche and other session players that if they wanted to work for him, they couldn't work for Melcher again (see McParland 2001).

As Columbia's only in-house producer, Melcher helped transform the prominent label's clean, staid "Easy Listening" image. Prior to his arrival, there were a limited number of releases on the label that fit the rock and pop groove, among them Carl Perkins. Melcher modernized the sound of some of Columbia's older and biggest selling artists such as Laine. He also began to chart Columbia's course through the hit single, record sale soundscape which had been largely defined by surf, the Phil Spector girl groups and the booming British Invasion. The Beatles alone held the first five spots on the U.S. Hot 100 singles chart. Melcher's main assignment was to foster a few fledgling bands—the Byrds and Paul Revere and the Raiders—which he had the business clout to recruit to Columbia. And he delivered results, orchestrating an impressive string of hits for both groups that checkered the charts, many reaching the Top Ten, during the next few years.

In the Jingle Jangle Morning

The Byrds' first hit single, a stunning transformation of Bob Dylan's seven-minute epic "Mr. Tambourine Man" from his *Bringing It All Back Home* (1965) album, may be conveniently considered Melcher's crowning contribution. The song was recorded on January 20, 1965, released in April, charted in May, and reached number one on the *Billboard* charts in June, giving Columbia its biggest hit for nearly three years. By July, the song had displaced The Hollies "I'm Alive" from the number one spot in Britain. The song's ascension was impressive considering the resistance and rejection it received before finally being recorded. "I didn't like it at all," said David Crosby. "I thought it stunk." Byrds' manager Jim Dickson initially approached one of his more established acts, The Kentucky Colonels, with "Mr. Tambourine Man." The group, whose line up featured eventual Byrds' guitarist Clarence White, rejected the offer (Hughes 2005: 28).

There are varying accounts of the recording session. Among the more notable are those by rock historian Geoffrey Stokes (Ward, Stokes, Tucker 1986) and *Rolling Stone*'s David Fricke in his essay in the first *Byrds Box Set* (1990). What may be most striking is that Columbia, despite its expectations for hit records, limited Melcher and the Byrds' studio time to three hours. Undeterred by his label's frugality and naivety, Melcher displayed some youthful savvy. He had learned from beach brothers Brian (Wilson) and Bruce (Johnston) that the end result was what really mattered, and to do what was necessary to achieve the desired sound, no matter the circumstances. Melcher daringly directed Jim (eventually Roger) McGuinn, David Crosby and Gene Clark to concentrate on the vocal lines, and proficient players Chris Hillman and Michael Clark to sit out the recording of the song. They were replaced by Nitzsche's core sessionists Larry Knechtal, Jerry Cole, Leon Russell, and Spector Wrecking Crew drummer Hal Blaine who were brought in to handle all the instrumentals except McGuinn's twelve-string. The arrangement created a lingering resentment. "I had a hard time getting friendly with any of the original Byrds besides Roger (McGuinn) because none of them had played on that record," said Melcher (Nolan 1974: 77). Though McGuinn and Dickson supported the session substitutes, agreeing that the group was not "ready," Melcher absorbed most of the blame.

Melcher utilized the same adventurous efficiency with Paul Revere and the Raiders when Columbia demanded a recording output incompatible with the band's tour schedule. Melcher frequently flew in lead singer Mark Lindsay from the Raiders' road locales to lay down vocals with studio musicians. The progressive practice of using a "ghost band" provided an early glimpse of the power of the record producer and anticipated creative-commercial conflicts as star power escalated. At a time when most record labels and producers treated pop performers as "haircuts-with-attitude," Melcher adeptly managed the likes of the egotistical Lindsay and complex Crosby, who in Bob Dylan's description, was "out of place in the Byrds" and "could freak out a whole city block by himself" (132).

McGuinn's opening chords of "Mr. Tambourine Man"—a reknowned 12-string Rickenbacker riff that blended Bach with the Beatles, with a brilliant bass line beneath—provided an eight second prelude to chiming, choir-like, three part harmonies, semi-military drum rolls and an overdubbed rock beat, threaded with what would become a signature electric jingle jangle. Melcher modified Dylan's 2/4 tempo up to rock's 4/4 time, adapting the rhythm of the Beach Boys' "Don't Worry Baby." Risking songwriter sacrilege, three of Dylan's verses were eliminated in order to emphasize the seductive reverie of the chorus and McGuinn's elliptical prayer-like delivery. The radical rearrangement confounded Columbia, which delayed the record's release for three months (see Hughes 2005: 28).

The striking synthesis of sound and spirit was epic, an automatic anthem-like imprint on the soul of the generational soundtrack, spinning beyond the studio and spilling into the streets. "No one could sound like that but Californians, but no Californians ever sounded like that before!" recalls Jim Bickhart (Byrds 1970). The ringing rendition of Dylan's hobo-two step was a historical hinge, a pivotal two minutes-twenty seconds brimming with musical, poetic and sociopolitical possibilities.

Melcher's Byrds' blend became an agent of awareness and transition on numerous levels. The innovative sound signaled the arrival of folk-rock as a major musical merger and mode. Artistically, the genre launched an era of lyrical and instrumental complexity as folk's outsider intellectualism became energized in a rock context. The Byrds made Dylan more accessible; their approach "galvanized the hopeful adolescent wanderlust in his lyrics" (Fricke 1990: 14), informed his words, and smoothed his rougher edges and eccentricities (Ward 1986: 304). Culturally, the "white pop" that aimed for and located itself in a conceptual gap between Dylan and the Beatles marked the first purely American response to the British Invasion. "Mr. Tambourine Man" reached out and consolidated that post pubescent generation the Beatles had first attracted with *A Hard Days Night* (Ward: 305).

A procession ensued. The Lovin' Spoonful, Association, We Five, and Sonny and Cher (who beat the Byrds to Dylan's "All I Really Wanna Do")[7] were among countless American artists who matched the Kinks, Herman's Hermits, Yardbirds and other imports, band for band, hit for hit. "Turn, Turn Turn," "Like A Rolling Stone," "The Sounds of Silence," and "California Girls" singled up alongside "(I Can't Get No) Satisfaction" and the best of the Brit hits in radio's rotations in 1965. Folk rock's inauguration via the Byrds' "Mr. Tambourine Man" became the sustaining sound of articulation, affirmation, and confrontation within the sociopolitical, countercultural and spiritual turbulence of the times. Cultural critic Greil Marcus provides his usual incisive characterization of the magnitude of the era's hit parade: "No one heard the music on the radio as part of a separate reality. Every new hit seemed full of novelty, as if its goal was not only to top the charts but to stop the world in its tracks and then start it up again" (2006: 4).

Melcher was unrelenting. The Byrds second album, *Turn! Turn! Turn!*, featuring the definitive cover of the Pete Seeger/Ecclesiastes tune, was released in December 1965, less than six months after the *Mr. Tambourine Man* debut. At the same time, the in-demand Melcher balanced producing, increased writing, and even singing as the "sixth Raider" with Paul Revere's outfit. There is a sense that 1965 was spinning fast, maybe too fast. The production pace was giddy, approaching out of control with a sense that everyone—labels, producers, and artists alike—was making it up as they went along. There was no precedent, no road map. Only the newness of notoriety. However, the "get it while you can" urgency may have been grim foreshadowing of the "too much too soon" cautionary tale. Star struck distractions, not to mention the motion of the turbulent times, made continuity a challenge even within the music and counterculture scenes which embraced values of "community." Personnel defections were steady, making a band's staying power improbable. The majority of popular groups from the period—the Turtles, Playboys, Raiders, Monkees, to name a few—did not endure beyond the accumulation of their hit songs. Once a greatest hits compilation was released, the collective began to slowly splinter. Dissolution became the pattern, if not the standard.

By 1967, rock music's mainstream marketability was amplified at Monterey Pop, a festival which Melcher helped organize and finance. Monterey marked the first of a three act play of festivals, followed by Woodstock's bliss and ending in tragedy at Altamont before fading into the disco inferno of the 1970s. The vibes and values rippled throughout music; community became more absorbed in commerce.

Raider Mark Lindsay's wife, Deb, provides a revealing retrospective passage on the "infectious and incestuous" way many records were made in California in

---

7   Cher characterized Melcher as "horribly competitive" and "a total asshole" after Melcher was upset that Sonny and Cher's version of "All I Really Wanna Do" scotched sales of the Byrds' single of the same song. See http://spectropop.com/Terry Melcher/index. htm).

18   *B-SIDES, UNDERCURRENTS AND OVERTONES*

the early 1960s. "Mark describes it as a free flow of ideas and musicianship across groups and labels, a practice that is nearly impossible today with all the legal mumbo-jumbo that has to be negotiated before the business affairs people will agree to anything. It was a kinder, simpler time then, a time when the Beach Boys could go over to Columbia Studio A with Capitol's blessing if Brian wanted to be there" (Lindsay 1998).

The times a-changed. Swiftly. *Sgt. Pepper* signaled a shift from surf to singles to the San Francisco sound, psychedelics and beyond. The Raiders peaked, saving their best for last with the richly produced Lindsay-Melcher composition, "Him or Me—What's It Gonna Be?" The Byrds withstood the convergence of industry, social and their own personnel transformations, at least for a short while. Amidst rumors of increasing tension with the Byrds' manager, Melcher became more detached from the group and gravitated to other projects. His longtime colleague and B-side companion Gary Usher stepped in and followed Melcher's two groundbreaking productions with a string of enduring Byrds' records: *Younger Than Yesterday* (1967), featuring the facetious (and what some read as a swipe at the Monkees) "So You Want to be Rock N' Roll Star;" the psychedelic opus *The Notorious Byrd Brothers* (1968); and the pioneering country rock *Sweethearts of the Rodeo* (1968) featuring Gram Parsons. Though mentor Melcher managed one more gem, *The Ballad of Easy Rider* (1969), Usher's triad trumped Melcher's late decade productions, *The Byrds* (*Untitled* (1970)), a double LP containing one live/one studio record, and *Byrdmaniax* (1971). The two recordings are generally regarded as some of the weakest entries in the Byrds' discography.[8] By 1970, the Byrds' signature 12-string sound was all but gone as were all of the band's original members and their replacements except for McGuinn. For the first time, Melcher's production and arranging choices became suspect. Longtime Byrd watcher Fricke writes how during the *Untitled* session, Melcher "drenched Dylan's 'Lay Lady Lay' in vocal gospel sugar" shortly before its release. The song was eventually remixed under McGuinn's supervision without the "offending female chorus" (Fricke 1990: 29) In 1973, Melcher and David Geffen reunited the original band for a reluctant final flight, *Byrds* on the Asylum label. The album, widely regarded as an uninspired work, included Neil Young and Joni Mitchell covers (see Hoskyns 2006: 157-158).[9]

Helter Skelter: The Byrds Flew Off...

Melcher may have been losing his gold touch, or had gradually grown distracted, discouraged or too spread out with multiple projects. Other indications were that

---

8   Los Angeles music scene chronicler Barney Hoskyns refers to *Byrdmaniax* as "Melcher's Folly" (1996).

9   Of that period, Melcher said, "I worked with the Byrds and got fired because I didn't get high. Then I worked with the Raiders and got fired because I did" (see Nolan 1974).

he may have been spooked by Charles Manson. The Melcher-Manson mystery qualifies as one of rock mythologies "lost episodes" with *Cold Case File* intrigue. Manson was a part of the L.A. scene and the Wilson brothers elite circle. Blurred communal L.A. lore suggests that Manson and some of his group lived in Dennis Wilson's mansion and recorded with the Beach Boys. "Never Learn Not to Love" on their final Capitol album *20/20* (1969), is a retitled Manson song, "Cease to Exist." When Dennis Wilson introduced Melcher and Manson, Manson asked the producer to listen to his demo tape that he had been shopping around Los Angeles. Like the other record labels that had roundly rejected Manson's music, Melcher was unimpressed. He refused to tout Manson at Columbia or sign him to a contract. According to several accounts, Manson became vengeful. "Charlie got pissed off that they didn't think he was a genius," said Denny Doherty of the Mamas and Papas. "His attitude was, 'Who the fuck is *Terry Melcher?* He can't even sing" (Hoskyns 2006: 95). In August 1969, Manson ordered some of his followers to break into the house on Cielo Drive where Melcher and then girlfriend Candace Bergen lived together. However, Melcher had rented the place to actress Sharon Tate and director Roman Polanski, who was out of the country at the time. The record rejection led to ongoing speculation that Melcher was the real target in the legendary, grisly mass murders that took place that evening. Susan Atkins, who was convicted of murdering Tate and her four friends, claimed that she and fellow members of the "Manson Family" were sent to the house to "instill fear into Terry Melcher, because Terry had given us his word on a few things and never came through with them" (Coleman 2004). Though there may have been a Manson motive, both Melcher and the police discounted the theory, saying that the frustrated musician and cult leader knew that the producer had moved to Malibu. The Manson massacre remains a peripheral, yet mandatory mention in the Melcher narrative (see Nolan 1974, Hoskyns 2006: 94-97, Walker 2006: 121-128).

Eight Miles High and Falling Fast

Enigmatically, Melcher's star flickered toward fading almost as fast as it had flourished. In 1968, he and Nitzsche collaborated on the sunshine pop duo Gentle Soul, which marked the last project the production team would work on together. Nitzsche became one of the most sought after producers in music, his distinctive arrangements and production signature appearing on records from the Rolling Stones to Neil Young. By the end of the decade, Melcher's surf-folk-rock arc diverged, perhaps out of desperation, disillusion, or the Doris Day gene. He veered outside the rock realm to Glen Campbell, Wayne Newton and Pat Boone. The transition was also personal necessity. Following the death of his step father, and Doris Day's final film, *With Six You Get Egg Roll* (1968), Melcher worked extensively with his mother, serving as executive producer of her CBS series *The Doris Day Show* from 1968-1972. Melcher re-entered the studio to record two solo records of "Beverly Hills country"—*Terry Melcher* (1974) and *Royal Flush* (1976).

20   *B-SIDES, UNDERCURRENTS AND OVERTONES*

The credits include the usual session suspects: Blaine, Knechtal, Johnston, Ry Cooder, and even Doris Day singing backup vocals on one tune. Dutiful and devoted, Melcher continued to work with his mother in many capacities during the 1980s—producing her cable show *Doris Day's Best Friends*, running her businesses, assisting her through personal and financial difficulties, supervising her charitable activities and foundations, and co-owning a small hotel.

Melcher never got the surf out of his songwriting system. His return to mainstream music in 1988 was a pseudo-tropical triumph. Melcher, along with California dreaming veterans John Phillips of the Mamas and Papas, and 1967 one hit wonder Scott McKenzie ("San Francisco (Be Sure to Wear Flowers in Your Hair))," were recruited to compose a song for the Beach Boys for the Tom Cruise bartender film *Cocktail*. The trio came up with the Caribbean sounding, "Kokomo," although the name has state of Indiana origins. Critically loathed, the syrup sopped song gave the label-less, surviving members of the Beach Boys their first number one hit since "Good Vibrations" and a Golden Globe nomination for best original song.

Rising Sons: Brink or Breakthrough

While "Mr. Tambourine Man" and "Kokomo" bookend Melcher's music biography, with "Hey Little Cobra" a preface, one of his most inconspicuous, yet consummate contributions as a mid-1960s sound shaper surfaced in 1992 with the release of materials which had been in a vault for nearly three decades. In mid-1965, around the time of the Byrds' baptismal albums, Columbia added another band to Melcher's hopeful hit list—the Rising Sons. The eclectic, interracial outfit was a small scale precursor to "super group" assemblies such as the Souther, Hillman, Furay Band, the Traveling Wilburys, Little Village and Golden Smog. The lineup was fronted by bluesman Taj Mahal and teen guitar virtuoso Ry Cooder, and backed by Beatle afficionado Jesse Lee Kincaid, Kevin Kelley (eventually a Byrd and Fever Tree), Gary Marker, a jazz bassist with a Berklee School of Music background, and briefly, jazz drummer Ed Cassidy (later in Spirit).

There were hints of an emerging congruity with rock and blues within the music movement. Elektra and MGM had signed white blues acts Paul Butterfield and Blues Project. The singles-minded Columbia hoped Melcher could get the Rising Sons to establish country blues the same way the Byrds displayed Dylan and folk rock. According to Melcher, the difference was that the Byrds "were all going in the same direction;" whereas the Rising Sons "had guys who should have been in two different groups" (Kirkeby 1992). Melcher favored the country blues sound for its uniqueness at the time. The group's multiple music agendas ultimately proved problematic for Melcher to meld into a marketable product on AM radio's pop rock rotations. Though they managed one single—a cover of Skip James's "The Devil's Got My Woman" with a B-side of Reverend Gary Davis's "Candy Man"—the Rising Sons never got that big push from Columbia and remained on the brink of a breakthrough. No one faulted Melcher or suggested Rising Sons was a low priority project to him. In Marker's view, Melcher "went out of his way to make us happy—within the scope of his knowledge" and "tried just about everything he could, including a live, acoustic session" (Kirkeby).

Rising Sons may have been a showcase for guitar interplay between Cooder and Taj Mahal, but it also provides perhaps the best capsule of Melcher's vision and versatility as a sound architect (see Metting 2001). Melcher encouraged instrumentation such as mandolin, dulcimer and bottleneck guitar which were not yet widely incorporated conventions in the rock realm. The 22 songs assembled from the sessions integrate Kincaid's Beatles demo sound (stunningly evident in "The Girl with Green Eyes") with borrowed blues, basement Bob Dylan and Brill Building. In between the band's rock originals, there are imaginative rearrangements of tunes by Sleepy John Estes, Robert Johnson, Willie Dixon, Willie McTell, and Jimmy Reed; the traditional standard "Corrin, Corrina; and "Let the Good Times Roll" which provides a trace of New Orleans R & B. Melcher proved to be an avid song searcher. He dug deeper into the Dylan songbook, excavating the obscure "Walkin' Down the Line" for a loose medley with Jackie DeShannon's "Walk in the Room," courtesy of an opening recognizable Ry Cooder riff. Melcher also realized the value of the most talented tunesmith teams, resourcefully retrieving the Gerry Goffin/Carole King composition, "Take A Giant Step," before the Monkees recorded it. Around the same time, he got Barry Mann and Cynthia Weill to provide the Raiders with two of their biggest hits, an antidrug song "Kicks" (originally written for the Animals) and the follow up, "Hungry."

The Rising Sons' fusion foreshadowed the sounds that surfaced between 1967 and 1968 and gradually steered rock away from AM Top 40 into FM formats, notably Moby Grape, the Buffalo Springfield, and Grateful Dead, whose "Friend of the Devil" mirrors of Rising Sons' "Tulsa Country." The musical mixture also embodies an enduring strand of antecedent Americana or alt.country, one of popular music's most thriving genres during past decades and in the wake of *O Brother! Where Art Thou* (2000).

Setting Son: The Melcher Myth

Rising Sons might be viewed as an incidental Melcher metaphor. Both linger, suspended in between lost and legendary. Even Melcher's most recognized credits remain relatively slighted. Two *Rolling Stone* special editions in 2004 underscored his unsung, B-side status. The Byrds' groundbreaking "Mr. Tambourine Man" ranked 79th among the "500 Greatest Songs of All Time" (9 December 2004); and its initiation of folk rock as a musical movement was not among the "50 Moments that Changed the History of Rock and Roll" (24 June 2004). Further, *Entertainment Weekly* demysitifed "Kokomo" with an essay entitled, "The Strange History of Summer's Most Annoying Song" (Brown 2004: 52). Melcher's death the same year did not activate instantaneous mythical ascension. Obituaries were predictably scant. Ken Barnes's appreciation in *USA Today* (22 November) and the ABC *Nightly News* were among the few eulogistic acknowledgements. Wire services, Internet news and entertainment web-site sources provided concise career capsules; most were misdirected with mandatory famous mother and Manson mentions. Random blogs also posted notice, with a number of entries expressing surprise at Melcher's November passing, with many unaware of his death until viewing the annual "wall of death" tribute during the February 2005 Grammy Awards ceremony.

The plausibility of Melcher's nebulous acclaim may lie in perceptions of his role as producer. Melcher is not credited with being a "pioneer" or founding father; perhaps at best he manages an occasional slight precursor or foster figure. Even mid-wife might be an appropriate analogy as he guided the birth of the Byrds from the Beefeaters. From Dickson to Dylan. Dylan and the Beatles. Bridging the Brill Building with the Beatles and other British sounds and back again. The sound reciprocation and ripples are evident in the Beatles Byrdsian guitar in "What You're Doing" on *Beatles For Sale* (1964), George Harrison's "If I Needed Someone," and to a lesser degree, the harmonies and bridge in "Nowhere Man" on *Rubber Soul* (1965). While Paul Revere and the Raiders may not have inspired the Rolling Stones and Animals, their garage sound is an occasional echo in their contemporaries' catalogs. "Visionary" may also be slightly overstating Melcher's musical legacy in the L.A. lineage. After all, it was Dickson who urged Dylan upon the Byrds. And Dylan himself was destined to be heard, with or without the Byrds as agents of adaptation, just as McGuinn's 12-string was too unique a sound to be silent. Further, the Paul Revere and the Raiders residency on Dick Clark's teen television show *Where the Action Is* may have been their key career catalyst. The Rising Sons sessions would have likely remained buried in the vaults were it not for the careers of Ry Cooder and Taj Mahal, whose musicology has always informed their music.

Demystification may be even more enticing when considering how Melcher's career context is conveniently linked to his lineage and the accompanying perception of privilege. In Melcher's view, being "Doris Day's son" hindered, rather than helped, his A & R job at Columbia, as many artists he attempted to sign did not take his approach seriously (see Prod. By Terry Melcher 2007). Whispers of entitlement accompanied Melcher mentions throughout Hoskyns' California chronicle (2006), overshadowing his quiet musical contributions. Whether juxtaposing Melcher with Lenny Waronker, John Phillips or Gram Parsons, the characterizations were consistent: "rich kid" (10), "trust-fund kid on the scene" (74), "moneyed and...debauched" (93), and "lived in tony property in Bel Air (95). Testimonials rang similar: "I enjoyed working with Terry. But he had this annoying thing of being a guy who didn't have to ever worry about time or money," said John York of his stint with the Byrds (94)[10]

---

10   The minimal Melcher mentions in the other notable L.A. music scene history, Michael Walker's *Laurel Canyon: The Inside Story of Rock and Roll's Legendary Neighborhood* (2006), are music and Manson related.

Despite the Doris Day dismissals, there is no denying or diminishing Terry Melcher's progressive presence as a producer in such a prolific era. One need only consider what he accomplished artistically by the time he was 25 years old. As a producer, Melcher possessed a knack and knowledge, and a feel for fitting sounds together. Surf and drag with layered harmonies. Folk with rock. Country with blues. Garage's edge with pop. Melcher's fingerprints may be peripheral, but they are imprints more than mere smudges on the grooves of the momentous 1960s soundtrack. As an early sound architect, Melcher was a musical matchmaker, a bridge builder, borrower and blender. Integration, instinct and integrity were among his key traits. More pivotal than prolific, Melcher's multiple musical personality anticipated sounds; he was at the forefront and middle of genre movements and mergers that became historical hinges. He orchestrated several sound syntheses that sustained.

Among the sound shapers and movers of the era, Melcher may not be regarded as giant or genius—that is clearly a thorny California crown worn by Brian Wilson. As Wilson's B-side, Melcher and his contributions seem to have gotten lost in the surf and the sun—both figuratively and literally—of the California scene, eclipsed and overshadowed, somewhere in between the jingle jangle morning and the helter skelter in the Summer of Love swelter of the circumstance that was the 1960s. Yet, Terry Melcher remains a bright B-side, a multimusical gem, glimmering anonymously, yet synonymously in the glow, the fine print and flow of the mid-1960s sound waves that we continue to ride.

Chapter 2

How the Midwest Was Won:
The Chicago Suburbs Seven,
a Mid-1960s Regional Rotation

And now I feel light years away / From the West side of Chicago.
Jim Peterik (Ides of March) "L.A. Goodbye" (1971)
© 2008, Jim Peterik Music

On Saturday, 2 July 2005, the crowd at the Chicago Cubs home game rose for the traditional seventh inning stretch and the celebrity-led sing-along inspired by late great broadcaster Harry Carey. Joining legendary Windy City radio personality Dick Biondi in the broadcast booth for the Wrigley Field rendition of "Take Me Out to the Ball Game" were Jim Peterik, Ronnie Rice and Carl Giammarese. For fans in attendance at the ballpark and those viewing the game on WGN's super station whose Wonder Years took place in the Chicago suburbs, the moment was a sentimental serenade that represented a retro regional rotation. The trio of local heroes alongside Biondi were the founders and fronts for the popular 1960s Chicago area bands—the Ides of March, New Colony Six, and the Buckinghams. Had Jim Fairs or Jim Pilster (J.C. Hooke) of the Cryan' Shames joined in the chorus, it would have been a grand slam. Add to that foursome other era area band leaders Gary Loizzo of the interracial American Breed, Jim Sohns or Warren Rogers of the Shadows of Knight and Jimy Rogers of the Mauds and a musical variation of the 1960s radical yippie "Chicago Seven" materializes as the "Chicago Suburbs Seven."[1]

A Prolific Pop Pocket

While there was an array of other eclectic local groups that emerged in the Chicago vicinity around the same time, among them Rotary Connection, the Flock, H.P. Lovecraft, Aorta, Saturday's Children, the Del-Vetts and Aliota, Haynes and

---

1   Many of the accounts, color, observations and backdrop in this chapter are based on my personal experience as these bands were central to my coming of age and musical maturation in the Western Suburbs of Chicago. Thanks also to Chuck Soumar of the Ides of March for his casual correspondence, retro reflections and gracious assistance with lyric permissions.

Jeremiah, the collective catalog of these seven bands comprises a notable cluster of garage, pop, rock, jazz and soul that was essential to the sound of the Chicago suburbs during the singles-rich era.

A Midwestern microcosm of the broader music scene, the string of singles produced by these seven bands mirrored the productivity and limited longevity of many higher profile hit makers of the time, from Garry Lewis and the Playboys, the Box Tops, Three Dog Night, Lovin' Spoonful, Grass Roots, Turtles, Association, Beau Brummels, Gary Puckett and the Union Gap, Classics IV to Motown to British Invasion groups such as Herman's Hermits, the Hollies, and Freddie and the Dreamers. The Chicago suburbs were well represented in the mid-1960s pop pantheon. Between 1966 and 1971, these bands, despite modest album sales and a shooting star, two-to-four year arc, permeated the local and regional Top Ten with their singles, with several breaking through to the national Cash Box and Billboard charts. A number of their singles, such as the Cryan' Shames "Mr. Unreliable" and the Mauds "Hold On," charted high locally without reaching the national Hot 100.

Collectively, nearly 40 songs from the Chicago Suburbs Seven charted during the five-year span, with 1966 to 1968 a particularly prolific parenthesis that featured 30 singles. The New Colony Six totaled the most with ten, followed by Buckinghams with seven, while four of the other bands had five songs each. The Mauds managed only one. The lone national number one hit among the groups was the Buckinghams' "Kind of a Drag" in 1966, which knocked the Monkees' Neil Diamond tune, "I'm a Believer," out of top spot. The following year, their' "Mercy, Mercy, Mercy" reached #5 and "Don't You Care" #6, while three of their others songs landed just outside the Top Ten. While the Buckinghams' chart saturation for that period may have approached a Beatles and Byrds benchmark, their secondary status aligned more closely with one of the most underrated bands of the British Invasion, the Dave Clark Five, who had 16 top 30 hits from 1964 to 1967. As a result of their five singles, the Buckinghams were named *Billboard*'s "Most Listened to Band in America" in 1967. The Ides of March "Vehicle" reached #2 in 1970, unable to unseat the Guess Who's "American Woman" from the top spot. Other Top Tens included the American Breed's "Bend Me, Shape Me (Anyway You Want Me)" which topped the local charts and reached #5 nationally in 1967, and the Shadows of Knight made it to #10 with "Gloria" in 1966.

Many of the songs also had respectable staying power that extended into double digit weeks on the charts. The longest run was the New Colony Six's "Things I'd Like to Say," which lingered for 16 weeks in 1968, despite a chart position peak at #16. "Bend Me, Shape Me" endured for 14 weeks while "Gloria" lasted 12. Five of the seven Buckinghams' songs that charted stayed between ten to fourteen weeks.[2]

---

2   Chart information is compiled from *Billboard* archives and discographies at individual band web sites.

The Sound of the Suburbs

The origins of these groups spanned Chicago's near western suburbs of Hinsdale, Berwyn and Cicero to Arlington Heights in the northwest region. The collective musical styles did not produce a signature suburban sound or groundbreaking genre that redefined the region's .musical map the way that the blues and jazz had. The closest to a commonality may be the horns utilized by the American Breed, Buckinghams and Ides of March. Each band incorporated the instrumentation differently—the Buckinghams punchy soul, the American Breed's polished garage, and the Ides of March a blend of folk, rock and jazz. The Ides of March's use of the brassy sound, notably Chuck Soumar's trumpet solos, intros and bridges, was a pop precursor to, rather than widely misperceived imitation of, bands such as Blood, Sweat and Tears, Lighthouse, Chase and local contemporaries Chicago Transit Authority, which became Chicago, one of the most popular and productive rock bands with a horn section.[3]

Beyond the inventive integration of trumpets and saxophones, the musical styles represented in the "Suburbs Seven" incorporated the popular American hooks and British roots of the time. The Buckinghams, originally The Pulsations, changed their name to reflect a more Englander image after a failed audition for a WGN-TV variety show. Producers said they "weren't British enough." Their music blended Dennis Tufano and Carl Giammarese vocals of Jim Holvay compositions with rock, soul and occasional psychedelia ("Susan"). The New Colony Six tried to fashion an anti-Brit style, adopting "uniforms" similar to Paul Revere and the Raiders. Their sound, initially exuberant garage rock with Farfisa organ and the unique Lesley guitar, evolved into pop/rock softness and harmonizing balladry that included strings. In addition to horns, the Ides of March combined complex jazz, rock, soul, folk stylings with occasional sprawling hippie-jam arrangements. The Shadows of Knight sound, self-described as an English version of the blues with a Chicago touch, is often compared to an amalgam of the Rolling Stones, Animals and Yardbirds (Unterberger 1995: 684), The Mauds' single, "Soul Drippin'," perhaps best characterized the band's gritty R& B, white soul sound. They, along with the Buckinghams, preceded the Rolling Stones as white bands to record at Chicago's renowned Chess studios. The Cryan' Shames' blended Beatlesque arrangements, the Byrds' jangling guitars and tambourine, and layered harmonies of the Beach Boys and the Association.

True to many band beginnings in garages with guitars, amps and a snare drum, these groups relied on cover versions during live performances, for album tracks and as singles. Before "Kind of a Drag" became a national hit, the Buckinghams' regional releases included versions of James Brown's "I'll Go Crazy," the Beatles' "I Call Your Name," and the Hollies' I've Been Wrong Before." They followed "Kind of A Drag" with Lloyd Price's "Lawdy Miss Clawdy" and Cannonball Adderly's

---

3 Buckingham James Guercio, who orchestrated the band's horn arrangements, eventually became a producer for Chicago.

"Mercy Mercy, Mercy," both of which charted. The American Breed's best known song, "Bend Me Shape Me" was actually a castoff from the Outsiders, best known for their hit "Time Won't Let Me." They also charted with Chip Taylor's "Step Outside Your Mind," and recorded Brill Building tunes, among them the Carole King/ Gerry Goffin gems "I Don't Think You Know Me" and "Don't Forget About Me," and Barry Mann/Cynthia Weill's Animals' hit, "We Gotta get Outta This Place." They also covered "Hi Heel Sneakers," Eddie Floyd's "Knock on Wood," and songs written by Paul Williams and Van McCoy.

R& B and soul tunes were commonly interpreted, particularly by the Shadows of Knight. In addition to their top ten hit with Van Morrison/Them's "Gloria," they charted with Muddy Waters' "Oh Yeah" and recorded songs by Willie Dixon, John Lee Hooker, Chuck Berry and Carole Bayer Sager. Bo Diddley's "Cadillac" was a B-side for the New Colony Six's "Long Time to Be Alone." The Mauds also recorded "Knock on Wood" and Sam and Dave's classic "Hold On," which WLS requested as a radio-friendly version which edited the chorus, "Hold on, I'm comin'/ Hold on, I'm comin" to "Hold on, don't you worry/Hold on, please" (Callahan, Edwards, Eyries 2005). The Ides of March, whose *Vehicle* LP featured jazzy extended Beatles ("Symphony for Eleanor (Rigby)") and Crosby, Stills and Nash variations (Wooden Ships/Dharma for One"), also included songs by James Brown, Arthur Conley, and Curtis Mayfield ("People Get Ready) in their regular set lists during live shows.

The Cryan' Shames, who had the least chart impact but most album appeal of the "Suburbs Seven," leaned on covers more than most of their colleagues, particularly on their three albums. As the Travelers, they recorded "If I Needed Someone" intent on the familiar Beatles song being their first single for the Destination label. George Harrison, apparently displeased with the Hollies version of his song despite it reaching the top 20 in England, refused to license the song (Besch 1992: 7). The Travelers' version was never released as a single, but was included on the Cryan' Shames debut album *Sugar and Spice* (1966). The album resembled a contemporary tribute/cover compilation, leading off with the single "Sugar and Spice," a Tony Hatch as Fred Nightingale composition popularized by the English group the Searchers in 1964. An array of interpretations of the 1960s playlist followed—"If I Needed Someone," Martha and the Vandellas' "Heat Wave," the popular "We Gotta Get Out of This Place," Gene Clark's Byrds' B-side gem, "She Don't Care About Time," and a requisite version of Jimi Hendrix's and the Leaves' "Hey Joe." The remastered edition of the *Sugar and Spice* album includes the Beatles "You're Gonna Lose That Girl" and Bread's "It Don't Matter to Me." Their two subsequent albums featured another Brill Building cornerstone, King and Goffin's "Up on the Roof," Hoagey Carmichael's "Baltimore Oriole," and the Youngbloods "Get Together." The Cryan Shames' final 45 single was also a cover, "Rainmaker," the B-side to Harry Nillson's "Everybody's Talkin'."

Vehicles, Baby

The bands benefited from Chicago's two, high-powered exposure vehicles—the legendary radio station WLS-AM and its arch-rival, WCFL. Both stations routinely raced to launch the latest singles from the locals. Promotion was further enhanced by the stations' impressive roster of popular radio personalities, among them Dick Biondi, Dex Card, Ron Riley, Clark Weber, Barney Pip and Art Roberts. Roberts also hosted an *American Bandstand*-style teen dance show, *Swingin' Majority* (see McWilliams 2007). Local bands appeared in "live" lip synch. The show originated from the WLS studio located at the top floor of the Chicago Board of Trade and aired on a UHF channel on Saturdays at 11 a.m. National appearances by the bands followed on *The Ed Sullivan Show, The Smothers Brothers Comedy Hour, Lloyd Thaxton's Showcase '68, American Bandstand*, and *Dick Clark's Caravan of Stars.*

As the exposure broadened and their singles started receiving airplay and appearing on the charts, major label deals awaited, luring the bands away from their smaller independents. The Buckinghams went from Chicago's U.S.A. Records (1966-1967) to the major Columbia (1967-1968). Columbia also signed the Cryan' Shames following their 1966 debut on Destination. The Ides of March began on their own label, Epitome, then went to Parrot (1966), which also had the Zombies on its roster, and eventually recorded two albums each for Warner Bros (1970-1971) and RCA (1972-1973). In between two successful singles on Sentar, and their final two singles on Sunlight, the New Colony Six recorded on Mercury, which also had the Mauds on their roster. The Shadows of Knight were on the Atlantic group's Chicago-based Dunwich label, while the American Breed was on Acta, a subsidiary of Dot Records

Despite the major label support, swift ascension and consistent presence on the charts, critical favor, and recognition beyond the region, the Chicago bands were seldom booked at big arenas or stadiums, other than as opening acts. Most of their live performances were along the smaller venue circuit, which, during the era, meant suburban teen clubs such as the Cellar and Wild Goose, dances and sock hops at high school gymnasiums, civic auditoriums, and church and community youth centers.

In One Ear and Gone Tomorrow

Consistent with the short term togetherness of bands during the era, the "Suburbs Seven" began to splinter by late 1968. The title of the Buckinghams' album, *In One Ear and Gone Tomorrow* (1968), foreshadowed the collective fade out. One year later, five of the seven groups had disbanded. Only the New Colony Six and Ides of March remained intact and continued to record into the early 1970s. In 1971, the Ides of March "L.A. Goodbye" became the 38th single from the Suburbs Seven to place on the charts. As the last band standing, the Ides of March's subsequent albums—*World Woven* (1972) and *Midnight Oil* (1973)—did not yield any singles. The Chicago Suburbs Seven chart run came to an end. The sentimental "L.A. Goodbye" stood as the final 45, a fitting farewell to punctuate the prolific pop/rock pocket.

Disintegrating harmony as a by-product of success was a familiar rock myth narrative. Record label meddling, commercial conflicts and creative differences, pressures of fame, line up changes that undermined the original sound, drugs, college, and the military draft were among the factors cultivating fragmentation among the Chicago Suburbs Seven.

In the immediate aftermath, many band members relocated to different groups and continued their musical careers. After being dropped by Dunwich, Jim Sohns and remaining members of the Shadows of Knight signed with Team Records which was part of the Jerry Kasentz and Jeff Katz "bubblegum empire" at Buddah Records. The band hovered in the shadows, contributing anonymously to hit songs "Quick Joey Small," "Yummy, Yummy, Yummy (I've Got Love in my Tummy")," and "Chewy Chewy" by Buddah bands the Ohio Express and 1910 Fruitgum Company. Earlier, other members relocated to the groups H.P. Lovecraft and Bangor Flying Circus. American Breeders' Kevin Murphy and Andre Fischer went on to form Rufus with Chaka Khan. Fischer eventually married singer Natalie Cole. Buckinghams' Carl Giammarese and Dennis Tufano formed a duo and recorded two well-reviewed albums for the Ode label during the 1970s. Perhaps the most notable career continuity belongs to Ides of March founder Jim Peterik. Following a few solo records, Peterik formed the band Survivor and co-wrote the jock rock hit "Eye of the Tiger," which became a *Rocky* soundtrack anthem. Peterik also co-wrote several of .38 Special's late 1970s, early 1980s hits, including "Hold on Loosely" and "Caught Up in You."

The individual body of works of many of the "Suburbs Seven" have been compiled by archival labels Rhino, Sundazed, Columbia Legacy, and Varese Sarabande, with many of the group's earliest recordings reissued and released in remastered packages

The resonance from the rich regional rotation of the "Suburbs Seven" remains a B-side, an undercurrent in the swell of the prolific playlist of the 1960s hit singles soundscape. Their songs are somewhat sparse in radio's retro rotations of Classic Rock and Oldies. The Buckinghams' hits, which may carry the highest degree of national notoriety beyond the suburbs, are among the most routinely played. Perhaps the most enduring song, not to mention horn hook, from the area and era is the Ides of March's "Vehicle." The song has been frequently covered in Fox's television karaoke spectacles, from *American Idol* to *America's Next Great Band. Idol* finalist Bo Bice performed "Vehicle" three times during the competition, and recorded the song as a B-side (though billed a "double A-side") to his 2005 single "Inside Your Heaven." "Vehicle" has also been a popular soundtrack choice for car commercials despite its lurking lead lyric about the "friendly stranger in the black sedan." The American Breed's Outsider take "Bend Me Shape Me" has also been adapted in an advertising campaign for the pharmaceutical product Flexon.

In 2001, "Gloria," without distinguishing between the Shadows of Knight or Van Morrison and Them versions, placed at number 81 in VH-1 music network's list of "Best Rock Songs."

The 1960s Chicago bands, with varying degrees of original representation, occasionally re-assemble for regional reunion concerts, benefits, festivals, mini-bookings in the casino and cruise circuit, and retro events with high baby boomer appeal, among them the "Solid Gold Sixties Tour" and 1985's highly successful "The Happy Together Tour," which traveled to 125 cities and featured a lineup of popular 1960s bands.

The productivity and distinctive chart presence of the Chicago's Suburbs Seven in the five year span between 1966 and 1971 represents a pop rock pocket that may be more a moment than a musical movement. The magnitude is not an overtone that approaches the level of other locales such as those of the fertile West Coast canyons, Topanga and Laurel, on the Los Angeles outskirts; sounds such as Seattle grunge, San Francisco psychedelia, or Athens alternative; or regional rotations of major metropolitan music scenes such as Memphis, Minneapolis, Nashville, Philadelphia, Detroit, Boston or Austin. Even within the Windy City vicinity, their accomplishments and identity were eclipsed, particularly on a national scale, by their long-playing resident contemporaries Chicago, playfully proclaimed as "the band so great they named a city after it."

The Buckinghams, Cryan' Shames, Ides of March, New Colony Six, American Breed, Shadows of Knight, and Mauds were an irrefutable defining component of the 1960s Chicago suburban scene and its "rock revolution." Collectively, they lived up to the 1967 *Billboard* ad for the Cryan' Shames' single, "Mr. Unreliable," that declared "How the Midwest Was Won." These bands were larger than local, yet smaller than sensations nationally, despite a comparable number of hits to many of the artists and groups they shared the charts with. There may have been no groundbreaking genre, singular sound or uniform stylistic identity that emerged in the catalog of music they produced. Yet, it is the concentration of singles and closeness in proximity that counts as context and makes the case for this unique Chicago cluster. The collective body of works and convergence of the "Suburbs Seven" represents a distinctive regional rotation that remains a meaningful marker of an era and an area of Chicago and the city's rich musical legacy.

Discography

The following discography chronicles the national singles and albums of the Chicago Suburb Seven between 1966 and 1973. (Total for each year is in parenthesis.) Among notable points are the concentration of charting singles (30) between 1966 and 1968; the solid longevity for many of the singles; the productivity of the Buckinghams in 1967; the groups' various record label transitions; the Cryan' Shames' moderate chart placement; and the four year gap between singles and labels for the Ides of March, from 1966 to 1970.

Singles

Song (Label)	Peak position	Weeks on charts
1966 (10)		
Buckinghams		
"Kind of A Drag" (U.S.A.)	1	13
Cryan' Shames		
"Sugar and Spice" (Destination)	49	9
"I Wanna Met You"/"We Could Be Happy"	85	4
(Columbia)		
Ides of March		
"You Wouldn't Listen" (Parrot)	42	7
"Roller Coaster" (Parrot)	92	1
New Colony Six		
"I Confess"/"Treat Her Groovy" (Sentar)	80	4
Shadows of Knight		
"Gloria" (Dunwich)	10	12
"Oh Yeah" (Dunwich)	39	6
"Bad Little Woman" (Dunwich)	91	2
"I'm Gonna' Make You Mine" (Dunwich)	90	1
1967 (9)		
American Breed		
"Step Out of Your Mind" (Acta)	24	9
"Bend Me/Shape Me" (Acta)	5	14
Buckinghams		
"Lawdy Miss Clawdy" (U.S.A.)	41	6
"Don't You Care" (Columbia)	6	14
"Mercy, Mercy, Mercy" (Columbia)	5	12
"Hey Baby (They're Playing Our Song)" (Columbia)	12	10
"Susan" (Columbia)	11	12
Cryan' Shames		
"It Could Be We're in Love" (Columbia)	85	8
New Colony Six		
"Love You So Much" (Sentar)	61	6
1968 (11)		
American Breed		
"Green Light" (Acta)	39	7
"Ready, Willing and Able" (Acta)	84	3
"Anyway That You Want Me" (Acta)	88	4
Buckinghams		
"Back in Love Again" (Columbia)	57	6

Cryan' Shames
"Up on the Roof" (Columbia)   85   3
"Young Birds Fly" (Columbia)   99   2
Mauds
"Soul Drippin'" (Mercury)   85
New Colony Six
"I Will Always Think About You" (Mercury)   22   13
"Can't You See Me Cry" (Mercury)   52   8
"Things I'd Like to Say" (Mercury)   16   16
Shadows of Knight
"Shake" (Team)   46   8

1969 (2)
New Colony Six
"I Could Never Lie to You" (Mercury)   50   8
"I Want You to Know" (Mercury)   65   6

1970 (3)
Ides of March
"Vehicle" (Warner Bros)   2   12
"Superman" (Warner Bros)   64   5
New Colony Six
"Barbara I Love You"/"You're Gonna Be Mine"   78   5
(Mercury)

1971 (3)
Ides of March
"L.A. Goodbye" (Warner Bros)   73   9
New Colony Six
"Roll On"/ "You're Gonna Be Mine" (Sunlight)   56   9
"Long Time to be Alone"/ "Cadillac" (Sunlight)   93   4

Albums

American Breed
American Breed (Acta/Dot, 1967)
No Way to Treat A Lady (Acta/Dot, 1968)
Lonely Side of the Street (Atlantic, 1968)
Bend Me, Shape Me (Acta, 1968)
Pumkin, Powder, Scarlet and Green (Atlantic, 1968)
Buckinghams
Kind of a Drag (U.S.A., 1966)
Time and Changes (Columbia, 1967)

34   *B-SIDES, UNDERCURRENTS AND OVERTONES*

Portraits (Columbia, 1968)
In One Ear and Gone Tomorrow (Columbia, 1968)
Greatest Hits (Columbia, 1969)
Cryan' Shames
Sugar and Spice (Destination/Columbia, 1966)
A Scratch in the Sky (Columbia, 1967)
Synthesis (Columbia, 1969)
Ides of March
Vehicle (Warner Bros, 1970)
Common Bond (Warner Bros, 1971)
World Woven (RCA, 1972)
Midnight Oil (RCA, 1973)
Mauds
Hold On (Mercury, 1967)
New Colony Six
Breakthrough (Sentar, 1966)
Colonization (Sentar, 1967)
Revelations (Mercury/Sentar, 1968)
Attacking A Straw Man (Mercury/Sentar, 1969)
Shadows of Knight
Gloria (Dunwich, 1966)
Back Door Men (Dunwich, 1967)
Shadows of Knight (Super K, 1969)

Chapter 3

Covering Outside the Lines:
Hans Fenger and the Langley Schools
Music Project

Scram Magazine: …hearing the kids sing "we are your friends" is very spooky.
Hans Fenger: It is. Because they are aliens…You know, kids are natural outsiders.

(Applestein 2002: 30)

In the film comedy, *School of Rock* (2003), struggling rock musician Dewey Finn (Jack Black) poses as a substitute teacher at an uptight prep school. As a self serving saboteur, the exuberant fraud Finn substitutes rock music lessons for the academy's traditional core curriculum. His ultimate aim is to groom his impressionable young recruits for a battle of the bands competition. In a scene from *In America* (2002), Christy (Sarah Bolger), the young daughter of an Irish illegal immigrant family in New York City, delivers a rendition of the Eagles "Desperado" at a school recital. And in the HBO surreal surfer series, *John From Cincinnati* (2007), Joe Strummer and the Mescalinos' "Johnny Appleseed" opening theme announces the arrival of a mysterious prophet dude washing strange and soulful wisdom onto the shores of a dysfunctional beach community "in their hour of need." Whether accidental or intentional, the prevalent innocence, iconoclasm, and "outsider" characterizations and themes in this trio of narratives provide a metaphorical glimpse and echo of Hans Fenger and his peripheral musical project involving four schools in the Langley district in rural Western Canada during the mid-1970s.

The Pied Piper of Langley

As much as Hans Fenger is a kindred spirit with the fictional Finn and John from Cinncinnati—a passionate outsider possessing unconventional methods—he was at once a pied piper[1] and Johnny Appleseed sewing seeds of song—organic, off beat and off key—in a choir rows of school children in a gymnasium near Vancouver, British Columbia. In the early 1970s, Fenger, a 24-year-old itinerant musician, was drawn to teaching out of necessity. Fenger was looking for steady

---

1   Outsider musicologist Irwin Chusid uses the term to characterize Fenger in the liner notes of the Langley School recording *Innocence and Despair* (2001: 3) which Chusid produced.

income beyond teaching guitar in a music shop and playing bars with a band at night. Stability became a priority following the birth of his son. Fenger, who already had a B.A. degree, enrolled at Simon Fraser University to earn his teaching certification. Following the one year program and teacher training, Fenger was hired to teach music and language arts in the Langley school district in British Columbia in 1974.

Fenger characterized Langley as "a single culture place, a sort of Canadian Bible Belt" (Fenger: 2001: 4). The rural region, located 45 kilometers southeast of Vancouver, was a conservative community consisting of many isolated family farms. In the mid 1970s, the region was experiencing a sudden burst of growth, with many areas being developed and subdivided. School was the center of social life for most children. Their music exposure and experience was limited to radio until Fenger arrived.

The school administrators were traditionalists whose outlook was as conservative as the locality. Fenger's progressive approach was a sharp contrast to the norm. "It was the mid-1970s; everything was kind of touchy-feely, and I was coming from Lou Reed, a different space," said Fenger (Applestein 2002: 28). His most enthusiastic support came from a rather unlikely source, Pat Bickerton, a 60-year old head teacher. According to Fenger, Bickerton was "different, a man of urban tastes" who loved Miles Davis and John Coltrane. Despite the contrast between Bickerton's sophistication and Fenger's guitar-strumming casual presence, the elder colleague was encouraging, as he recognized the music Fenger taught "had a feeling that was different from other programs" (Fenger: 3).

In 1975, Fenger was assigned to teach just music at three schools in the Langley district, grades 4 through 7, with children ages 9-12. The Lochiel School was a small, rustic facility of 50 children; South Carvolth elementary was a 4-room schoolhouse located out in the country where horseback was a primary means of travel; and the largest was Glenwood School. Fenger was eventually assigned to a fourth school, Wix-Brown.

Fenger's approach to teaching music was more subtly subversive than Finn's over the top method in *School of Rock.* "I always liked the homemade approach to music—the idea that anybody can do this," said Fenger. "Musicality and music ability are two different things" (Applestein: 27). Because Fenger had no experience teaching music and relied largely on his instincts, he naturally formed the kids into a band. Fenger did not employ professional techniques or music theory, but emphasized "music feel:"

> Of course I had no idea what I was doing. I knew virtually nothing about conventional music education, and I didn't know how to teach singing. Above all, I knew nothing of what children's music was supposed to be.
>
> But the kids had a better grasp of what they liked—emotion, drama and making music as a group. Whether the results were good, bad, in tune or out was no big deal—they had élan. This was not the way music was traditionally taught, but I never liked conventional "children's music" which is condescending and ignores the reality

of children's lives, which can be dark and scary. These children hated "cute." They cherished songs that evoked loneliness and sadness. (Fenger: 7)

Fenger's unusual method encouraged the children to sing and play songs they liked and which reflected their emotions, interests, environment and experiences.

Kids have absolutely no power. They're malleable, and people do that with them all the time. They're small, they're not really articulate, they have to behave in obnoxious ways to get all they want...they really have nothing. I think what I'd been doing with them gave them a voice, a way of expressing that. This was purely fortunate; it wasn't as if I'd been thinking of that. (Applestein: 30)

According to Sheila Behman, one of Langley's soloists, "the majority of us in the '70s came from troubled families," and the music "was to express our torments" (*Weekend Edition Saturday* 2001). "What was going through me was coming out through the music" (Applestein: 31).

Fenger's meticulous choice of songs was rooted in his instincts that "these children liked to sing songs that gave them the feeling of heaviness." (Applestein: 27; Cosh 2001) His primary source was the rich 1960s and 1970s pop playlist, including songs by the Beatles, David Bowie, the Beach Boys, Eagles, Fleetwood Mac, Neil Diamond and others. The students' familiarity with the music and songs enabled them to sing and play spontaneously. Fenger's instruction began with "Bad Bad Leroy Brown" but quickly gravitated to more serious subject matter:

And I tried to find material that was a little bit more philosophical in nature rather than the standard children's songs, which tended to be more descriptive or tended to be about, you know, animals or peace in the world that sort of thing. And I was more interested in children singing songs that were more introspective and more philosophical. (*Weekend Edition Saturday*)

Brian Wilson's reflective "In My Room" was emblematic of the emotive approach. Fenger considered the song "the ultimate children's song," perfectly introspective for a nine-year-old. "There's nothing esoteric about the concept of being in your room and being alone, feeling safe and secure there, and I think that children just naturally sort of understood that," said Fenger (*Weekend Edition Saturday*). "Children are people with the same emotions as the rest of us. They know nothing of the way adults feel love, fear, loneliness and loss, but an eight-year-old whose parents are divorced knows loneliness. An eight-year-old who's alone in a room with someone picking on them knows fear" (Price 2002).

Even songs with traditional children subject matter emanated with emotional resonance. Fenger's students related to Michael Murphy's mystical "Wildfire," a tragic pony tale about death and a horse lost in a blizzard. Horse farms and hitching posts were a prevalent part of the Langley landscape, and it was not uncommon for many children to ride horseback to their schools.

Wilson's Beach Boy compositions—"Good Vibrations," "God Only Knows," "In My Room," "I Get Around," "Help Me Rhonda," "You're So Good to Me," and "Little Deuce Coupe"—comprised one-third of the songs Fenger taught his school children.[2] He playfully and reverently tapped into the children song sensibility that Wilson had ingeniously embedded into the classic surf sound. The songs were effective in demonstrating basic music lessons beyond feeling. "God Only Knows" embodied classic construction and elements of Bach. Fenger used "Good Vibrations" to praise the inventiveness of the theremin and strange sounds, and "Help Me Rhonda" and "I Get Around" to teach harmony, bass guitar riffs, repetition and rounds. Repeating "Help Me Rhonda" 47 times replaced "Row, Row Row Your Boat" in Fenger's music class. Similarly, Fenger presented Paul McCartney's Wings hits "Band on the Run and "Venus and Mars" as classical music forms, and David Bowie's "Space Oddity" as opera. "Everything, in my mind, had an extremely valid reason," said Fenger (Applestein: 27)

Fenger's mindfulness of the conservative community and child sensibilities shaped some of his song selections and how they were presented and interpreted. In addition to "Space Oddity," he wanted to use Elton John's "Rocket Man," another popular outer space song from the *Close Encounters of the Third Kind* era. However, Fenger chose not to because "hell" is in the lyrics. He also cut out the second verse of "I Get Around" about "never messing with the girls we meet."

Fenger often taught laterally rather than literally. Rather than treat Barry Manilow's "Mandy" as an overt love song, he emphasized the melody and told the children to imagine that it was about a pet. Fenger presented Carole King's composition, "I'm into Something Good," as a kindred spirit to her "The Loco-Motion," with the "woo-woo-woo's" a delightful diversion. "I thought it was important that they understand what they were singing about, which usually had to come from experience," said Fenger. "Strangely enough, I thought the kids could relate to lost astronauts, but I didn't think they could relate to "messing" with girls. The weirder the song, the better they could relate" (Applestein: 28).

Because of the children's limited frame of reference, there was an inherent purity in their interpretations that transcended the originals. They delivered versions without artifice, experience or mannerism. Qualities of authenticity were particularly evident in solos by Joy Jackson ("The Long and Winding Road") and Sheila Behman's "Desperado." Fenger discusses the performances:

> Joy sang it in a way that even Paul McCartney couldn't. When we hear the original, we think of the Beatles at the time, it's so sad they were breaking up. With Joy we hear the song in a purer way. And the same with Sheila. She knew none of the literary references, films like *Shane*, the lone cowboy riding into the sunset (Price 2002). You can see it as a cowboy romantic story but that's not the way Sheila heard it. She couldn't

---

2   In addition to these seven songs that were recorded, "Do You Wanna Dance?" was part of Fenger's Beach Boy lesson plan.

articulate it metaphorically what the song was about…It's not as if the kids were trying to be somebody else. They were just trying to be who they were." (Applestein: 27)[3]

Fenger was inspired "not by people who broke rules but by those who never realized there were rules." Among his favorite composers and arrangers were Wilson, Sun Ra, and Phil Spector, "people who just did music that was in their head." Fenger drew extensively from Spector's "little symphonies for the kids" Wagnerian approach to rock and roll and the orchestral, layered arrangements of Wilson's *Pet Sounds* and his "teenage symphony to God" in *Smile*. He considered Wilson the "ultimate outsider musician in many ways" (Applestein: 27)

A more inconspicuous musical muse for Fenger outside the pop realm was the German composer and children's music theorist Carl Orff. The "Orff Approach" was a significant component adapted into Fenger's teaching technique, particularly the simple instrumentation and adventurous arrangements. Fenger discovered Orff's developmental approach to Music Education during his teacher training. Orff was a major proponent of alternative music instruction education for children, a method that treats music as a basic system similar language. Within this framework, rudimentary activities and primal behaviors of children such as clapping, chanting, dancing, rhyming, banging a beat—or "body music"—can be more effective educational building blocks than formal music training and emphasis on technical proficiency. Once children learn to appreciate fundamental music making, rhythmic activities and games, they were more responsive to learning to read and write notation (www.keyofz.com).

In 1924, Orff and Dorothee Gunter founded the Gunterschule in Munich, where dance, music and gymnastics were the core curriculum. Orff and Gunild Keetman further developed the philosophy into a more formal doctrine recognized as the "Schulwerk" (translated means "school work"). The approach focuses on creative and educational activity through language, speech, music and movement, and encourages listening, cooperation, improvisation and an awareness of the ensemble sound.

An important dimension of the "Schulwerk" was an "instrumentarium" which fostered an expressive environment of rhythm and melody for children. Orff considered the percussive rhythm as a natural and essential form of human expression. Orff incorporated exotic Indonesian gamelan orchestra and early African percussion with diatonic and chromatic xylophones, glockenspiels and metallophones. These were complemented by an array of rhythmic noisemakers and devices including bells, drums, claves, resonator bars, jingle rings, temple blocks and shakers. The aim was to generate music with simple, yet forceful variations on rhythmic patterns. The simple-to-play Orff instruments are designed to make the music learning experience fun and exploratory, and help develop motor

---

3   Critic Robert Christgau's critical view of the "Desperado" version is just the opposite, writing that "a ten-year-old who doesn't seem to have any idea what the song means, which is to her credit as a human being but not as a singer."

skills. Children have to concentrate on repeated pulses and melodic patterns, and at the same time are encouraged to improvise (www.keyofz). "The beauty of his instruments is that you can remove notes that don't fit harmonically in a piece, so it's impossible to hit a 'wrong' note," said Fenger. (Fenger: 10)

Improvisation and feeling the song dynamic were priorities in Fenger's "organic" Orff approach. Singing out of key and hitting correct notes did not matter. Fenger taught "head arrangements" that were not on paper, but only explained orally and by example. Many sounds were spontaneous and accidental. During "Space Oddity," a student took out a Coke bottle from his lunch and intuitively ran it up and down the fretboard of a steel guitar to create the sound of a rocket taking off following countdown. Fenger further distorted the sound effect by manipulating the volume controls (Applestein: 29).

Fenger organized pep rally sized sing-alongs and concerts in the Glenwood gymnasium that were small scale, contemporary pop variations loosely modeled after the Gunterschule.[4] The Langley instrumentarium reflected Schulwerk's profound simplicity. In addition to Orff instruments—wooden xylophones and metallophones[5]—which the school had purchased at Fenger's request, the choir used "whatever was available:" an electric bass, with a student plucking one open-tuned string,[6] with a Marshall amp "bigger than she was;" a stripped down drum kit, a bass drum on a pedestal, hand cymbals and percussion, tambourines, claves, and a 1940s vintage National Steel laptop electric, wired through a tremelo. Fenger accompanied the children with acoustic rhythm guitar and piano (Chusid 2001: 5).

The Langley project was not only unusual by children's music standards but in Fenger's loose application of the strict Orff techniques. "I liked the instruments, but I hated the method exactly because it was so rigid" said Fenger (Applestein: 29). Fenger modified the Orff approach from being learning-centered to performance-oriented. Rather than being used to play any songs the way Fenger did, the tuned percussion was designed to provide a "sound carpet" for vocalizing and expressive movement. The method required certain songs played in certain ways with a very specific sequence. The use of the instrumentarium to render contemporary pop music was rare. The Schulwerk almost exclusively utilized indigenous folk music, with blues or jazz improvisations occasionally attempted by upper level students.[7]

---

4 Logistics were problematic as many children had to be driven significant distances by parents.

5 The metal bars on metallophones sustain resonance longer than wood. A unique characteristic of this pitch percussion is that bars can be removed from the tonal array, thereby guiding children to hit the right notes. As Fenger observed, "even a little kid can jam."

6 Fenger said he only trusted them with one string.

7 Somewhat striking was the Orff-Schulwerk Association's total lack of support, if not denunciation of Fenger's musical method. The AOSA Executive Director wrote: "It is very evident that the [Orff] instruments were not used as they would be in the

Fenger further integrated Guntershule principles by adding gymnastics, dance and drama to the music performance during his Wix-Brown Elementary assignment in Langley. Students staged a gymnastic interpretation of "Space Oddity," with constellation slide shows, black lights, a disco ball, costumes and day-glo paint. The mini-musical also dramatized the Klaatu and Carpenters song "Calling Occupants of Interplanetary Craft" and Kansas's "Dust in the Wind."[8]

"Wall of Sound Made of Lego Bricks"[9]

In 1976, Fenger thought it would be fun to record an album of the children's pop performances. "We didn't have a studio, but we had a big empty gym. With a whole load of reverb" said Fenger (Price 2002). The motivation for recording was as pure as the project itself. There was no pretension or posturing. The goal was not to achieve fame or fortune, to compete in a contest or produce a demo to shop to a record label, to uncover a singing star or even generate support as a school fundraiser. Fenger simply thought it was a unique opportunity to expose students to the recording process. The "market" for the exclusive record was strictly local, limited to the child performers, their parents, classmates, and school faculty. Fenger collected seven dollars per record from his students and pressed an estimated 300 copies of the 12-inch vinyl LP.

Rehearsals and preparation were minimal. The only practice was at a performance in a small school concert weeks before the recording. Fenger's friend, Greg Finseth, engineered the first session at the Glenwood gymnasium, using a Revox two-track deck and two Shure microphones. They recorded nine songs, each in one take, with no live audience and no mixing. The following year, Fenger was assigned to the Wix-Brown Elementary School where he recorded a second album of twelve songs. Fenger engineered the recording, using a Teac open-reel deck. Each session involved approximately 60 students. As Fenger had hoped, the recording activity was a vital part, if not highlight, of the children's educational experience:

> They were very thrilled by the whole process. It was unusual. It was something that happened in their life that was out of the ordinary. It's like anything in school. I mean, a field trip in school is exciting because you're out of school that day. And making a

---

Orff-Schulwerk approach. AOSA has no desire to be connected with this recording...Thank you for your interest in the American Orff-Schulwerk Association" (www.keyofz.com).

8 "Dust in the Wind" and the traditional "Amazing Grace" were among songs Fenger taught but were not recorded for the Langley albums.

9 Price (2002) uses this nifty phrase to characterize the lo-fi majesty of the arrangements.

record was something that was different. It was a unique experience for them, so it was a very exciting experience. (*Weekend Edition* 2001)

They had a record, Shaun Cassidy had a record, therefore in their heads, they were just like Shaun Cassidy. Making a record put them in the same league. And I would tell them, "Of course you are. He makes a record, you make a record. What's the difference? (Applestein: 27)

Outing Outsiders

Recording the performances preserved the music class project, while pressing the music into vinyl provided imprints of Fenger's fingerprints in an artifact that would sustain over time and place. For the next 25 years, the Langley project remained a local legacy. In June 2000, the obscure recordings were flipped from their B-side periphery to the precipice of the popular sphere. The uncommon journey of the audio artifacts which began in a school gymnasium passes from a thrift store in western Canada to a New Jersey radio station and into the mainstream across the international music market.

The discovery of the Langley children's music project was initiated by Brian Linds of Victoria, British Columbia. Linds was a devoted Internet listener of the *Incorrect Music Hour* on free form radio station WFMU in New Jersey. The show, hosted by Irwin Chusid and Michele Boule, featured audio odds and ends, curiosities and found music. Linds burned a CD of various artist obscurities from his collection, inlcuding Little Marcy, Smilin' Johnny, Nashville Country Singers, Think and Superman, and sent a copy of the compilation to Chusid to consider for the radio show's idiosyncratic playlist. Among the 16 songs on Linds's mix was the Langley kids choir (credited as the Locheil and South Carvolth Schools Greenwod Region Music Group) version of Bowie's 1969 glam-rock classic, "Space Oddity." Lind culled the cut from a copy of the Langley album he had found in a local thrift store.

Chusid, his station staff and listeners, were immediately captivated by the "slightly sinister" and "charming" rendition. "I flipped over the unique, haunting arrangement and gave it immediate airing," said Chusid. "It was one of the strangest school recordings I had ever heard—and I've heard hundreds. I recognized this as more than just a cute, sloppy school band relic" (www.keyofz).

Chusid may have been the ideal recipient for Linds's song solicitation. The radio personality was a notable outsider musicologist, journalist, archivist and preservationist. Chusid had an ear and knack for salvaging overlooked gems. He authored *Songs in the Key of Z: The Curious Universe of Outsider Music* (2000), which profiles 26 artists, among them Tiny Tim, Daniel Johnston, Syd Barrett, and sister aboriginal rockers The Shaggs. Chusid also compiled and produced two companion volumes of music from the outsider artists featured in the book in 2002 on the Gammon label. Chusid's other notable "revival" missions include the space age bachelor pad music of Juan Esquivel, which sparked a 1990s retro resurgance of exotica and lounge music, and electronic music pioneer and bandleader Raymond Scott and his Orchestrette.

Chusid is credited with adapting the "outsider" term to music in a 1996 article in the Tower Records publication *Pulse!* Chusid uses "outsider" to loosely identify "crackpot and visionary music where all trails lead essentially to one place: over the edge" (www.keyofz.com). The "outsider" label was a significant part of the cultural lexicon during the mid 1980s and into the 1990s largely due to its broad application in the visual arts. Reverend Howard Finster, whose works were widely exhibited, from his Paradise Garden home in Georgia, to the Talking Heads' *Little Creatures* (1985) album cover to books, museums and galleries, was the archetypal folk figurehead of the stylistic movement which peaked in popularity during the era. "Outsider" became a catch-all phrase synonymous with "self taught," "untrained," and "primitive," and conveniently stretched to characterize much of what is considered folk art. The term predates its 1990s popularity and is rooted in the French counterpart "l'Art Brut." In the early 1970s, Roger Cardinal introduced this French view to American culture but adopted a more catchy term "Outsider Art" (1972). "Outsider" was a purist concept that covered the work of mental patients and children exclusively. The term was too appealing to remain that strict and narrow in its application. As "outsider" was expanded, its mystique grew along with its over use of synonyms and loose treatment. In the process, "outsider's" original meaning has been considerably distorted and its significance diminished (see Prince 1995).

Unlike outsider art, "outsider music" is not necessarily related to folk music. However, using "outsider music" as a catchall category for odds and ends that are naïve to the idea of 'good' music and its techniques, serves a purpose similar to its visual cousin (Hagan 2001). Chusid avoids interchangeable, synonymous use of terms and allows for only slight overlaps. He draws several distinctions between terms such as "incorrect" and "outsider" as they are used in music. Chusid employs "Incorrect music" as a radio concept referring to "musical wrongness," often expressed vocally or instrumentally by individuals who should have known better or whose sincerity was questionable. In contrast, "outsider music" is more sincere in Chusid's view. The individual artists who create the musical forms and expressions operate outside the mainstream and are often termed 'bad' or 'inept' by an audience who evaluate and judge them by standards of mainstream popular music. These musicians, often untrained and self taught, distinguish themselves by their earnestness, passion, absence of pretense, inventiveness and originality (see Chusid 2000).[10]

After listening to "Space Oddity" on Linds's homemade compilation, Chusid inquired about additional recordings by the school band. Linds responded by burning a CD of the album's entire nine-song set which included "Rhiannon,"

---

10   Chusid's web site (www.keyofz.com) features a page devoted to defining "outsider music."

"Band on the Run," Phil Spector's "To Know Him is to Love Him," and a rollicking rendition of the Bay City Rollers "Saturday Night." Chusid was convinced the sparse 30 minutes of music had to be made available commercially.

With album credits limited and the grainy, reduced Xerox barely legible, Chusid began seeking sources. After "embarking on some Internet sleuthing," he contacted the Langley school district. School officials were not familiar with the recording, nor did they recognize the name "Hans Fenger" who was listed as "music supervisor." Finally, one administrator knew the name "Pat Bickerton" to whom the record was dedicated.[11] Bickerton's son, Mike, was a teacher in the Langley district. According to Chsuid, Mike Bickerton vividly recalled the project, provided background and helped locate Fenger. Fenger left the school district in 1979 because he wanted "to go back to playing in a band" (*Weekend Edition Saturday*). He eventually returned to teaching in Vancouver.

Fenger appreciated Chusid's enthusiasm and interest in releasing the album commercially. "No one had brought up the record in decades; it was ancient history to him," said Chusid. Fenger casually mentioned the second album he had recorded at Wix-Brown, cautioning Chusid that the recording was "not as interesting" as the first because he had been trying to be more controlling with the arrangements. Fenger himself no longer had the original tapes, however his mother had clean copies of the vinyl LPs. He sent Chusid a DAT copy of the twelve song LP, which Chusid liked better than the first. The second album featured a wider range of material and arrangements, and included solo performances of "Desperado," "The Long and Winding Road," and Klaatu/The Carpenters' "Calling Occupants of Interplanetary Craft (The Recognized Anthem of World Contact Day)."

Six months after Chusid's discovery of the Langley recordings, his fascination continued. Chusid's determination to release the records commercially became an obsession. He discussed royalties, licensing and scholarship funds[12] with Fenger and the school district and approached record labels hoping to find one interested in recording and distributing the unconventional children's collection. Skepticism was common among A & R executives who routinely dismissed the albums as novelties with little repeat listen appeal. Basta Audio-Visuals in the Netherlands agreed to release the record, but Chusid was not satisfied with the company's United States distributor.[13] With Basta's cooperation, Chusid continued to search for a label to cover the North American market. The project was rejected

---

11   Bickerton was diagnosed with cancer and was no longer teaching when Fenger began the recordings. He died a short time later. Fenger dedicated the album to the memory of his supportive colleague, "a lover of all music."

12   The Langley School District agreed to serve as trustee for royalties for the recordings, applying the income towards music scholarships or purchase of instruments for music education. Langley also agreed to pay pro-rated royalties to participating students.

13   Chusid said it became apparent to him that Basta's U.S. distributor "would not fully understand the nature of the release." He had Basta's cooperation with a U.S. label search (see www.keyofz.com).

by ten domestic labels, among them Artemis, Luaka Bop, Nonesuch, Rhino, and Astralwerks. Matador expressed interest but could not fit the release into its short-term schedule. Frustrated, but persistent, Chusid turned to a hometown Hoboken, New Jersey friend at Bar None Records, Glenn Morrow, who he had worked with in the mid-1990s on two Esquivel packages. The label happened to be looking for a Fall release for its 2001 schedule and agreed to be the Dutch label's North American distributor for the record.

Innocence and Despair

The two albums were compiled into one collection of 19 songs entitled *Innocence and Despair* under the composite credit The Langley Schools Music Project. The original albums did not have titles, only the names of the four participating schools as identification. The title phrase derived from Fenger's characterization of nine-year-old Sheila Behman's vocal solo of "Desperado," which emerged as the album's single. The title signified the pervasive premise of the project that was not only present in the song selection, but magnified in the liner notes. The centerpiece of the CD's booklet featured "Innocence..." on one page, "Despair..." on the opposite side, with selected lyrics and motifs from the songs reflecting each theme. On "Innocence," there is "the blossom world" ("Good Vibrations"), spring becoming summer ("Sweet Caroline"), holding hands ("I'm into Something Good") and "dancing to the rock and roll" on "Saturday Night," hope of contact and friendship ("Calling Occupants of Interplanetary Craft"), understanding ("You're So Good to Me") and Silly Willie and the Philly Band ("Venus and Mars/Rock Show"). There is "Despair" in being "stuck inside these four walls" ("Band on the Run"), floating wayward in a tin can in space ("Space Oddity"), "crying in the night" ("Mandy"), dying in winter in a chilling frost ("Wildfire"), shattered plans ("Help Me Rhonda"), a "prisoner walkin' through this world all alone" ("Desperado"), and wondering if "you will ever win" ("Rhiannon"). Lyrics from "In My Room" and "The Long and Winding Road" appear on both pages. The 16-page package also includes an essay by Chusid, reminisces by Fenger and photo collages of the children performing during the music classes and recording sessions.

The song order of the original albums was resequenced for the CD version. Seven songs from the Lochiel, South Carvolth and Glenwood schools in 1976 were shuffled with 12 from the Wix-Brown session in 1977. The import edition on the Dutch Basta label includes two additional tracks, the Beach Boys "Little Deuce Coupe," and "You're Sixteen," the Sherman brothers tune popularized by Johnny Burnette in 1960 and later by Ringo Starr. Some audio restoration was required, as the album was mastered from vinyl LPs since the original tapes were unavailable. However, there was no studio enhancing of the majestic lo-fi "outsider" sound. The recording captured a minimalist convergence of garage and Gregorian chant, with splendid eruptions, wobbling rhythms, off beat banging percussion, exuberant shouts and off key melodies and melancholy, and the "ineffable sound of wistfulness"[14] wrapped in 1960s and 1970s pop songs echoing in the odd acoustics of the cavernous gymnasium setting; the "Wall of Sound made of Lego bricks" (Price 2002).

Innocence and Despair was released 23 October 2001. The collection surpassed a "children's music" brand and was a natural fit in a music market that had been steadily proliferating with a vast array of cover compilations and tribute records since the early 1990s. Benefits, genres, regions, parodies, soundtracks, record labels, individual songs and albums, artists, bands and composers were among the many bases for individual and multi-artist cover and tribute albums. The Langley project's novel nature and narrative was a curiosity among the boundless variations of the saturated subgenre. Coverage was widespread, with positive critical and commercial responses to the record. Reviews and interviews spanned the rock press such as *Rolling Stone* and *Spin* to major metropolitan newspapers in New York, Washington D.C., Seattle, and Philadelphia, to trade and popular press sources such as *Entertainment Weekly*, and media outlets including National Public Radio. "Haunting," "heartbreaking," "charming," "wistful" and "otherworldiness" were among common critical characterizations of the record, with "kitsch" and "campy" convenient tags as well. In *Scram*, the Canadian 'zine of "unpopular culture," Mike Applestein may have provided some of the more imaginative observations. He suggested the record conjured images of "Shaggs and Danielson presiding over an elementary school assembly," and that the spooky "we are your friends" chanting of "Calling Occupants of Interplanetary Craft" "sounds like a delegation of extraterrestrial children sent to Earth on a goodwill mission" (26). Venerated *Village Voice* critic Robert Christgau was among the few who were unimpressed. Reviewing the record as his "Dud of the Month," he recognized Fenger for being "a gifted teacher on a mission," but labeled Chusid "a tedious ideologue with a hustle." "Turning that vinyl into a collectible CD is the latest way for him to remind the converted that artistic intention is reserved for the beholder in these postmodern times—especially if the beholder has a hustle." Christgau's grade for the record was a "C-minus." He wrote that "a few of the songs were great, a few sucked, and every one more innocent and/or desperate than its original;" "Desperado" was a "special annoyance," and Brian Wilson "the sole revelation whose six songs still sound like themselves" (see www.keyofz.com). A few of the artists whose songs were covered by the children's choir complimented the innocent interpretations. Among them was David Bowie commenting on "Space Oddity": "The backing arrangement is astounding. Coupled with the earnest if lubrigous vocal performance you have a piece of art that I couldn't have conceived of, even with half of Columbia's finest export products in me."[15]

---

14   The phrase was used by National Public Radio's *Weekend Edition* host Scott Simon to characterize the record during his interview with Hans Fenger, 27 October 2001.

15   A representative sampling of "Press Quotes," general quotes, letters to Hans Fenger from students, and a letter from Fenger to students are among the Langley lists and resources available at Irwin Chusid's www.keyofz.com.

COVERING OUTSIDE THE LINES

Sales of the record eventually approached 100,000 units, split between 50,000 copies sold in the U.S. and the other half from distribution in the U.K., Canada, France and Japan. The extensive coverage culminated with a 25-year Langley children's music class and choir alumni reunion special produced and aired on VH-1 cable music network in 2002.[16]

Lost and Found

> I didn't look for this, it found me.
>
> Hans Fenger (Applestein: 27)

The Langley Schools music classes' record release and reunion generated ripples of reference and replication internationally. The VH-1 commemoration was instantly enshrined in a three part series in the You Tube video archive on the Internet. In 2002, the school choir of St. Jude's Primary School in London's Herne Hill recreated the Langley Project. When David Bowie was invited to be the guest curator of the 2002 Meltdown festival in London, he commissioned Laka D to arrange and conduct "Langley Schools Revisited" (Price 2002).

In film, Sarah Bolger's innocent immigrant recital rendition of "Desperado" in *In America* (2002) is more a vision of homage to Sheila Behman's Glenwood gymnasium rendition than it is a cover of the Don Henley/Glenn Frey Eagles' original. When *School of Rock* was released in 2003, there were scattered allusions of inspiration attributed to Fenger and the Langley schools, though the film's director, Richard Linklater, and its star, Jack Black, never confirmed the connection or primary influence. Aware of the association, Fenger said, "The difference between this and *School of Rock* is that I didn't teach kids rock and roll riffs. I didn't teach them Deep Purple songs; I didn't put them in rock and roll bands" (Buium 2008).

Despite the belated, widespread music appreciation and scattered references, the Langley School's Music Project's lasting legacy may be limited to a momentary mark more than a redefining touchstone of popular culture, music education or the arts empowering children.[17] Fenger has consistently downplayed his teaching

---

16 The VH-1 reunion was an upbeat, sentimental gathering that reflecting a similar range of warmth and emotion as in the student letters to Fenger and his written response as listed in keyofZ.com. website. Prior to the event, many of the interviews with Fenger and his students in print and other media outlets such public radio revealed an undercurrent of discomfort with the attention. Fenger routinely referred to the project as "bittersweet." Soloist Sheila Behman was notably uncomfortable on the NPR *Weekend Edition.*

17 Greg Buim's CBC News article, "Kid Stuff: Art projects empower children and make adults think" (4 February 2008) explores connections between children's art projects, juxtaposing music (*The Langley Schools Music Project*), performance (*Haircuts*

legacy as an "Orff pop" experimentalist, crediting metaphysical forces and synchronicity for the unintended, but fortuitous end result.

Without suggesting a "one of a kind" quality to his Langley music explorations, Fenger expressed doubt that such an album could happen in current cultural conditions. While he observed that kids in music classes still respond to "Help Me Rhonda" the same way, the technology and marketplace, cluttered with karaoke machines, MP3 players, downloading and distractions, is a vastly different world. In addition, he laments changes in attitudes toward the value of music education that have occurred during the 25 years since his Langley teaching experience. "I'm not optimistic. There's a lot of lip service paid, but in actual practicality, computer labs put hundreds of thousands of dollars into schools, and the music teacher teaches with three broken guitars. I'm not happy about it, and I have a feeling I'm a bit of a dinosaur. I don't think it's going to get better" (Applestein 2002: 30).

Fenger's concerns have been affirmed in the United States during the "No Child Left Behind" era's increased emphasis on math, reading and a teaching-for-testing approach. In the process, the arts have been widely devalued. According to the non-profit center for Education Policy, an estimated 16% of schools have cut back on art and music programs since 2003.[18]

Perhaps the most enduring aspect of the Langley Schools Music Project is its path of peculiarity. Langley's "outsider" narrative, featuring a folk hero figure in Fenger and a merry band of followers, is standard B-side process. The arc demonstrates passage from the peripheral to the popular, an undercurrent becoming overtone, and returning to settle into the margins. The music class's anonymous gymnasium renditions were never intended to be heard beyond the school district and the borders of the Langley provincial region. Fenger's decision to record the performances was an auspicious act of preservation that provided a souvenir set of songs for his students and their families. However, the audio artifact permitted the possibility of discovery and diffusion. In typical B-side progression, a curious disc jockey flips the thrift store relic into revelation. In a serendipitous sequence twenty five years after its conception, Irwin Chusid uncovered the conspicuous collection of cover songs. The subsequent commercial compilation in 2001 distinguished

---

by Children) and painting (My Kid Could Paint That), the 2007 documentary on 4-year-old "artist" Marla Olmstead).

18   There have been significant efforts to slow the art erosion. In 2007, E Street Band guitarist, Underground Garage host and Soprano cast member Little Steven Van Zandt initiated "Rock and Roll High School" within his non-profit Rock and Roll Forever Foundation. The project echoes VH-1's Save the Music Foundation, which was established in 1997 and designed to restore instrumental music education and awareness in public schools. Van Zandt's program, a cooperative with publisher Scholastic InSchool Division, aims to introduce a new generation of teenagers to rock and roll music and culture. The partnership will distribute a 40-chapter curriculum that includes teachers' guides, lesson plans, media and Web-based resources, DVDs and CDs at no cost to middle and high schools. The program, endorsed by the National Association for Music Education, is scheduled for implementation during the 2008-2009 academic year.

itself among the glut of cover and tribute recordings of the era. Rather than being dismissed as a one hit wonder or novelty album, *Innocence and Despair: The Langley Schools Music Project* remains a worthwhile rarity, a B-side musical memento of a choir of natural outsiders, lost and found, during a few afternoons in a gymnasium in Canada during the mid-1970s.

Chapter 4
Geffen Records v. Neil Young:
The Battle of the Brands

But if you want to sing your own song / You're gonna have to lose a few.

Mose Allison "If You Only Knew"
©1969 Audre Mae Music BMI

Success is simultaneously desired and feared. On the one hand it promises the means to survive and go on working, on the other it threatens corruption. The most frequently heard criticism is that, since his success, X is repeating himself, is merely picturemaking. But the problem is often seen too narrowly as one of personal integrity, it is suggested, one should be able to steer an honest course between success and corruption. A few extremists react so violently that they actually believe in failure. Yet failure is always a waste. The importance of Picasso's example is that it shows us how this fundamental problem of our epoch is an historical and not a moral one.

(Berger 1965:204)

During his 1979 "Rust Never Sleeps" Tour, Neil Young could be seen (in Rust-O-Vision) on stage dwarfed by oversized amplifiers, instruments and stage props, a visual statement by Young that the music was getting so huge, performers could feel like little kids. Nearly ten years later, in July, 1988, MTV refused to air Young's music video, "This Note's For You," another Youngian state-of-the-music/commercialization comment aimed at artists who endorse products.[1] "What does the "M" in MTV stand for: music or money?" wrote an agitated Young in an open letter to MTV, calling the cable network "spineless jerks" (McDonough 2002: 619). In between, in November 1983, Young was sued by his label—Geffen Records—for producing "non-commercial records." During the 1980s, Young appeared to adapt his punk proverb from "better to burn out than to rust" to "better to burn out

---

1   Young's video parodies several television commercials and features Michael Jackson, Whitney Houston and Spuds McKenzie look-alikes, and lists Pepsi, Coca-Cola Miller and Budweiser beers among those he "ain't singin for." MTV feared advertiser backlash and claimed the clip violated their policy of mentioning products. They also refused a substitute video of Young performing "This Note's for You" on stage. The policy appeared to be inconsistent as MTV aired other videos which mentioned product lines, notably DJ Jazzy Jeff & Fresh Prince's, "Parents Just Don't Understand" which reveres Adidas, Big Macs and Porsche (see Goodman 1988: 25).

52 B-SIDES, UNDERCURRENTS AND OVERTONES

than to be branded." Young's unusual situation during the era provides a useful text for examining shifting cultural values and vision of the artist, creative control and autonomy, and the relations between artists, organizations and commercial imperatives in the popular arts. As an undercurrent, the case foreshadowed the emphasis on product "branding" and the convergence of a company trademark and artist identity.

Rock Reaganomics and the Big '80s

Rock critic Dave Marsh echoed Young's oversized stage iconography, suggesting the music industry itself may have been the biggest star the 1970s created, as the business had become more potent than any of its parts (Marsh 1980: 1). As the recording industry enjoyed unprecedented profits during the decade, artists and businessmen had to reconcile the music with the commerce it had inspired. While some took big business for granted, others, like the Punks, rejected the industry entirely. Artists were forced to look for ways to pursue their musical and aesthetic goals while remaining mindful of the surrounding commercial sprawl. Record companies, on the other hand, increasingly emphasized categorization of artists to achieve easy marketing.[2]

The industry's star, however, soon faded. Increased costs, declining sales, and an undeclared war with radio over programming and promotion, began to plague the music business by the early 1980s. A revenue decrease from $4.31 billion in 1978 to $3.52 in 1982 had a devastating impact on the artist-industry relationship. As production costs escalated increased, record companies—almost totally dependent on proven superstars—were less inclined to invest in marginally commercial acts; nor would they push hard to break new ones because of cutbacks in promotion and advertising.

The recession also reached the concert arena. Promoters reported their business down 30 percent from 1979. The youth audience—with less disposable income, and spending much of what they had at video arcades—were more selective in the concerts they attended. As a result, even superstar acts struggled to fill large arenas. Many tours were cancelled, some performers opted for the small club circuit, and tour support from record companies became scarce, particularly for medium level acts.

Standards also changed, and there were soon distortions other than those on Neil Young's stage. "Suddenly records were judged not on their artistry—or even whether they're hits—but on their chances of putting the machinery back into gear," wrote Marsh in his "State of the Music Industry" address in January, 1980.

---

2   There are several useful rock histories which document the record industry during the 1970s, among them R. Serge Denisoff's sociological inquiry *Tarnished Gold*, New Brunswick NJ: Transaction (1986) and a more popularized account, Ed Ward, Geoffrey Stokes, and Ken Tucker, *Rock of Ages*, New York: Summit (1986).

Fleetwood Mac's *Tusk* (1979), for example, sold 2 million units but was not considered a "hit" because their *Rumors* (1977) sold six times that many.

With the music itself and its finances scraping rock bottom, artists, executives, critics, and the rock audience struggled with the downward spiral. Many predicted a demise, fearing the Punks' basic premise to be true—the industry could not keep getting bigger and more complacent about its importance and its audience. Others felt the problem could be summed up in one word—marketing. By the 1980s, rock had become a marketplace dominated by entrepreneurs who were united by their focus on product units sold. Commodity ruled any sense of oddity as the vanguard concept had been traded in for good marketing strategies. "Almost nowhere, and from no one, does anyone presently feel a sense of reaching," wrote Marsh (1980: 2). As a result, record companies began to take an even more active role in record making and creative decisions. Ironically, the industry was most prosperous in the mid-1970s when there was the least creative interference by businessmen.

The critical consensus lamented the loss of community and any commitment to unconventional values in the music industry. It was a confusing, passionless time for rock and roll, with many artists lost in the shuffle. Many argued that spontaneity was missing, and the creative process had become more stylized, structured, formulaic and routinized. "In the process, it has become easier for business men and behind the scenes manipulators to structure their approach to merchandising music," wrote critic producer Jon Landau (1972: 40). Greil Marcus suggested that the goal of most bands was "to simply find the right already-marked-off plot of ground and occupy it—ideally forever." Marsh added, "In the short term, the safely marketed superstar may be more profitable than the artists who take chances, but in the long run, the audience, the artist, or both will become bored and process will disintegrate. Enter a new cycle of stars, who will play out the string, to be replaced by the next batch and the next—ideally forever (1980: 2).

MTV's arrival in 1981, coupled with megastars Prince, Michael Jackson, and Bruce Springsteen a few years later, led to an economic recovery with emphasis on media synergy and savvy. Despite the widespread optimism, some ills lingered and others were masked by the industry's revitalization. MTV's powers proved just as creatively seductive as they were economically vital. Accompanying the emerging music network was a new set of criteria for music and its creators. Songs were judged on visualization and artists signed to labels for their "video potential."[3]

While music video may have forged a valuable new aesthetic, it hardly represented a musical Renaissance. There was still little experimentation on any front as both record companies and artists—now committed to perfecting their video images—were reluctant to explore new musical directions.[4] The primary

---

3   The best source on MTV arrival and impact is R. Serge Denisoff's *Inside MTV*. New Brunswick, NJ: Transaction, 1988.

4   In the popular market, some major innovations in musical style may not have developed without MTV. New Wave (Talking Heads), New Romanticism (Duran Duran), and R & B crossover (Prince, Michael Jackson) were MTV aided phenomena.

focus remained on the safest formula and easiest marketing; any departure from the norm was likely to be deemed risky business or taken as an affront rather than a challenge.

While the industry's recovery reaffirmed the premise that "rock and roll is here to stay," another message was loud and clear—rock and roll is here to pay. Music video and superstar success might have dominated music headlines in the early 1980s, but tidbits of other cases also surfaced, quietly drawing attention to the plight of several artists and their struggles with their labels and commercial imperatives. Casualties were not limited to new acts or critical favorites with small, loyal audiences and modest record sales. Many well-known performers, such as Young, who had been recording for nearly twenty years, were also affected.

As cut-out bins slowly expanded with the catalogs of labelless artists, some larger rumblings were heard by 1984. In July, the unprecedented housecleaning by one of the industry's largest companies—Warner Brothers—magnified the seriousness of the situation. Van Morrison, Bonnie Raitt, Arlo Guthrie and T-Bone Burnett were among the 30 artists dropped from the Warner roster.[5] In all cases, the song remained the same—unit sales. "The record companies have to sell a million or two million records to even show a profit, which is death to the artist," said Burnett. "If you don't have the freedom to fail, you don't have any freedom at all" (Flanagan: 1987: 55).

Record companies were not supportive of experimentation or creative exploration. Any sense of the avant garde was discouraged because it was not saleable; call it "original sin". U2's Bono offered this view on music's industrialization and corporate state of affairs during the 1980s: "Taking chances is not high on the list of priorities. There is an environment in which music can live and breathe, and right now the environment is suffocating. When we look back at this decade, we'll have to say that in the Eighties rock and roll got up at 6:00 a.m. to go jogging. And it wasn't just to keep fit. It was to get ahead: to improve the prospects of the corporation" (Breskin 1987: 284).

Critic Jon Pareles labeled the process taking place in music, "rock Reaganomics,"

> As the richest part of the record business pulls rapidly away from the rest of it. Chart toppers, with enough capital behind them to market across the universe, blanket the media and make a humongous profit. Down below, the also-rans starve or scrape by, minus a safety net: don't look for independent labels in the Top 200 without a magnifying glass. Apparently record companies aren't willing to take many chances on unexposed music. Just as in the supply-side economy, nothing trickles down from the top. (1984:137)

---

5   See (Connelly 1984: 41) for Warner Bros President Lenny Waronker's views, and (Schruers 1984: 61-62) for Morrison's reaction.

Artistic Freedom, "Institutional Individuality" and the "Organizational Imperative"

"Art" is just a dog on my porch.

> Neil Young (Crowe 1979: 42)

"Art" is just short for "Arthur."

> Keith Richards (Flanagan 1987: 207)

The state of relations in the music industry during the 1980s illustrates facets of the enduring struggle between art and commerce as it adapted to the postmodern era. In the often contradictory union of aesthetics and business in the popular arts, the industry, on one side, values proven products that generate profits; while the aesthetic appreciates experimentation, courage, risk, and emotional involvement. Two concepts, in particular, are evident: " institutional individuality" and "the organizational imperative."

Since the influx of the mass media, the cultural vision of the artist—closely bound to romantic ideals of the independent, alienated, solitary creator—has been modified to include the individual artist absorbed into the collaborative expression of the organizational structure. Within such a context, several issues, dichotomies and recurring themes emerge with relevance to the music industry and the relationships between individual artists and their record companies, among them creative control, company involvement, autonomy, marketability, conditions for compromise, artist longevity and loyalty.

As the marketplace and distribution outlets expanded, emphasis continued to shift to commerce and conformity. Artists learned to strive along an imposed scale of career values and strategies for security or risk displacement. Perhaps the most significant source of subversion of the individual is the modern organization in which the moral burdens of autonomy are traded in for the comforts of security. In *Has Modernism Failed?* (1984), Suzi Gablik identifies the rise of a new psychological type of artist: "the bureaucratic or organizational personality who lives in a condition of submission to a cultural and economic power system" (62). Also emerging is a new value system—"the organizational imperative"—which functions on the premise that whatever is good for the individual comes from the modern organization (see Scott and Hart 1980). The suggestion is that artists need organizations—galleries, studios, networks, record companies, etc.—more than the organization needs the artist. A record company may be more likely to survive more easily and longer than the individual artists who may be forced to choose between repaying their dues, sometimes for years until they can get another contract, or repositioning themselves as a another brand in another market or role. Some established artists, such as Neil Young and Van Morrison, actively resist conformity to the organizational imperative, while the less established artist often has little choice but to compromise. The pressure to conform usually transcends the importance of trying to achieve consistency between one's beliefs and actions.

This view—that the artist cannot function without the aid of the organization—is rather incongruous in a society which constantly proclaims values of freedom and independence for the artist.

In the gradual shift in the cultural value scale, bureaucratic rules and procedures seem to have taken the place of personal morality. Gablik writes:

> The old values of individuality, indispensability, and spontaneity are replaced by new ones, based on obedience, distensibility, specialization, placing, and paternalism. The goal is security: to be a part of the big powerful machine, to be protected by it and to feel strong in the symbiotic connection to it. In the case of artists, these values are hostile to all that we know about the nature of creativity. And within the service in the new order of things, all must conform to the requirements of the modern organization—therein lies the problem. (62)

The "institutional individuality" that demands conformity can hinder the creative process and frustrate the artist, as systematic constraints are often understood as counter-creative forces. This is not to imply that the organization cannot be a valuable catalyst and support system for creativity or that the only significant individualism is that which is solitary, uncompromising, and alienated. Tension, regardless of the source, is a necessary ingredient in the livelihood of the artist. The dilemma Gablik refers to arises when creativity of the least resistance becomes the standard mode of operation, and experimentation and discovery do not receive the same emphasis as conformity and commercialism. When artistic standards are centralized and the creative process routinized, the artist's imagination is inhibited and schematized even before the process begins.

Being an artist has traditionally meant maintaining a certain independence of mind and spirit. Accepting societal or organizational emphasis on achievement and economic growth has always provoked a crisis for creators, challenging the ways in which they value art, their work, and motives for creating. The hidden pressures, although in the Geffen-Young case a lawsuit is hardly subtle, make submission the easier response than experimentation. How is it possible, then, for creators working within the popular arts organizations with its increasing emphasis centered on production, consumption, and marketability, to achieve and maintain any degree of creative control and autonomy? Is even the self-determined, independent-minded artist confined to a prescribed route?

Gablik sees the future of art dependent upon how artists themselves define and interpret their own needs, aspirations, interests and situations within their organizations. "Only perhaps, by the willingness to apply an inner brake that says "no" to the dominant claims of our times, even when everybody else says "yes." Rather than vainly attempt to abolish the system, it will mean altering the values that motivate one's striving" (71).

While being a resistor and "singing one's own song" may retain a piece of one's soul, that choice often results in paying a price or even "losing a few." It may be convenient or simplistic to criticize the postmodern mode, the system and its structures, demands, and lack of compromise; or too romantic and naïve a lament to say there are not enough courageous artists willing to challenge that system; that too many artists are resigned to punching a clock at the factory, having lost sight of the fact that they are to be engaged in something more than a commercial enterprise. In *Organizational America*, William Scott and David Hart emphasize that the culture as a whole must share the blame for allowing the organization, management, and commerce to dominate aesthetic considerations:

> We did this because we believe that the modern organization would provide us with the material affluence, physical safety, and peace of mind. We were not aware that we would have to buy a whole sack full of new values in the process. But something does not come for nothing; once the organizational imperative was set in motion, it became so powerful that we lost our sense of how to control it, let alone how to turn it off. (Gablik 71)

For any artist in the popular arts it is challenging to locate a situation that allows for an appropriate degree independence within an organizational framework. Even the most solitary creators will discover barriers to autonomy and the necessity of dependence upon other individuals as well as a structured system which imposes constraints on personal artistic vision. In short, individuality compromises its quality of freedom. Is this a grim view of culture or a grim culture to view? According to Gablik, perhaps both:

> As a society, we have become so hooked on environmental and bureaucratic artificiality that there seems little chance of escape from it. The agonies of even partial withdrawal are more than most of us dare contemplate. It must be said, however, that at this point the machine can be controlled only by people willing to change their whole value system, their whole world view, and their whole way of life. (72)

The Geffen-Young Courtship

> David Geffen missed his calling in life. He should have been a dictator in an art colony.
>
> Neil Young (McDonough: 610)

> It was starting to feel like Neil Young was on a kamikaze mission.
>
> Jimmy McDonough (2002: 593)

"Institutional individuality" and "organizational imperative" were at the core of the music industry's development and value shift during the 1980s. The concepts became even more magnified when the artist-organization relations became tangled in a litigious twist, the result of a curious lawsuit involving Geffen Records and Neil Young. In November 1983, Geffen filed a $3.3 million suit against Young, claiming that his first two records for the label—the techno *Trans* (1982) and the retro rockabilly *Everybody's Rockin* (1983)—were "non-commercial." Geffen alleged that the records were "musically uncharacteristic of Young's previous recordings." The company wanted "Neil Young records."[6] By Geffen's standards, "characteristic Neil Young" was tantamount with Young's most commercially successful, widely accessible and critically acclaimed albums from the previous decade—*Harvest* (1972), *Comes A Time* (1978) and *Rust Never Sleeps* (1979).

Dating to the Buffalo Springfield in the 1960s, Young established a characteristic acoustic-electric pattern with his record releases, alternating between folk rock and country tinged strumming, piano and harmonica, and rock and power chording with Crazy Horse. During the post-*Rust* 1980s, Young abandoned that blueprint and charted an erratic stylistic course of extreme genre deviations that included, overdubs, robotic voices, minimalist lyrics, "weird sequencing" and "synth shit" that were widely dismissed by his label, fans, critics, and even his band. "They played on the stuff but they didn't think it was music," said Young sessionist Frank "Poncho" Sampedro (McDonough: 552).

Young's artistic approach may have reflected not only his professional conflicts but personal struggles as well, particularly caring for sons Zeke and Ben who were stricken with cerebral palsy. Young began the era with *Hawks and Doves* (1980) and *Re-ac-tor* (1981), then began a downward spiral that would last through the remainder of the decade. According to longtime producer David Briggs, Young "lost control of his personal life, and everything went along with it" (McDonough: 550). After thirteen years and seventeen records, a disgruntled Young left legendary producer Mo Ostin and his Reprise label and signed with the newly formed Geffen Records.[7]

David Geffen was a captivating character who brought an intriguing personal and professional context to the Young lawsuit. Geffen was one of the most prominent non-artist figures of the Southern California music scene during the 1960s and 1970s.[8] Geffen swiftly ascended from a William Morris agent to establishing himself as one of the leading record industry entrepreneurs and eventual multi media mega mogul. He created Asylum Records in 1970, which merged with Elektra in 1972, and became a touchstone label of the thriving

---

6   Jimmy McDonough provides the most insightful, detailed account of the Geffen-Young lawsuit, their relationship and personal and professional circumstances in the Neil Young biography *Shakey* (2002: 544-618).

7   Young's financial woes worsened as he was unable to tour to promote *Re-ac-tor* due to the consuming work with his sons Zeke and Ben's pattern program for cerebral palsy. The label did not know of the extent of Young's personal situation. Young and Reprise argued over several things, including the release of a triangle-shaped single for the album (see McDonough: 554).

8   Hoskins' *Hotel California* (2006) subtitle reinforces this premise: *The true life adventures of Crosby, Stills Nash, Young, Mitchell, Taylor, Browne, Ronstadt, Geffen, the Eagles and their many friends.*

Los Angeles vicinity singer-songwriter scene, particularly the folk rock/country signature sound.[9]

During that time, Geffen connected with Young's manager Elliot Roberts of Lookout Management. Lookout morphed into the Geffen-Roberts Company, a partnership which sought to reinvent the business to become more artist-friendly in its dealings both creatively and financially. Geffen and Roberts refused to repeat the fleecing of rock's first generation by agents, managers and record labels. They were committed to providing a nurturing, protective, indulgent environment for new and young artists. The agency became the core of the music scene, selling millions of albums and extracting better royalty rates and prerequisites from record labels for artists. "Everywhere you looked, it seemed, there was evidence that Los Angeles, thanks in no small measure to the Laurel Canyon/Geffen Roberts stable [of artists], had eclipsed San Francisco as the music capital of America," writes music historian Michael Walker (2006: 114).

The Geffen-Roberts relationship was a swaying factor in Young's decision to sign with the new label. Geffen offered Young the same financial deal he had at Warner-Reprise—one million dollars per record. The promise of total creative control was the most appealing part of the package. Despite dissent from some who encouraged Young to sign the more lucrative offer from RCA, Geffen seemed the safe, familiar and obvious choice to Young. In a 1982 interview with the fanzine *Broken Arrow*, Roberts' positive projection of the partnership reveals a better understanding of Young than Geffen:

> David has worked with Neil for a very long time. He totally relates to Neil as an artist and has no preconceived notions. He knows that he's capable of doing anything at any point in time...Neil's not concerned with selling large numbers of his records, he's concerned with making records he's pleased with. Unfortunately they are not always commercial from the record company's point of view. David Geffen relates to that. (McDonough: 554)

In addition to Young, Geffen recruited Joni Mitchell from Asylum, followed by Elton John from MCA and Donna Summer. They all received the same million-dollar deals and were the anticipated star cornerstones of the new label. When their debuts fell flat in sales, Geffen immediately felt pressure, both financial and peer.[10] According to Roberts, Geffen felt the inauspicious start was a reflection on him, "that he was a failure...and couldn't handle it. That he wasn't as good as

---

9   In addition to McDonough (2002), Hoskins' *Hotel California* and Walker's *Laurel Canyon* (2006) provide fascinating accounts of Geffen's personal and professional presence in the L.A. scene before rising to greater mega mogul prominence as part of the DreamWorks trinity with Steven Spielberg and Lawrence Katzenberg.

10   Summer's *The Wanderer* (1980), Elton John's *The Fox* (1981), and Mitchell's *Wild Things Run Fast* (1982) preceded Young's *Trans* (1982).

60 B-SIDES, UNDERCURRENTS AND OVERTONES

Mo (Ostin), because Mo made successful records with these people and he didn't. David is not used to losing—and he's not a very good loser" (555).

Geffen's frustration filtered down to the artists where creative tensions soon developed. "David's a very controlling person, a very powerful person, and he's got his own ideas about what people should do and what they shouldn't do," said Elton John. "And no artist likes to be told what to do. They can be told what to do if someone knows what they are talking about—they'll listen to a producer for example—but if they're being told what to do by someone they have no respect for on any musical level, I think things start to get a little uncomfortable" (McDonough: 555).

Young's work was clearly the most conspicuous. With Geffen Records, Young swerved from his 1970s sounds into a series of stylistic extremities, beginning with the techno *Trans* (1982) and retro roots *Everybody's Rockin'* (1983), that lasted through the decade. On the surface, the projects appeared random and experimental, with B-Side characteristics. Young assumed different personas and bands for each record—abandoning Crazy Horse for the Vocoder and "Neil 2", the Shocking Pinks, International Harvesters, Bluenotes and back to Crazy Horse.

Young began tinkering with *Trans* and mechanical voices at the end of his Warner Reprise term.[11] His initial Geffen sessions focused on mellow, acoustic ballads with Hawaiian flavored, bongo rhythms intended for an album to be called *Island in the Sun*. Young decided to combine the materials from the two divergent sessions for *Trans*. The placement of three songs from the Geffen session—one to lead off each side of the album and "Like an Inca" to end the nine song cycle—gave the impression Young was using the acoustic, human voiced numbers to hide the computerized material in between.[12] The fusion was a predictable stylistic collision that surprised Geffen and the music audience, with critical *Trans*lations ranging from "*trans*ition" to "*trans*gression." While Young admitted *Trans* was "definitely out-there," he felt his "big concept"—computers and heartbeat, chemistry and electronics meeting—was completely misunderstood (556). He was disappointed that Geffen refused to provide money for an accompanying video, which Young felt would have helped explain the concept. After one record, Young expressed regret for leaving Mo Ostin and Reprise, saying that he made a big, stupid mistake and was "totally fucking wrong." Young's claims that Reprise was "the greatest

---

11   Young's interest in integrating technology into his music was clearly linked to his sons. The *Trans* sessions marked the beginning of Young's "search for a way for a...severely physically handicapped nonoral person, to find some sort of interface for communication" (McDonough: 556).

12   *Trans* also included a computer transformation of Young's Buffalo Springfield classic "Mr. Soul." Inversely, Young's lovely acoustic rendition of the computerized "Transformer Man," a song about Young's son, on *Unplugged* (1993) demonstrates a trace of some of the intended musical compatibility from the late Reprise, early Geffen sessions.

record company" and that they would have supported any of his projects "whether it was commercial or not," amplified the widening Geffen-Young divide (557).

The tension carried over into Young's next record *Everybody's Rockin'* (1983), which Young "almost vindictively gave Geffen" after he denied Young studio time and rejected his plans to record a country album.[13] Geffen wanted more rock and roll. Young and a pared-down version of his Nashville lineup dubbed the Shocking Pinks turned out an album of authentic, minimalist rock and roll roots sound "in about two hours" (McDonough: 571). The sparse album—five songs on each side totaling 25 minutes—was true to the early era as well.[14] Despite some merits, notably the tribute to Alan Freed in "Payola Blues," and covers of "Mystery Train and Slim Harpo's "Rainin' in my Heart," the pink retro gimmick loosely rendered a B-side approach that continued to emphasize concept over content. Even with the exposure from an MTV "pink Cadillac" contest, the album flopped.

Whereas *Trans* was greeted with indifference and mild derision, *Everybody's Rockin'* was roundly rejected by the record buying audience and critics, who grew increasingly bewildered by Young's musical directions. Reviewers shrugged— "Well, Mr. Weird is at it again"—and wondered, "What's next? Rap? The Nelson Riddle Orchestra?" (McDonough: 617). The few who were willing to attribute any value to the records rationalized them as products of Young's singular vision and exploration as an auteur.

Young routinely engaged the rock press trying to explain himself. His openness with the media during the Geffen years was as uncharacteristic as his records. Producer David Briggs thought it was a mistake, and that Young was selling his mystique: "Neil went chasin'. The one thing you can't do is chase. You gotta keep standin' in your spot, swingin' that bat, hopin' that other people will catch up to you sooner or later—but if they don't, buddy that's what art's about" (McDonough: 559).

Young's audience appeared to be less forgiving than the critics, which confirmed Geffen's worst fears regarding sales. The extreme stylistic journey alienated his most devoted listeners who apparently shared Geffen's preference for recordings that aligned along Young's 1970s stylistic axis more so than his early 1980s directions. During the period, Young's accompanying tours fared just as poorly. They were commonly characterized as a debacle, chaotic, disastrous and out of control. Many dates were cancelled and Young was often booed as his stylistic shape shifting and unpredictability wore thin on booking agents and faithful fans. "There was a new Neil every year," said Roberts. "Not only did you not know which Neil you were going to get, you didn't even know if you were gonna get Neil" (587).

---

13   Some of the material from that January 1983 session survived for Young's next Geffen record, *Old Ways* (1985), his most straightforward country album. Young considered the finished product "*Old Ways II*" and the original session that was rejected by Geffen "*Old Ways I*.".

14   The sequencing was structured for vinyl which was still the primary music format. The compact disc had only been in the market for a year.

Young resorted to playing his country material at outdoor arenas and state fairs, which ended up being some of his most successful gigs of the era.

Predictably, the longstanding, tense triangulation between Young, Geffen and Roberts promptly collapsed under mounting pressures. Trust and communication disintegrated. Both sides felt betrayed. Young had been in a difficult place personally dealing with finances and his sons' condition. Geffen was not only working to establish a new company within a highly competitive industry, he wanted to build an empire. Geffen dramatically altered his brand from Asylum's nurturing artist trademark during the 1970s. He signed Young to be a megastar, not an unpredictable artist who expected total support to do the kind of music he wanted to do no matter the commercial consequences. Geffen gave Young $1 million each for two unusual albums that alienated listeners and systematically dismantled his record sales base.

By all accounts, both Geffen and Young took the failures personally. Roberts, hopelessly caught between his strong willed friends, said they all handled the situation badly and overreacted. In its simplest sense, Roberts attributed much of the conflict to what had become a widespread notion, that "Neil has this album—*Harvest Two*—in his pocket and is capable of taking it out at any time" (579, 580).[15] Geffen was convinced Young was taunting him and deliberately producing esoteric albums of substandard material. Upon realizing that no one, including Roberts, could ever approach Young about the kind of material he should write and record, Geffen decided he had no option but to pursue legal action.

Considering Geffen's reputation for providing a supportive environment for his artists, not to mention his friendship with Roberts, a lawsuit seemed as extreme as Young's random musical directions. The Geffen stance may have been an overreaction that was part panic, fear and confusion, but also a last resort means of making a point to Young.

Young responded to the litigation with a counter suit and sarcasm: "That was confusing to me because I'd always thought that I *was* Neil Young. But it turns out that when I do certain things, I'm not Neil Young. Well, to get sued for being non-commercial after 20 years of making records, I thought was better than getting a Grammy" (Flanagan 1985: 34).

Young adamantly refuted suggestions in the rock press that he was deliberately trying to be different to draw attention to himself, saying he made the records that he made simply because he wanted to. However, Young admitted reaching a stage where he was questioning where he fit in musically, comparing himself to a moth banging against a light, "flitting from one thing to another." Young viewed his exploration as part of a natural, inevitable progression as an artist:

---

15 "Harvest II" finally arrived in 1992, twenty years after *Harvest*, when Young recorded *Harvest Moon* for Reprise. *Silver and Gold* (2000) further expanded the series of recordings into a trilogy.

Rather than a conscious effort to do different things every time, maybe it's just a sign that I was lost and searching for new directions, wondering about my own relevance and the continuance of my work; all of the things that one would think about when they've been doing something as long as I have. (Flanagan 1985: 34)

Ironically, Young's self-doubts in the 1980s came at a time when his stock was extremely high, commercially and critically. He was named Rock Artist of the Decade (1970s) by the *Village Voice* and had back-to-back Top Ten albums with *Comes A Time* and *Rust Never Sleeps*. Paul Nelson's *Rolling Stone* review of *Rust* was representative of the high praise the record received: "For anyone still passionately in love with rock and roll, Neil Young has made a record that defines the territory. Defines it, expands it, explodes it. Burns it to the ground. *Rust Never Sleeps* tells me more about my life, my country, and rock and roll than any music I've heard in years."[16] And Nelson was not the only one impressed. In *Rolling Stone*'s 1979 Readers Poll, Young won the Best Album, Male Vocalist, Songwriter, and Artist of the Year (tied with The Who) titles. Likewise, the critics named Young their Artist of the Year and *Rust* Best Album.

Yet, commercial success and mainstream acceptance have tended to make Young artistically uncomfortable throughout his career. Young's "dark period" in the early 1970s following the platinum *Harvest* reveals a creative reaching on his part similar to that of the 1980s, only less extreme. Young knew what others suspected—that he could do another *Harvest* or *Rust* at any time. Yet, Young resisted repetition, seeing it as artistic decline rather than development:

After I have a big peak, it seems like I don't want to be there anymore. It's too dangerous. Sure, I can do this over and over for a while and that would be an easy way out. Financially, I'd have everything I wanted because the idea, business-wise, is to go with a winner. But even more than the money and everything, I hate being labeled. I hate to be stuck in any one thing. I just don't want to be anything for very long, I don't know why. I'm just very extreme." (Flanagan 1985: 34)

Prisoners of Rock and Roll

They didn't look at me as an artist. They looked at me as a product and this product didn't fit with their marketing scheme.

Neil Young (Henke 1986: 46)

The Geffen-Young conflict lingered for several months. While the case may not have been a sensational headliner, it did provide the rock press with an engaging short term narrative with long term implications. Geffen was cast as the corporate

---

16   Nelson's excerpt appeared in the "Artist of the Year" supplement in *Rolling Stone* 4 June 1987.

villain and Young the iconoclast artist and victim. The publicity was some of the best Young had received during the early 1980s. Young continued to openly criticize Geffen, a tactic widely interpreted as an attempt by Young to get released from the label. He remained cantankerous with Geffen about creative control, threatening to "play country music forever," taunting "And then you won't be able to sue me anymore because country music will be all that I do so it won't be 'uncharacteristic' anymore, hahahaha. So stop telling me what to do or I'll turn into George Jones" (592).

Perhaps due to the unfavorable attention brought on by the ongoing discord, Geffen eventually changed his mind about pursuing the lawsuit. In the compromise, Young was to complete a new version of his country album, and agreed to make a "real" record that was more "characteristic Neil Young" at some point. Geffen was apologetic, saying that his approach to handling Young was wrong. He mainly regretted suing Young to try to bring him "back to track" (594). Young softened momentarily, saying that his embattled times with David Geffen were no worse than his worst times with long time producer David Briggs. The lawsuits were dropped, with the dismissals filed in Los Angeles Superior Court fittingly on April Fools Day 1985.

The most unusual part of the settlement was that Young instructed manager Elliot Roberts to change his deal from one million dollars to $500,000 for his three remaining records for Geffen. An artist surrendering half a million dollars per record was unprecedented. The move pained Roberts as a manager, but he understood Young's idiosyncratic position. Young was essentially buying creative control. "Neil was on a such a trip about the money and about the pressure it brought him," said Roberts. "Neil felt that for a million bucks, maybe they're right, but for five hundred thousand, I should able to do whatever I want to" (593).[17]

Young considered the lack of support from Geffen the source of a chip on his shoulder that he carried from record to record during the era. Young understood the record company's economic position, but resented the creative meddling that accompanied it:

> But they (Geffen) are still worried about my career. They think I should have a huge pop record. They think if I really applied myself to doing one that I could. David (Geffen) is genuinely worried about me. He wants to see me succeed just as much as he wants himself to succeed. So he's not coming from a bad place, but they did it in a way that I couldn't compromise myself on. They pushed me into a corner and that was a bad idea (Flanagan 1985: 36). The more they tried to stop me (from doing the music I wanted to do), the more I did it. Just to let them know that no one's gonna tell me what to do. (Henke: 46)

---

17   Young's manager Elliot Roberts and David Geffen's longtime friendship ended as a result of the conflict (McDonough: 580).

The tension did not subside, but remained an undercurrent during Young's post lawsuit recordings. *Old Ways* was a project that was initially rejected by Geffen in 1983 following *Trans*. At one point, Geffen even denied Young recording studio permission during a tour. Only two cuts survived the original Nashville sessions, with the rest of the new version of the record reshaped into a sound described by band members as "absurdly country" and "countrypolitan" (McDonough: 596-597). For a third consecutive album, Young was in extreme stylistic overdrive and continued to exasperate not only his audience and label, but his band members, particularly those exiled from the second *Old Ways*. Producer Elliott Mazer was dumbfounded and angry. He threw the record away and accused Young of "deliberately trying to give Geffen a piece of junk" (597). Geffen apparently agreed, and pressed only 80,000 copies for the August 1985 release. Young's commercial and critical decline continued into free fall.

Following *Old Ways,* Young recorded two more albums for Geffen. Though neither were particularly strong records, they provided the music community with encouraging signs of a more conventional stylistic approach. *Landing on Water* (1986) was primarily guitar rock, though Young considered the work an overdubbed "piece of crap," and *Life* (1987) was an uneven reunion with Crazy Horse. In 1987, Elliot Roberts completed negotiations between David Geffen and Mo Ostin for Young to leave his label for the one he abandoned at the beginning of the end of the 1970s. However, Young's return to Reprise was a Geffen hangover as Young's genre sampling continued, this time a ten-piece horn based, rhythm and blues album *This Notes for You* (1988). It was not until the end of the decade with *Freedom* (1989) that Young returned to his original "brand" and more closely resembled Neil Young.

The "Invisible Shield": Better to Burn Out Than to be Branded?

> There was a huge abyss between me and everybody (543). Peaks and valleys, as opposed to deserts, that's the way I look at it. Long, flat expanses of professionalism bother me (562). That whole era [the 1980s] there's always something between me and what I was trying to say. The invisible shield. (543)
>
> Neil Young (McDonough 2002)

The 1980s were unquestionably Neil Young's most difficult decade. Young's genre exploration during the era represents a B-side of his prolific musical career. The obligatory "greatest hits" compilation of the Geffen Years, *Lucky Thirteen* (1993), which was part of Young's buyout deal with the label, resembles a B-sides, demos, rarities, outtakes collection. While the subtitle, *Excursions into Alien Territory*, is fitting, the songs are an odd assortment that under represents Young's experimental era. There is no cut from *Everybody's Rockin'*, yet a song from Young's Reprise return *This Note's for You*. A more revealing narrative of Young's troubled Geffen years can be found on Young's album covers from the period. *Trans* depicts dual images of Young as a roadside hitchhiker on a contrasting two lane highway. The approaching side is a futuristic metropolis and jet age transport, the opposite direction a tail finned Cadillac and tall spruce forest. On *Old Ways*, the cowboy Young, wearing an old felt hat that belonged to his bus driver's father, walks down a winding road at his ranch, his back to the camera, and thus the world. *Landing on Water*'s cover, an illustration from an airliner emergency manual of crash survivors crowded into a little raft, conveyed hopelessness and sinking. "It didn't look like they had a chance. I kind of felt that way myself," said Young (McDonough: 608). The most telling is *Life*'s parting shot. The shadowy, sepia tinted design depicts two blurred hands gripping prison cell bars. In the background, a photo of Young in electric guitar stomp pose slants sharply on the wall. Subtly scratched into the surface below it are five score marks, a "sentence" representing the number of records Young made for Geffen. The cover composition complements the album's defiant garage song, "Prisoners of Rock 'N' Roll," with lyrics about not "taking orders from record company clowns."

The immediate impact of Geffen v. Young was minimal, the long term effect more principle than practical. A lawsuit was a new and unusual dimension to the proverbial predicament over creative control. The dilemma caused distress among artists, most who sympathized with Young. Those signed to the Geffen roster, such as Elton John, were particularly uncomfortable.[18] In 1988, R.E.M. admitted the Geffen-Young case was a factor in their signing a major label deal with Warner Brothers rather than Geffen Records following their indie I.R.S. years. Geffen Records survived, with an impressive roster that featured Don Henley, Guns N' Roses and Nirvana and commercial appeal of bands such as Asia and Quarterflash. Though David Geffen's reputation may have been tarnished, he joined with Steven Spielberg and Jeffrey Katzenberg to form the multi media empire DreamWorks in 1994.

The case did not set a precedent one way or another, encouraging or deterring established artists' from atypical musical ventures. There was no standard; conditions varied between artists and their record companies. Paul Simon's exploration of African and Brazilian musical styles on two consecutive records, the Grammy-winning *Graceland* (1986) and *Rhythm of the Saints* (1990), were certainly high profile and striking departures from his signature approach. The response was contrary to what Young had encountered. Though exotic, Simon's albums were less drastic than Young's deviations and more accessible as reflected in their commercial success and critical acclaim.

There is little evidence to suggest that Simon's travels across the musical map were inspired by Young's genre explorations earlier in the decade. Young's extremes stirred mocking and amusement more than they did praise as musical muse. David Briggs suggested Young deserved more credit, particularly for his courage:

---

18   Joni Mitchell's relationship with Geffen disintegrated as she blamed him for her commercial failure and for withholding royalty payments. She also returned to Reprise in 1994 (Hoskyns: 265-266).

You tell me any artists that did anything new and different in the eighties. Nobody was doin' that vocoder stuff, and that's what artists do—they go out there and plow new ground, and in rock and roll it's hard to find new ground. *Trans* was a success in the fact that a major established artist took music to a place that was as abrasive and grating to listeners as *Tonight's the Night*. When a major established artist puts his whole career on the line to go to new ground, the critics should at least applaud the guy—as opposed to dismissin' it. (McDonough: 557)

The tumultuous period did not alter Neil Young's status or progression as an artist. His prolific career continued, mostly following its original course alternating between guitar rock with Crazy Horse and country folk rock. Though he never revisited a similar series of stylistic extremes, Young still explored boundaries, whether a utopian rock novel (*Greendale*, 2004) or political statement (*Living with War*, 2005). Young also intermittently surrendered *Harvest* sequels that "he carried in his pocket" (*Silver and Gold*, 2000, *Prairie Wind*, 2005), and gradually began to release a long awaited series of recordings from his vast archive in 2006.

The ongoing conflict between Young and Geffen during the 1980s stands as a mythical B-side, a peripheral case that never ascended to a landmark lawsuit in the rock annals. The circumstance, with its captivating conflict and willful characters, was defined by incompatible brands and extremes—Young's musical disparity and Geffen's overreaction to it. Had Geffen v. Young advanced to court, the proceedings may have qualified for inclusion among the nine music cases involving management rip offs, copyright infringement and merchandising deals presented in Stan Soocher's *They Fought the Law: Rock Music Goes to Court* (1998). Nonetheless, the undercurrent of creative, economic and legal implications derived from Geffen v. Young demonstrates the enduring and intricate relationships between artists and their record companies, exploration and exploitation, and creative control and commercial imperatives. The Geffen-Young dissonance during the 1980s foreshadowed the increasing importance, complexities and convergence of artist, genre and record company branding in the music marketplace and its expanding niches.

Chapter 5
Music and Movie Mutuality:
Ry Cooder, the Involved Bystander

I'm just an involved outsider here. An interested innocent bystander. I provide a kind of service. Similar to the one I used to provide the record industry—except the record business wasn't as receptive…Doing these movies, I've learned so much I never knew before. It's hit and miss, hunt and peck. Hollywood's been a giant hands-on nursery school for me…it's all Ry Cooder music. It's just that the jar's changed.

Ry Cooder (Scherman 1985: 56, 75)

And I'm thinking to myself, "I could almost disappear from the street and no one would ever know."… At the tail end of everything, I see myself as someone going through all these little towns on the observation platform. I'm just the guy on the back of a speeding train.

Ry Cooder (Hoskyns 2005: 67, 70)

Between 2005 and 2008, Ry Cooder released an ambitious series of recordings—the pre-baseball progress report *Chavez Ravine* (2005), the populist parable and animal allegory *My Name is Buddy* (2007) and a petrol head novella, *I, Flathead* (2008). The "California trilogy" is quintessential Cooder—multicultural, curatorial, and courageously non-commercial. The factual and fictional narratives are as cinematic as they are literary and musically diverse. Images and characters abound within the rich soundscapes—hobos and trains, dragsters and "klowns," cats and cool cats, homies and old timers, UFOs and bulldozers. Tonal travelogues convey an acute sense of time and place. Depression era tunes, Dust bowl ballads, country, rock, blues, Tex-Mex and Western Swing strands conjure a sense of place and displacement, from barrios, alleyways and jukejoints to roadsides, neighborhoods and a hillside community.

Though high concept, Cooder's California trilogy reflects continuity between the series of distinct, yet interconnected stanzas that comprise his forty year music "Quest…being led into strange, new territory" (Scherman 1985: 56). Cooder's conceptual direction was preceded by extended cross cultural collaborations in world music during the 1990s, initiated with V.M. Bhatt in India and Ali Farka Toure in West Africa and culminating with recordings with Cuban artists of the Buena Vista Social Club (see Chapter 6). From the late 1970s until the late 1990s, Cooder's interests shifted exclusively to recording film score and soundtracks following his eleven solo albums between 1970 and 1987 and extensive session work during the 1960s. Cooder's catalog of film music, dating from *The Long Riders* (1980) and compiled in *The Music of Ry Cooder* (1995), is not only a bridge between his musical periods, but a signature stage that embodies the most characteristic Cooder qualities and colors, and provides a thread of continuity through his recordings.[1]

Mutuality: A Music Manifesto

Despite six Grammy awards and ten nominations in an impressive array of categories including Pop, Latin, World, Children's, Instrumental, Country Western, Contemporary Blues and Contemporary Folk, the versatile virtuoso Cooder remains one of the most understated musicians in popular music.[2] Throughout his career, Cooder has demonstrated a preference for the peripheries, the backgrounds and fringes. More comfortable in the studio than on the stage, he has toured minimally, and remains as intentionally inconspicuous as he is inventive, intuitive and inquisitive as an artist.

In addition to being a skilled string slider, picker and player, Cooder is widely regarded as a knowledgeable, reverent ethnomusicologist who seeks "mutuality in music." Cooder uses the term "mutuality" to describe years of work, friendship and a real understanding among a diverse assembly of musicians.[3] "Mutuality" has become Cooder's music manifesto and method, marking every stage of his musical progression, from studio session and solo to score and soundtrack to world music collaborations and concept trilogy.

Mutuality is evident in Cooder's ethnographic approach, his resourcefulness and reverence for music, his extraordinary level of technical instrumental proficiency; and his understanding of diverse musical forms. Cooder's commitment to and pursuit of the qualities of music mutuality provide an identity that sets him apart from other contemporary artists, such as Randy Newman and Stewart Copeland, who have crossed over into film scoring and composing.[4]

---

1 I have previously written about Cooder's film work in "The Long Ryder: From Studio Sessions and Solo Artist and Score and Soundtrack Specialist: Ry Cooder Musicological Quest," *Popular Music and Society*, Volume 22: 2, Summer 1998: 49-65.

2 Cooder won Grammys for Best Pop Instrumental Album (*Mambo Sinuendo* with Manuel Galban, 2003); Best Traditional Tropical Latin Album (*Buenos Hermanos*, Ibrahim Ferrer 2003); Best Tropical Latin Performance *(Buena Vista Social Club*, 1997); Best World Music Album (*Talking Timbuktu* with Ali Farka Toure, 1994) and (*A Meeting by the* River with V.M. Bhatt, 1993); Best Recording for Children (*Pecos Bill* with Robin Williams, 1988).

3 Cooder introduces the term in the liner notes of *Chicken Skin Music* (1976).

4 The list of prominent soundtrack specialists and score composers with pop and rock roots also includes Danny Elfman (Oingo Boingo), Hans Zimmer (Buggles) and Mark Mothersbaugh (Devo).

Across the Borderline

The mutuality Cooder seeks is rooted in "the only style he knows—exploratory and intuitive." His musical understanding and multi-instrumental mastery of slide guitar, bottleneck, saz, banjo, tiple, mandolin, slack-key, dulcimer, among other stringed things, enable him to weave together such distinct genres and styles as rock, gospel, Norteno or Tex-Mex, Dixieland, jazz, ragtime, Hawaiiaan, blues, vaudeville, gospel, soul, rockabilly, calypso, reggae, country and western, Middle and Far Eastern.[5] While Cooder's exotic music tastes were magnified in his world music explorations during the 1990s, his "strange musical energy" has always been deeply embedded in indigenous American music traditions, particularly folk and the blues.[6] Producer Kavichandran Alexander acknowledged Cooder's often overlooked native roots during the V.M Bhatt session, which began Cooder's world music expedition:

> Long before there was such a term as "world beat," Ry Cooder has proved that within the American context there was much that was as exotic as anything from Africa, Asia, or South America. He has shown that in the barrios and in the back alleys there is great music, as rich and poignant as any from the sub-Saharan regions or the Amazonian rainforests. (1993)

Cooder's curiousity extends to corners well beyond many borders. He has always responded to diverse outside ethnic influences, and the unique contexts and collaborative potential the musical forms and their musicians hold. In addition to Tex-Mex accordionist Flaco Jimenez, Bahamian guitarist Joseph Spence and Hawaiiaan slack-key father Gabby Pahinui are Cooder's self-described "musical beacons." "They had what I call high-Zen understanding," says Cooder. "If you hear the sound they make, you know right away it's the Sound. It's always r-r-ight there, in everything they play. Those are the great masters, the people that, you know, are cool to know about" (Scherman: 56).

---

5   See Fred Metting's fine critical musical biography *The Unbroken Circle: Tradition and Innovation in the Music of Ry Cooder and Taj Mahal.* Metuchen, NJ: Scarecrow Press 2001.

6   The compilation *The Roots of... Ry Cooder* (Catfish Records (U.K.), 2002) features songs by Woody Guthrie, Leadbelly, Mississippi John Hurt, Skip James, Blind Blake, Sleepy John Estes, Charley Patton and others that inspired Cooder's music and compositions.

Coloring an Ensemble: Sessions and Solo

> Nobody was ready for this weird thing we did.
>
> Ry Cooder (Santoro 1986: 28)

Cooder, who prodigiously picked up his first guitar at age four, began his musical "apprenticeship" in the 1960s in Southern California, where he was active in blues and folk circles. He soon emerged as a popular studio musician, accumulating an impressive list of session and backing credits that included Jackie DeShannon, Paul Revere and the Raiders, Gordon Lightfoot, Van Dyke Parks, Randy Newman, Maria Muldaur, the Everly Brothers, Arlo Guthrie, and Little Feat, among others. Among Cooder's more notable early projects are Captain Beefheart's Magic Band; Rising Sons, a group formed with fellow archivist Taj Mahal in 1966 (see Chapter 1); and sessions with the Rolling Stones following guitarist Brian Jones's death. Cooder recorded extensively on the Stones' *Let it Bleed* (1969) album—although he is credited only for the mandolin on "Love in Vain"—and later plays on *Sticky Fingers* (1972).[7]

Cooder's approach to playing sessions foreshadowed his full-time film work years later. "My job seemed to consist of taking strange instruments which were not as yet clichéd in the rock field—like mandolin and dulcimer, even bottleneck guitar—and pump 'em up, play 'em hard, and integrate myself into the ensemble as a color or sound effect," explains Cooder (Santoro 1986: 27).

Cooder's eleven solo albums, beginning with his self-titled debut on Reprise in 1970 through *Get Rhythm* (1987), reflect distinctive musicianship and fanciful curiosity. His quirky, catchy, ethnographic eclecticism, reverence, and delight in discovering and preserving music is apparent in his range of inventive crossbreeds and covers of songs by Leadbelly, Bobby and Shirley Womack, Ben E. King, Burt Bacharach, Woody Guthrie, Chuck Berry, Otis Blackwell, Jelly Roll Morton, Elvis Presley, Willie McTell, Arthur Blake, Mort Shuman, Doc Pomus, Joe South, Carl Perkins, Bob Dylan, Curtis Mayfield, and Willie Dixon, among others.

Critical responses to Cooder's collection of generic collisions and cultural collusions contain descriptions ranging from "charming eccentricity" and "intriguingly experimental" to "misguided," "found weirdness" and "false nostalgia." With the exception of *Bop Till You Drop* (1979)—the first rock album to be digitally mastered—which sold 300,000 copies, and the moderate success that followed with *Borderline* (1980), Cooder has never dented the commercial market. Interestingly, European audiences respond far more favorably. For example,

---

7 Much of Cooder's session work with the Rolling Stones is documented on *Jamming With Edward*, recently reissued by Virgin Records. Other Cooder/Stones lore suggests Cooder could have replaced Brian Jones, but chose not to; and that it was Cooder who provided the main riff for "Honky Tonk Woman." Cooder taught Keith Richards to play slide and the open G tuning favored by John Lee Hooker. Richards once said, "I took Ry Cooder for everything I could get" (Harrington 2003: G4).

Chicken Skin Music (1976), which peaked at # 177 on the U.S. charts, went gold in Holland and earned a German Grammy.[8]

Get Rhythm (1987) punctuated "Ry Cooder records," marking a significant shift from solo recordings that would last until the beginning of the California trilogy in 2006. Before relocating in world music projects that defined his discography through the 1990s and into early 2000s, Cooder joined longtime cohorts John Hiatt and Jim Keltner, and Nick Lowe in 1992 to record as Little Village, a poorman's Traveling Wilburys "supergroup" assembly. Although Cooder experienced the familiar creative-commercial struggles artists often encounter within organizational structures, his "quest" remained clear during solo projects. "I've tended to look at my albums as research and development. I was just trying to get some place new on each one," says Cooder (Jerome 1986: 128). The "rock ethnographer" image of Cooder often overshadows his practical approach to music. "A hopeless antiquarian...that's not the point at all," says Cooder. "I've just been looking for what I can use, absorb into my own playing. With me practicality is everything. I've got to know how to do something" (Scherman 56). Cooder elaborates about the misperception:

> Everybody got the wrong idea...including Warner Brothers. They thought, "Well, this guy's a musicologist, a collector freak" which really wasn't so. I just happened to be looking to learn and do something, but what I didn't realize fully in those days was that Warner Brothers was not in the business of subsidizing my personal interests; it seemed to me that they should be, but they definitely weren't. I was trying very hard to get somewhere with musical understanding and using the records as an excuse, and you're not supposed to do that...After a while it became hard to say just what I was accomplishing. I thought the music was the thing to be served. I just kept thinking of the synthesis you could make, which seems to be the American musical heritage, the point of the whole thing anyhow—that everybody puts together something that wasn't there before. (Santoro: 27-28)

Score and Soundtrack

Cooder's exploration of new musical territory resulted in an industrial shift from the record companies to movie studios. The transition seemed a natural direction, especially when considering Cooder's marginal record sales, and that his singing and songwriting were widely regarded as subordinate to his extraordinary musical skills. Critics' descriptions of Cooder's vocals range from Robert Christgau's

---

8 The chart figures for other Cooder records further demonstrate the striking contrast of his European and U.S. followings: *Bop Till You Drop* (1979): UK #36, US #62; *Borderline* (1980): UK #35, US #43; *The Slide Area* (1982): UK #18, US #105; *Get Rhythm* (1987): UK #75, US #177; *Little Village* (1992) UK #23, US #66. Cooder routinely tours in Europe, often with fellow instrumental virtuoso David Lindley.

brutal "ugly voice" to a kinder "somewhat slurred resonant baritone" (Santoro: 27). Film appeared to present an ideal medium for Cooder's versatility and intuitive, exploratory style. The mutuality Cooder attained shaped an expansive, expressive, supple musical language that translated seamlessly into film narratives and their settings, moods and characters.

Cooder's earliest soundtrack experience dates to *Candy* (1968). He also "tagged along" with producer/arranger Jack Nitzsche, who integrated Cooder's bottleneck guitar throughout *Performance* (1970), a film best known for being Mick Jagger's acting debut, and *Blue Collar* (1978), Paul Schrader's directing debut. "I'd wanted to do film work, and I knew I could do it, if there was the opportunity to do it in the right way, with the right context," says Cooder. "So I began to do a little bit, and a little bit more, until it became a full-time job" (Santoro: 28).

It was not until Cooder connected with director Walter Hill in 1980 that film composing became a full-time endeavor. After hearing the lovely country-marching band, early-jazz flavor of Cooder's album *Jazz* (1978), Hill was interested in Cooder doing music for his film, *The Long Riders*. Despite studio resistance because Cooder had no film credits, the project initiated a special film-music mutuality as the first of nine scores Cooder produced for the director between 1980 and 1996. Their enduring partnership provides Hill with a unique perspective on Cooder's approach to scoring:

> With someone like Ry, you don't ask how, you just admire. Ry's a great artist, nothing less. Face it, ninety-six percent of all movie scores are corny beyond belief. Ry has always had this ability to be touching—but with sophistication. (Scherman 56)

> Ry's film music…doesn't work in the traditional manner; doesn't underscore, as much as it envelops; doesn't heighten the moment as much as it adds atmosphere—surrounds the story—supplies missing information—champions the mood rather than the event. (Hill: 1995)

What Cooder aimed to accomplish during his session work and solo projects— "integrating into the ensemble as a color or sound effect"—translated well into film ambience. Among the moods, textures, and backdrops he has shaped with sound are: dry, plaintive Tex-Mex (*The Border* (1982)); desolation and vague ennui (*Paris, Texas* (1984), *Last Man Standing* (1996)); eerie swamp (*Southern Comfort* (1981)); traditional, outlaw, march, elegiac and playful Wild West (*Pecos Bill* (1988), *Geronimo: An American Legend* (1993), *The Long Riders* (1980)); and inner city ghetto (*Trespass* (1992)). Cooder is particularly adept at providing atmosphere for rural, Southwest and Deep South settings. The three-inch, sawed-off sherry bottle neck he uses with his slide guitar provides a rich tone that evokes the scorching heat, backroads dust, and menace of the South. In addition to mood and locale, Cooder's instrumentation fills in spaces and provides character sketches without intruding on the narrative. Though the music may not infringe, critical consensus is that that Cooder's soundtracks often stand by themselves and are more complete and focused than the films themselves.

While Cooder's respect for the music seems to layer a score with conviction, his compulsive inquisitiveness as an artist and accumulated musical knowledge make Cooder a resourceful soundtrack composer. For example, on *Southern Comfort*, he blends his trademark bottleneck with appropriate ethnic instruments, and a shakuhachi, a Japanese flute. And his reworking of the Robert Johnson classic that gives *Crossroads* its title features an edgy bottleneck opening, uneven bar patterns, powerful vocals, and a gospel-style breakdown. "You can always find someplace to go with this material especially after having lived with it so long—you want to make a contribution," says Cooder (Santoro: 28).

The blues, which has always been a staple of Cooder's repertoire, underscores much of his soundtrack work, the most obvious being *Crossroads* (1986). "I know it, I play it, I understand it. The trick is to apply it. Not to be too literal but to be `blues-inflected.' The blues is so expressive—nostalgic but not sentimental, mournful but not pathetic, so humble and close to the earth. It's a nuance filled thing. I don't let myself be frontal about it. You got to know when the sun's going down, the music needs to sound like this. When it's raining, like that" (Jerome: 128).

Cooder elaborates further on producing music for films:

> A soundtrack is a glue. Music gives the audience subliminal cues. It can anticipate something they're about to see or stir a memory of something they saw an hour before. It's a continuity beneath the linear continuity of the film. When a picture's got room for that kind of subtext…(Scherman 56) …an ambience to create with sound, I can do…but if what they want is laugh music…or space…or fright…or guy-sits-on-a-cake music, I can't figure that stuff out so good. (Jerome 127)

Cooder's preference for ambience and "serious" sound is evident in his soundtrack catalog. *Brewster's Millions* (1985), his only comedy credit, reflects the musician's awkwardness with the genre. Cooder's attempt at substituting a contemplative score for "funny" is not compatible with the conventional comic expectations of the film.

"The Last Refuge of Abstract Music"

> What I was trying for in *Paris, Texas* was simple—the musical equivalent of Harry Dean Stanton's walk. That lonely walk.
>
> Ry Cooder (Scherman: 56)

Cooder views soundtracks as "the last refuge of abstract music." His musical methodology for film relies on intuition rather than actual composing:

> Composition is what's it's all about, so even in a blues context you have to think conceptually. I do this more naturally. I'll be looking at the film and thinking, 'What do I hear?' You just have to sit there and listen for it. I'm not trained for composition, so I have to work intuitively. Hopefully, that's why the director hired me because he's of like mind. But every film is obviously   different, how you put it together, which frees my mind up from patterns and cliches. (Santoro: 28)

Cooder begins the process by studying a rough cut of a film for at least two weeks, "waiting for a feeling, a way in, a way to tricking myself to finding any kind of handle I can get" (Scherman: 56). Eventually, he hears a chord that defines the movie. "The movie starts hovering in tonality. *Paris, Texas* was an E-flat. You get the movie's key from the wind. The ocean. Air noise. Easy if it's being shot in the countryside. City pictures, it's hard to pin the key down. I have to throw out that whole methodology and look for other hints. Tempo, attitude, emotion (Scherman: 56).

Cooder draws on images, associations, and "stuff" he has heard, imagined and retained over the years for soundscapes. For example, in *Crossroads*, he says he hears a "shout" and sees church imagery. "That stuff is ready to go, pops into my head," says Cooder. "You can't mastermind everything; it needs to be cathartic, intuitive, spontaneous. What kills music in films is when it's done as performance, drawing attention to the fact that someone in the background's playing it" (Jerome: 127).

As a musician, Ry Cooder is unlikely to ever arrive at a final destination on his musical quest. But film has provided a vehicle and peripheral, behind the scenes, B-side place—that strange, new territory—which allows him to continue to explore, refine and expand the mutuality, rather than the marketablity, in music. Cooder's crossover to the reel world has been both a learning experience—a "hit and miss, hunt and peck giant hands-on nursery school"—and a liberating one that enables him to dig deeper into musical roots and "extend his reach into the American backwaters of sound" (Mitchell 1986: 76). "It's music freed from the constraints of the four-minute song…the horrors of 'How do we sell it?' [and] the demands of the marketplace, says Cooder. "And I just like it better" (Scherman: 75).

In addition, the focused demands of film-scoring have made Cooder a better, more dexterous player. He says his guitar playing is "galactically improved" and his music has "come alive" and is "universally better" than any of the material on his solo recordings. For Cooder, soundtrack work is closer to being the kind of music he likes to make and no less personal statement than his "Ry Cooder" records.[9] "Everyone talks about personal vision. Personal vision is in the notes.

---

9   One of Cooder's favorite pieces of music he created is not on one of his records, rather music he did for a Levi's commercial. "Thirty seconds of utter perfection…Now that made me very happy, says Cooder. "I don't play my old records for anyone. But I'll play that ad for anybody (Scherman: 75).

The little notes, the sounds. The notes are the notes are the notes. If you wanna call it a Ry Cooder album, call it that" (Scherman: 75).

Slice of Ry: Singles, Scores, and Soundtracks, An Annotated Discography

The discography chronicles Ry Cooder's film music contributions from 1968 to 2008. Included are original motion picture soundtracks and scores, songs, and concert performances with record label, film director and studio citations. The discography does not provide a close reading of the film/music text, rather capsules of Cooder context. The commentary highlights the distinctive and diverse musical styles utilized for each film; the settings and atmospheres created by Cooder's soundscapes; and the producers, directors, and familiar players who are a part of the Cooder musical ensemble. The discography also illustrates Cooder's ability to capture cultural clashes, the "two sides to every war" conveyed in *Last Man Standing*. In addition, the overlapping projects magnify Cooder's work ethic. For example, in 1984, he was simultaneously working on the scores to *Streets of Fire*, *Paris, Texas*, and *Alamo Bay*, for three different directors. Finally, the insightful observations and comments from critics, musical and film collaborators, particularly director Walter Hill, and Cooder himself, provide a frame of reference for Cooder's music and movie mutuality.

The soundtrack chronicle is followed by a discography of Cooder's solo recordings, backtracking from *I, Flathead* (2008) to his self-titled titled debut in 1970.

Candy (1968) (U.S.-Italian-French). Dir. Christain Marquand

Ry Cooder's first dabbling with film music features his trademark bottleneck guitar in this sexual satire about a woman who is attacked by every man she meets.

Performance (1970) (British). Dirs. Donald Cammell. Nicholas Roeg

While "tagging along" with arranger/producer Jack Nitzsche in London in 1969, Cooder sits in on some sessions with the Rolling Stones following guitarist Brian Jones's death. The connections led to his work on the psychological melodrama about a criminal on the lam hiding out with a rock performer played by Mick Jagger in his acting debut. Cooder contributes bottleneck and dulcimer to the score. Randy Newman also contributes.

Blue Collar (1978). MCA Records (out of print). Dir. Paul Schrader. MCA/ Universal

Another Nitzsche project that reunited Cooder with late 1960s collaborator Captain Beefheart. Together they deliver blues based tracks, such as the growly

78   *B-SIDES, UNDERCURRENTS AND OVERTONES*

"Hard Working Man," that magnify auto workers' struggles with management and their union.

Goin' South (1978). Dir Jack Nicholson. Paramount Pictures

Director and star Nicholson uses the song "Available Space" from Cooder's debut album *Ry Cooder* (1970) in this Western comedy that features the acting debuts of John Belushi and Mary Steenburgen. "The song stood out like a natural gem amidst all the forced musical and theatrical capering." (Mitchell 78).

No Nukes: The MUSE Concert (1980). Music from The MUSE Concerts for a Non-Nuclear Future. Asylum ML-801. Dirs. Julian Schlossberg, Danny Goldberg, Anthony Potenza

Concert film documentary of Madison Square Garden gathering from September 19-23, 1979, by Musicians United for Safe Energy, an all-star cast that includes James Taylor, Carly Simon, Bonnie Raitt, Bruce Springsteen, Jackson Browne, Crosby, Stills, and Nash, and many others. Cooder performs his biggest hit, "Little Sister," from his record *Bop Till You Drop* (1979).

The Long Riders (1980). Warner Bros. Dir. Walter Hill. United Artists

What most consider Cooder's initiation into full-time film soundtracking, and the first of nine scores he produces for Hill. Familiar Cooder ensemble that includes David Lindley, drummer Jim Keltner, and Jim Dickinson fashions a traditional Western style music, rich with fiddle, banjo, mandolin, harmonium, and dulcimer, that resonates with a burnished, old-fashioned lyricism. Other Western variations surface in numerous other Cooder scores. "The score is almost an outlaw among formula scores..with a sharply controlled sense of irony. [The] spare…slightly mournful tone conveys and comments upon the end of an era, while simultaneously celebrating the raw nobility of the James and Younger families," writes critic Elvis Mitchell (1986: 76). "Ry has a way of reaching into traditional sounds, re-interpreting and making the result singly his own," adds Hill in a note on the album's jacket cover. Winner of a Los Angeles Film Critics Award for Original Score.

Southern Comfort (1981). (No soundtrack release). Dir. Walter Hill. United Artists

An exquisite and powerful score of thick compositions and spare finger picking. Cooder's langorious chords and muted gourd pounding "suggest a bastard mutant version of music from the American Southeast" (Mitchell: 76). The haunting sound is an eerie reflection of the National Guard unit that is lost in the Louisiana bayous. The troop upsets the sleepy life of the locals and triggers their fury in the film. His integration of a Japanese flute (which he uses in numerous scores) with his bottleneck guitar creates a sense of spiritual grimness. "The swamp to me was an interior space, a state of mind," explains Cooder. "I thought the sound had to be lonesome, dangerous, pastoral and ominous" (Jerome 1986: 129). Although a soundtrack was never released, three tracks are included on the compilation *Music by Ry Cooder* (1995).

The Border (1982). Backstreet Records. Dir. Walter Hill. Universal-RKO Pictures

The Tex-Mex sound Cooder affectionately highlights in much of his solo recordings translates into a plaintive backdrop for this south of the border struggle to reach the promised land that stars Jack Nicholson. Cooder's musicological knowledge and reverence is apparent in his choice of legendary Norteno singer Freddie Fender for the evocative, heartbreakingly apt theme, "Across the Borderline," co-written by Cooder, Hiatt, and Dickinson. Fender's bright, bitter vocals, and Cooder's subtle musical trim lay a subdued blanket of gloom tinged with hope over the closing credits.

Paris, Texas (1984). Warner Bros. Dir. Wim Wenders. 20th Century Fox

An eloquently atmospheric tone poem (in E-flat). Cooder based his music for the movie on Harry Dean Stanton's lonely walk. Cooder's languorous acoustic slide in the film's forlorn theme "creates just the right ambience for endless stretches of late summer blacktop" (Mansfield 2005: 1D). There is a shimmering sense of alienation, wandering, solitude, secrets, desert expanse and barren landscape in the lush, evocative, score. Cooder, accompanied only by Lindley and Dickinson, also rearranges Blind Willie Johnson's aching blues in "Dark Was the Night" as a starting point for this Sam Shepard story.

Streets of Fire (1984). MCA Records. Dir. Walter Hill. Universal-RKO Pictures

Unfortunately, Universal never released Cooder's pulsating rock score for this epic, operatic, comic, action-adventure, B-flick-like "rock and roll fable" about a female rock star kidnapped by sadistic bikers. "Bomber Bash" from the score is one of the "previosuly unreleased" highlights on the *Music by Ry Cooder* (1995) compilation. Jimmy Iovine produces the soundtrack, which includes Cooder performing "Hold That Snake."

Alamo Bay (1985). Slash Records. Dir. Louis Malle. Tri-Star Pictures

Cooder's protean soundtrack for Malle's pastoral treatise on ignorance and bigotry embraces the clash between two cultures—Vietnamese immigrants and American fisherman on the Texas Gulf Coast. Compositions ranging from the festering

"Klan Meeting" to the sweet harmony of "Quatro Vicios" to the punkish "Gooks on Mainstreet," forge an unusual synthesis: "Asian cowboy blues" (Mitchell: 78). John Hiatt contributes a vocal, and members of Los Lobos join Cooder's ensemble of players.

Brewster's Millions (1985). MCA Records (out of print). Dir. Walter Hill, Universal Pictures

A handsome score, but at odds with the purpose of the movie. Cooder's contemplative, cool sound sets the wrong mood for the diversionary, wish-fulfillment comedy starring late greats Richard Pryor and John Candy.

Blue City (1986). Warner Bros. Dir. Michelle Manning. Paramount Pictures

Based on a Ross MacDonald novel about a young man who returns to his Florida hometown to avenge his father's murder. Cooder and his longtime studio session stand-bys (Keltner, Dickinson, Bentmont Tench, Jorge Calderon, David Paich, Steve Porcaro) create a predominatly electric rock soundtrack. "[Ry's] guitar speaks for Billy's feelings with an understanding a director often thinks only she has," says director Manning on the album jacket notes.

Crossroads (1986). Warner Bros. Dir. Walter Hill. Columbia Pictures

Perhaps the soundtrack he is most widely and conveniently identified with. Cooder rearranges and synthesizes traditional gut bucket blues into a newer strand for this contemporary version of Robert Johnson's legendary "crossroads" deal with the devil. "It's got a lot of church imagery to it, especially the way they developed it in the film," says Cooder of the music (Scherman: 56). Gospel vocals of longtime Cooder backing singers Willie Green, Terry Evans, and Bobby King enhance the religiosity of the songs. "Too heavy on overstuffed blues," says critic J.D. Considine of the film. Climactic showdown features guitar duel between ex-Zappa and David Lee Roth guitarist, Steve Vai, and Cooder-enhanced actor Ralph Macchio (*The Karate Kid*) wielding their instruments like weapons. During the shooting, Cooder's pursuit of musical mutuality led him to Frank Frost and his band, John Price and the Wonders. The Greenville, Mississippians contribute two songs to the soundtrack. "I told him I never heard a white man could fit in so quick and so good with my blues," recalls Frost. "He just look at me and say, 'You're a musician, I'm a musician,' and that was that" (Scherman: 56). Musicologist Cooder considers the "low, wonderful, de-tuned" sound of John Price's drum set his "personal payoff" for doing the film.

Cocktail (1988). Elektra Records. Dir. Roger Donaldson. Touchstone Pictures

Features Cooder's version of "All Shook Up" culled from his album *Get Rhythm* (Warner 1987), another example of the record and film industries' marketing synergy that was a by product of music video during the 1980s.

Pecos Bill (1988). Windham Hill Records. Story by Brian Gleeson. Showtime Productions

A Grammy winner for Best Recording for Children, Cooder's playful picking creates a Wild West setting and appropriate backdrop for Robin Williams' narration on this cable television presentation. The project spawned a children's recording series, "American Heroes and Legends," for Windham Hill's Rabbit Ears Productions. *The Song of Sacajawea* (1994) (Rabbit Ears, featuring Cooder's kindred spirit, David Lindley providing instrumentation for Laura Dern's narration, is a nice musical companion piece to *Pecos Bill* and *Geronimo*.

Johnny Handsome (1989). Warner Bros. Dir. Walter Hill. Tri-Star Pictures

A sobbing, bluesy score accents the film noir atmosphere and gritty loneliness of Mickey Rourke's disfigured character. Moods range from the ominous quiet of the "Main Theme" to the jaunt of "Clip Joint Rhumba." Prominent piano and horn arrangements by Van Dyke Parks enhance the New Orleans setting. Cooder adds accordian to his personal musical repertoire.

Steel Magnolias (1989). Polydor Records (out of print). Dir. Herbert Ross. Columbia Pictures

Another Louisiana setting, the Cajun flavored soundtrack features Zydeco musicians Jo-el Sonnier and Zachary Richard, Hank Williams' "Jambalaya," and Cooder's "I Got Mine," an old pop song from the minstrel and medicine show tradition, which appears on Cooder's *Chicken Skin Music* (1976).

Cadillac Man (1990). Polydor Records. Dir. Roger Donaldson. Orion Pictures

If ever a Cooder song contained marketing merit as a single, either off one of his records or a soundtrack, it may be "The Tattler," one of the limited number of (non-instrumental) original songs Cooder has written from what many consider to be his masterpiece, *Paradise and Lunch* (1974). (His cover of "Little Sister" on *Bop Till You Drop* (1979) came closest to being considered a single). On a soundtrack with tunes ranging from "Stayin' Alive" to "Hit the Road Jack," "The Tattler" underscores Robin Williams' character's redemption, and continues over the closing credits. Cooder is detached from the hit-making strategy that accompanies soundtracks. "That's product. A decision: 'We need a hit.' That's

82   B-SIDES, UNDERCURRENTS AND OVERTONES

why they stick those songs on now at the end of movies. That's packaging. I know nothing about packaging," he says (Jerome: 128).

Trespass (1992). Sire/Warner Bros. Dir. Walter Hill. Universal Pictures

A funky, chunky, and foreboding score that captures inner city slum setting ("East St. Louis") and complements Hill's cat-and-mouse style narrative involving two firemen seeking ancient treasure buried in a decrepit building, not knowing that the structure is the headquarters for a band of menacing drug dealers. A trumpet provides fitting urban angst underscoring. Jr. Brown's fiddle and steel guitar-driven "Party Lights" is countrified, if not comic, contrast as the closing track.

Geronimo: An American Legend (1993). Columbia Records. Dir. Walter Hill. Columbia Pictures

The Long Ryder goes West again for Hill's chronicle of the legendary warrior. "How to put music to a drama about two cultures? How to find sounds that valorize both sides?" wonders Hill in the soundtrack's liner notes. "The answer was simple. I called Ry Cooder." Cooder delivers an elegant and elegaic score that blends and juxtaposes Native American throat singing, chants, water pipes, flutes, and tombaks, with accordian, banjo, mandolin, cello, Lindley's masterful bouzouki, orchestration, and a brass band.

Dead Man Walking (1995). Columbia Records. Dir. Tim Robbins. Gramercy Pictures

David Robbins, the composer and music supervisor for the death row film, explains in the liner notes that he was seeking a wide variety of musical styles from all over the world. One of the earliest indications that the "universal, spiritual feel" was right for the film was "Isa Lei," from Cooder and V.M. Bhatt's Grammy-winning *A Meeting by the River* (1993). The elegant blend of Cooder's bottleneck (glass against steel strings) Bhatt's Mohan Vina (steel rod against metal strings), and Joachim Cooder's soft tapping percussion, resonates with sweet sadness and calm resolution. Cooder also plays bottleneck on several tracks of the film's World Music dominated score.

Music by Ry Cooder (1995). Warner Brothers

This two-CD collection gathers primarily instrumental excerpts from 11 soundtracks Cooder produced between 1980 and 1993. The anthology contains "previously unreleased" tracks—three from *Southern Comfort* and "Bomber Bash" from *Streets of Fire*. Cooder cultists may lament the omission of finer film musical moments, and the removal of the songs from their soundtrack contexts. (The majority of Cooder's soundtrack recordings remain in print and have been reissued.) Though Cooder's movie music may be worthy of a box set, this is a good representation of his film contributions. The 34-song collection captures Cooder's diversity and evocative soundscapes (there are only a few vocals in the set). Co-produced by Cooder and his son, Joachim, who accompanies dad on many of his 1990s projects as a percussionist.

Last Man Standing (1996). Verve Records. Dir. Walter Hill. New Line Cinema

Cooder's ninth score for director Hill, who considers it one of the best. The adaptation of Akira Kurosawa's masterpiece The Seven Samurai combines conventions of film noir, Samurai movies, dime novels, and comic books into a 1930's hardboiled, prohibitionist gangster piece disguised as a Western. Despite the cluttered aims of the project, Cooder provides what Hill envisioned: "a hymn to the tradition of fictional tough guys." Sounds range from the edgy (sampling, saxophone, synthesizer) to the exotic (flutes), and Cooder even slips in a two-step. Once again, Cooder demonstrates his adroitness at conveying distance ("Five Mile Road") and the dusty desolation of a Texas hellhole.

The Wizard of Oz in Concert: The Dream Concert (1996). Rhino Records. Turner Pictures Worldwide, Inc.

A benefit concert at New York's Lincoln Center for the Children's Defense Fund that features actors Debra Winger and Joel Grey, and recording artists Natalie Cole, Jewel, Jackson Browne, Roger Daltrey, and The Boys Choir of Harlem as Oz characters. Cooder is among a supporting cast that includes David Sanborn, Images, Phoebe Snow, Dr. John, and Ronnie Spector. His crisp instrumental accompaniment can be heard on "If I Only Had A Brain" and "We're Off to See the Wizard."

The End of the Violence (1997). Outpost Records Dir. Wim Wenders. MGM Pictures

Cooder's second galvanizing score composed for a Wenders film (see *Paris, Texas*). Cooder's thematic, "Define Violence," is featured throughout the film. The soundtrack also includes previously unreleased songs from U2, Sinéad O'Connor, Michael Stipe with Vic Chestnutt, Tom Waits, Los Lobos, DJ Shadow, Eels, and Latin Playboys.

My Blueberry Nights (2007). Blue Note Records. Dir. Wong Kar Wai. The Weinstein Group and Block 2 Pictures

Cooder returns to movie music following a ten-year soundtrack sabbatical. Cooder collaborates with his son Jaochim and mixer Martin Pradler to compose, perform and produce the travelscapes "Ely Nevada," "Long Ride," "Bus Ride" and "Devil's Highway." Cooder also produces Mavis Staples track, "Eyes on the Prize," for the soundtrack that includes Cat Power, Otis Redding, Cassandra Wilson and Norah Jones, who appears in the film in her acting debut.

Solo Recording Discography

The Ry Cooder Anthology: The UFO Has Landed (Rhino, 2008).
I, Flathead (Nonesuch/Perro Verde, 2008).
My Name is Buddy (Nonesuch/Perro Verde, 2007).
Chavez Ravine (Nonesuch/Perro Verde, 2006).
Mambo Sinuendo (with Manuel Galban) (Nonesuch/Perro Verde, 2002).
Buena Vista Social Club (with Cuban musicians and composers) (World Circuit/Nonesuch, 1997).
Music by Ry Cooder (soundtrack compilation) (Warner Bros., 1995).
River Rescue: The Very Best of Ry Cooder (Warner Bros., 1994).
Talking Timbuktu (with Ali Farka Toure) (Rykodisc, 1994).
A Meeting by the River (with V.M. Bhatt) (Water Lily Acoustics, 1993).
Rising Sons (with Taj Mahal) (Columbia Legacy, 1992).
Little Village (with John Hiatt, Jim Keltner, Nick Lowe) (Reprise, 1992).
Get Rhythm (Warner Bros., 1987).
The Slide Area (Warner Bros., 1982).
Borderline (Warner Bros., 1980)
Bop Till You Drop (Warner Bros., 1979).
Jazz (Warner Bros., 1978)
Show Time (Warner Bros., 1976).
Chicken Skin Music (Reprise, 1976).
Paradise and Lunch (Reprise, 1974).
Boomer's Story (Reprise, 1972).
Into the Purple Valley (Reprise, 1972).
Ry Cooder (Reprise, 1970).

Chapter 6

World Music Missionaries:
Cross Cultural Convergences

> Anybody is entitled to record with anybody else. Anywhere. You don't erect barriers
> between cultures; you tear down barriers between cultures.
>
> Paul Simon (Steinberg and Lacy 1992)

From the mid-1960s until the mid-1970s, certain segments of the music world strived to achieve a synthesis by attempting to bridge elements of jazz, rock, and blues with music of Europe, Asia, Africa, and South America. Soloists such as Miles Davis and Gato Barbieri, and groups from Weather Report to Shakti succeeded at creating highly evocative music. One such intersection could be seen in Bossa Nova, characterized by Arto Lindsay as "a revolution of sophistication." Bossa Nova combined certain strains of traditional Brazilian popular music and the advanced harmonies of American cool jazz." Like Miles Davis and Gil Evans, Antonio Carlos Jobim, the composer of the classic "Girl From Ipanema," was influenced by classicists such as Debussy, Stravinsky, and Bartok. Singer Joao Gilberto's rendition uses the cool stylings of vocalist and trumpeter Chet Baker to create an intensely swinging vocal style.

Such exploratory efforts raised widespread hopes that a "new music" would emerge. While the concepts and artistic intentions may have been filled with promise and possibility, the East-West musical experimentation was never fully realized, but for a few exceptions. The Beatles and Canned Heat were among those who integrated Indian strands into their music during the 1960s. Broader attempts at synthesizing Western music's linear qualities with, among other forms, the ethereal strands of Eastern classical traditions too often resulted in cultural collision rather than collusion, and convergences that some critics considered more comic than creative.

During the late 1980s, "World Music," or "World Beat" as a concept and genre became increasingly drawn from the peripheries into the American musical mainstream and vernacular. Record retailers, which had for years struggled to categorize releases from international artists representing many countries, adopted the umbrella term "world" to accommodate the expanding import selections. Gradually, diverse global samplings could be heard bedded in commercials, on collections and compilations, soundtracks, and Muzak-like packages from Putumayo piped into hip clothing stores. Further evidence of the growth and recognition of these long-established musical styles could also be found throughout the voluminous 720 pages of *World Music: The Rough Guide* (1994).

Among the chief contributors to the wave of greater world music awareness were several American recording artists who might be viewed, among other things, as "musical missionaries" and "disc-coverers." These musicians have explored, compiled, and integrated traditional, classical, and modern African, Asian, Middle Eastern, South American, and numerous other regional rhythms, arrangements, sounds, and styles from the peripheries into recordings that have been made available and become popular in the United States.

Continental Drifters and Disc-Coverers: Diamonds in the Rough

One of the earliest album-length experimental endeavors that integrated world music into the pop music realm originated from a somewhat surprising source— Neil Diamond. Diamond's impressive string of Top 20 songs, among them "Kentucky Woman," Cherry Cherry," "Thank the Lord for the Night Time," "Sweet Caroline," and "Holly Holy," and "I'm a Believer," which reached number one on the charts with The Monkees, were collectively part of a catalog that was a defining dimension of late 1960s pop. In 1970, Diamond released *Tap Root Manuscript*, which led off with another gold single, "Cracklin' Rosie" and a Top 20 Hollies cover "He Ain't Heavy, He's My Brother." However, what made the record distinctive was its side-long suite entitled "The African Trilogy." Conceived by Diamond as "a folk ballet," the six songs represented an "attempt to convey my passion for the folk music of that black continent" (Diamond). The rootsy, rhythmic blend of blues, gospel, and folk music featured primitive, percussive pop instrumentation and a child choir. The centerpiece of the twenty-minute musical narrative, "Soolaimon," became another Diamond hit.

Reviews of the record were mixed. To some critics, the ambitious recording was an artistic breakthrough for the commercially successful Diamond. To others, such as Dave Marsh, the record marked an identity crisis and Diamond's peer pursuit of the songwriting realm of Dylan and Paul Simon (Marsh and Swenson 1983: 39).

Whether viewed as a novelty, artistic diversion or pioneering effort, *Tap Root Manuscript*'s immediate influence was minimal. Few artists took a continental cue from the album's inventive Side Two suite. Diamond himself never followed his own foreign footsteps on subsequent recordings; *Tap Root Manuscript* appeared to be a one trick pony. During the next ten years, World pop music quests on any scale were sparse at best.

Beginning in 1982 with his pivotal role in the WOMAD festival and organization, and continuing through other efforts working with musicians such as Youssou N'Dour, Peter Gabriel has made ethnic world music a major focus of his work. Via the Real World label, he has showcased recordings by artists from a wide variety of cultures. At the same time, his own music became increasingly intertwined with traditional styles well outside Western norms and forms. While composing the musical score for Martin Scorsese's film, *The Last Temptation of Christ* (1988), Gabriel assembled many location field recordings, traditional music, and sources of inspiration into an accompanying record for the movie's soundtrack. *Passion Sources* (1989) features singers and soloists of Pakistan, Turkey, India, Ivory Coast, Bahrain, Egypt, New Guinea, Morocco, Senegal, and Ghana performing over a backdrop of North African rhythms and sounds.

David Byrne's artistic attentions have also spanned the globe, to Asia and Africa, before settling into Brazil. With the Talking Heads, he showed an inquisitive, intelligent interest in unusual applications of, and exploratory cultural variations on, pop music. Likewise, much of his solo work, particularly *Rei Momo* (1989), utilizes extensive Spanish and Latin styles, rhythms, and instrumentation. Byrne eventually was involved in compiling four volumes of contemporary Brazilian pop and dance music for the Luaka Bop label (*Brazil Classics: Beleza Tropical* (1989), *O Samba* (1989), *Tom Ze* (1990), *Forro Etc./ Music of the Brazilian Northeast* (1991)).

Jamaica's rich roots attracted singer-songwriter Jules Shear and Rolling Stone Keith Richards for a series of primitive projects. Shear's B-side career is highlighted by his songwriting credits for Big 80s hits by the Bangles ("If She Knew What She Wants"), Cyndi Lauper ("All Through the Night") and Alison Moyet ("Whispering Your Name"). The host of the earliest installments of MTV's *Unplugged* series, and the bittersweet subject of the 'Til Tuesday tune, "'J' for Jules," written by his ex, Aimee Mann, Shear has recorded nearly 20 albums since 1976, either solo or with Jules and the Polar Bears, The Funky Kings and Reckless Sleepers. In Jamaica, he added The Jolly Boys to his recording resume. Through these four elder musicians, Shear uncovered "mento," an African ancestral form rooted in English and French folk music and Afro Caribbean rhythms. During the 1930s and 1940s, mento was the island's most popular music, until it was exiled to the B-side around the 1950s, overwhelmed by electronic instrumentation and the arrival of reggae, ska and bluebeat. Between 1989 and 1991, Shear produced three live recordings with the funky, strumming Jolly Boys—*Pop 'n' Mento, Sunshine 'n' Water*, and *Beer Joint and Tailoring*. The traditional trilogy never reached revival or *Graceland* proportions, but, like many of the other world music missionary explorations, the series of recordings provided important small scale, B-side exposure and documentation within the global and American music marketplaces.

Richards joined the musical missionary ranks in Jamaica with the Wingless Angels, a seven member Rastarfarian drum and chant chorus. Richards's relationship with the dreadlock devotees dates to 1972 when they met at his restful retreat following the Rolling Stones's *Goat Heads Soup* recording session. Named by Richards because "they sing like angels but can't fly," the assembly of accomplished musicians includes St. Ann's first pop star, ska pioneer Justin Hinds and Winston Thomas, who has played with the Talking Heads and Bad Brains.

The group's African chant and a capella deliverance transcend local "Johnny Too Bad" dread heads covering Marley and Cliff classics for a case of Red Stripe and some island herb. Whether chants of praise or rhythms of resistance, invocations of spirituality pervade. The group reinterprets many traditional tunes, ranging from the familiar "We Shall Overcome" and "Rivers of Babylon" to more obscure Wesleyan church hymns brought to the island by missionaries. Though co-producer Richards removes the music from its original context for some studio enhancing, the sound retains its primitive rather than polished sound. The field recording character from the sun setting sessions in Brother Keith's Ocho Rios yard, complete with the noise of night insects and nature's nuances, remains. *Wingless Angels* (1996) marked the first release on Richards's Mindless Records label.

Without question, the most widely recognized accomplishment among the cross cultural collaborations, both critically and commercially, is Paul Simon's *Graceland* (1986), which emphasizes "township jive," the street music of Soweto, South Africa. "I couldn't figure out how they were doing what they were doing," explains Simon about his attraction to the African musical forms. "It was so different, so rhythmically sophisticated" (Steinberg and Lacy 1992). Several years later, Simon sought a similar rhythm method fusion with Brazilian interpretations that resulted in *Rhythm of the Saints* (1990).

The African and Brazilian dance rhythm uncovered by these recordings transcended the language barrier more easily than the lyric-oriented songs, melodic folk tunes, and dense trance pieces that also abound in the regions. These forms found a comfortable cultural and commercial niche, and largely defined the first wave of World Music imports to land on North American shores.

The second surge carried a far more diverse sampling to the United States. Though more anonymous enterprises with a B-side spirit, the musical pilgrimages to exotic locales by American musical missionaries reach such distant destinations as India, the island of Madagascar, Norway, and the more adjacent Cuba. These expeditions, led by eclectic, innovative multi-instrumentalists David Lindley, Henry Kaiser and Ry Cooder have yielded some of the richest, most impressive, intriguing conceptual and musical collections of any cross cultural convergences.

Henry and David's Excellent Adventures

> It might sound like seventeenth-century French music, Hawaiian music, African music and South American music all being played at the same time. It's really strange.
>
> Henry Kaiser (Goldberg 1991: 28)

California-based guitarists Henry Kaiser and David Lindley are considered "musician's musicians." Kaiser, characterized as a "brilliant post modern guitar hero," (Gehr 1989: 360) has appeared on more than 50 records since the early 1970s. His strange-ranging repertoire is both rootsy and electronically experimental, as it includes blues and jazz constructions, disjointed bluegrass, progressive rock, dazzling textured architechtronics, ethnic strands and total improvisation.

Lindley, characterized by one critic as a "phenomenon," may be one of popular music's most eclectic, exotic, eccentric and extraordinary musicians. Best known for being a session magician string master and Jackson Browne's sideman, Lindley, like Ry Cooder who began playing at an early age, was virtually born with an instrument in his hands. His uncle, a world-class concert pianist, and a violinist from the string quartet he rehearsed with, helped Lindley pick out a violin—a Sears Silvertone—when he was four years old. "I couldn't put it under my chin because I was so small, so I played it like a cello, a Viola da Gamba," recalls Lindley (Mr. Bonzai 1990: 108). At 14, he picked up a baritone ukelele, and soon after a Paracho Especial Flamenco guitar. "One of the reasons I picked up the guitar was so I could play Vietnamese zither music," claims Lindley (Wildfeuer 1993: 92). By age 18, he had won five consecutive Topanga Canyon Banjo and Fiddle competitions. His first band, the Mad Mountain Ramblers, played at Disneyland. In 1966 in Berkeley, he formed Kaleidoscope, an appropriately named psychedelic cult group that combined rag, jug, jazz, Cajun, boogie, bluegrass, blues, acid rock, with Near, Far, and Middle Eastern sounds. During the 1970s, Lindley was an integral part of Browne's band, and in the 1980s, he released five funky solo albums with his band El Rayo-X. Since then, Lindley has continued recording and touring with percussionists Hani Naser and Wally Ingram. Lindley has compiled one of the most exhaustive lists of session credits of any musician during the past 40 years (see Forte 1982; Kotapish 2000).

A casual survey of Lindley's recording credits reveals an astonishingly eclectic and unusual collection of instruments that reinforces frequent collaborator Cooder's claim that "David can play anything:" (Forte: 50) tambur, fiddle, citern, harpolek, psaltery, mandocello, pennywhistle, "Kona" koa lap steel and Hawaiiaan lap, vena, keyboard, banjo, bouzoukis, chumbas, guitorgan, mellobar, slide, mandolin, Divan and electro saz, saz bow, violin, six string bass, banduria, harp, chord zither, autoharp, dulcimer, oud, and Kora, Weisenborn Hawaiiaan, Silvertone, Goya Danelectro, Fender, National, Supro and "cheapo" pawn shop electric, acoustic, lead, rhythm, slide and slack-key guitars.[1]

Lindley's mastery of a multitude of instruments, combined with his tastes and knowledge of musics from many cultures, help account for "genre-blending mutations" (Grula 1988: 48) that "runs the gamut from Long Riders to low riders, traditional to radical, funk to chunk.mixes Okinawan, Korean and Chinese music with reggae, ska and rock and roll" (Bradley 1983: 29).[2]

---

1   Lindley's colorful collection of vintage, exotic stringed instruments and "cheapo" guitars is on display at his website, www.davidlindley.com.

2   After being in the audience for a 1994 Washington D.C. small club performance by Lindley with Jordanian hand percussionist, Hani Naser, American Studies scholar Greg Metcalf wrote: "There's almost nothing in this world that, once I've seen it or heard it, I can't figure out how the creator got there. Lindley is the transcendent exception. I ended up reacting to his performance as if he was a juggler or magician; I just couldn't believe what he was accomplishing both technically and conceptually. Shifting back and forth from

In October 1991, with the support of Shanachie Records and Yamaha Corporation, Kaiser and Lindley packed up their instruments, and, along with a two-person production team with state-of-the-art portable digital recording equipment, departed on the first of a series of expeditions to explore some of the farthest fringes of international music and culture. Their first destination was Madagascar, the planet's fourth largest island. Lindley and Kaiser had long been fascinated with the Malagasy people, their music, the rich and distinctive culture, and the isolated island's endemic plant and wildlife species. To them, it represented an ultimate fantasy island, an end of-the-world exotica and "world out of time."

The American explorers, or "vazaha" (the Malagasy term for foreigners or strangers), had arranged musical meetings with all of the major Malagasy musicians—popular, folk, traditional, electric, acoustic. Together they recorded for 16 to 18 hours a day over a two week period, resulting in five discs' worth of music. Shanachie refined and released the Kaiser/Lindley Madagascar collection in two thorough sets, *A World Out of Time* (1992) (18 tracks, 66 minutes), and *Volume 2* (1993) (17 tracks, 73 minutes), followed by a thinner *Volume 3* (1996).

Unlike Paul Simon, whose Third World collaborations were as a singer-songwriter, the Kaiser/Lindley approach was almost exclusively as pickers and players. Throughout, the pair respectfully tried to remain faithful to the Malagasy musical and cultural traditions in both feeling and content. The methods, circumstances, nature and results of the collaborations were wide ranging. The majority of the repertoire and arrangements were Malagasyan, with Lindley and Kaiser adapting to those roots. On some occasions, the two stayed out of the way entirely because they felt they had nothing to contribute to the music as it was being played in its purest forms. At other times, they overlayed their own elegant and unusual musical ideas, and were not bashful about inserting a slide-guitar solo, Celtic fiddle break, or suggesting everyone experiment by playing an Okinawan love song.

As a result, Kaiser's experimental impulses and Lindley's "genre-blending mutation" signatures surfaced on occasion in the cultural exchange. The island's most popular and eclectic electric band, Rossy, reinterprets the Sonny Curtis American standard popularized by the Bobby Fuller Four, "I Fought the Law," in a Malagasy mode. The group also joins Lindley in a wild, cross-cultural reggae, valiha (a tubular zither of the highland plateau constructed with bamboo with metal strings) and bouzouki version of Merle Haggard's #1 country hit from 1966, "I'm A Lonesome Fugitive."

Many of the magical musical moments from the meeting were spontaneous occurrences. Two involved Rakota Frah, a 70-year old sodina (Malagasy flute constructed from aluminum tent or ski poles) master who draws comparisons to Western instrumental masters such as Ornette Coleman, Miles Davis, and John Coltrane. Rakota Frah unexpectedly joined Lindley during a break while he

---

Turkish to Bluegrass, with stopovers in Reggae and Mariachi in the same song" (personal correspondence April 1994).

was playing a Weissenborn slide guitar version of Ray Price's 1956 hit (and later the Everly Brothers), "You Done Me Wrong." The recording engineer had left the DAT machine running and the impromptu track was preserved. "The Rakota Frah Two-Step" is the result of the Malagaysan master again instantly joining Lindley as he was picking out a New Orleans type groove on his Weissenborn. Kaiser contributed an electric kabosy, a strange, partially fretted mandolin-like guitar; and Rakota Frah's two drummers provided a rhythm that Lindley and Ry Cooder have been trying for years to get people to play during Los Angeles recording sessions.

From their arrival until their departure, the Americans appeared committed to capturing every sound of the expedition. In addition to the diverse music sampling that includes lullabyes, ballads, instrumentals, village roots and dance music, there are field recordings which further capture the Malagasy culture and accent the collection. Among the naturalistic sounds are "The Welcome Party," recorded upon the vazaha arrival in the island's capital, Antananarivo; "Kabary," a public speech or poetic proclamation that is a living art on the island, used during various religious and cultural ceremonies and rituals; and "Lemur Rap," a recording that inadvertently, but perfectly, mixed drum tracks onto a tape that had previously captured the indri lemurs of Madagascar's rainforests "singing" together in groups at dawn and dusk on another track.

Following the unprecedented project, and the critical and commercial acceptance of the *World Out of Time* recordings, Lindley and Kaiser were committed to pursuing similar musical expeditions to other locales. Following months of research, planning, and careful consideration of various destinations, the two chose another "world out of time"—Norway. The isolated, sparsely populated, narrow region is one of the most northerly parts of the world with deep cultural and musical traditions.

In the summer of 1994, Lindley, Kaiser, and their production team departed for Norway, where they spent three weeks in a rented worker's dormitory, musician's homes, and the natural environments of the mountains and valleys, collaborating with 61 of the region's diverse and expressive artists. The conditions were rather unusual due to the typical Norwegian summers which consist of long days with only one or two hours of darkness.

The beauty, depth, and pleasure of the sessions with the Laplanders and locals are apparent in the music on the resulting two volumes, *The Sweet Sunny North* (1994, 1996). Many of the 28 tracks of each album emphasize Norway's national instrument, the hardanger fiddle. In addition, there are the requisite Kaiser/Lindley American exchanges that evolve into unsusual cross-cultural hybrids. For example, they perform "Drunken Hiccups," a well known, traditional American fiddle piece, with master musician and silversmith Halvard T. Bjorgum. "The Pilgrim Song," based on an old religious folk tune, combines the Norse funeral and New Orleans funeral brass band traditions. Teenage singer, Deepika, covers Lindley's "Alien Invasion" alternating verses in Norwegian and English, with a Pakistani style, with Lindley accompanying her on bouzouki, oud, and background vocals. And Lindley and Kaiser do a version of the classic American Civil War ballad,

"The Sweet Sunny South," with Tone and Hans Frederick, who lead the musicians into Norwegian cow call variations at the end of the song.

From Ganges Delta to Buena Vista

> Music is a treasure hunt. You dig and dig and sometimes you find something.
> Ry Cooder (1997: 3)

In addition to being one of the most skilled and versatile players in popular music, Ry Cooder is commonly regarded as a knowledgeable, passionate musicologist and ethnographer, descriptions he readily dismisses. Cooder's ceaseless curiosity of American musical traditions precedes his world view (see Chapter 5). Though deeply rooted in the American musical idiom, Cooder has always responded to outside ethnic influences and the unique collaborative potential the musical forms and their musicians hold. A unique opportunity arose in 1993 when Cooder heard a recording of Hindustani, or North Indian Classical music, performed by young instrumentalist V.M. Bhatt. Cooder was not only impressed with Bhatt's playing, but intrigued by the haunting clarity that was both lively and lovely, of the Mohan Vina, a slide-guitar variation of Bhatt's own design. According to Alexander (1993), it is quite possible that the "slide" technique as it was initially done in Hawaii and later by Delta bluesmen could have been influenced by these North and South Indian musical instrument models.

The two master musicians connected for a spontaneous session in which they explored surprising common ground without imitating each other's traditions. Bhatt's playing is highly nuanced, whereas Cooder works in the loose-jointed, slip 'n' slide style. Blending the contrasting sounds of Bhatt's Mohan Vina (steel rod against metal strings) with Cooder's bottleneck blues (glass against steel strings), made the collaboration conceptually challenging. "With no planning whatsoever, and no preparation, the musicians soon established a dialogue through which they could probe each other so as to know where the bends in the river were going to be, or how deep, or how swift the waters," writes Alexander (1993), who arranged, recorded and produced the meeting. Percussionists Sukhvinder Singh Namdhari and Cooder's 14-year-old son, Joachim, accompanied the side players, providing an extra dimension of complex Indian rhythms with the tabla and dumbek, a Middle Eastern drum.

The resulting recording, *A Meeting by the River* (1993), is a blend of American grit and Indian stateliness, a mutuality best expressed in the song title "Ganges Delta Blues." Musically and metaphorically, Cooder and Bhatt represented two streams hoping to form, or flow into, a river. The record's sonic and symbolic pleasures are an expansive musical landscape that resonate beyond its forty minute running time; the four songs contain celebration, sweet sadness, and calm resolution, and "represents a tone poem side of Cooder not heard since his music for the soundtrack to *Paris, Texas*" (Woodard 1993: 110).

The record, which was awarded a Grammy, marked a pivotal point in Cooder's career. Following his film soundtrack period, Cooder's cultural quests continued to move him farther away from the musical mainstream. From Little Village, Cooder's 1992 commercial co-op with John Hiatt, Nick Lowe and Jim Keltner, to global village, Ry's residency in the world music sphere became more permanent during the next 13 years.

Following *A Meeting by the River,* Cooder sought another exotic organic union, this time with Mailian guitarist Ali Farka Toure, as the two blended Delta blues with traditional West Africa music on *Talking Timbuktu* (1994). Later, Cooder paired first with Indian flautist Ronu Majumadar for electric genre-defying compositions and Indian folk melodies on *Hollow Bamboo* (2002), then with Cuban guitarist Manuel Galban on *Mambo Sinuendo* (2002), a record which features an elaborate, eclectic stylistic range from sultry bolero and mambo jazz to go-go funk and sock hop shuffle.

Mambo Sinuendo[3] was a by product of Cooder's Cuban connection which had been evolving since 1996. Cooder's fascination with Cuban music dates back to a 1976 visit to the republic as part of a touring clandestine jazz outfit which featured Dizzie Gillespie, Stan Getz and Earl Hines. Twenty years later, Cooder returned to Cuba seeking to reunite the "son de Cuba," retired African and Cuban musicians and composers from the 1940s and 1950s. Most of the veterans, whose ages ranged from the mid to late-seventies to the nineties, had for the most part been forgotten in their homeland. Among the elder musicians were 89-year old guitarist Compay Segundo, pianist Ruben Gonzalez, who no longer even had a piano, vocalist Ibrahim Ferrer, who was shining shoes for a living, trumpeter Manuel "Guajiro" Mirabel, and bolero and *feeling* singer Omara Portuondo, the only woman in the ensemble.

Once assembled, the group named their improvisational sessions in honor of the Buena Vista, an iconic members-only social club in the hills of east Havana. Accompanied and augmented by the versatile Cooder and his percussionist son Joachim, they recorded 14 songs that provided a composite of a rich Cuban heritage, its dancehalls and clubs. Many of the songs were rooted in turn of the century compositions, their lyrics drawn from folklore, romantic ballads, patriotic hymns, Spanish traditions and *guajiro* (peasant) backgrounds. The instrumentation, rhythms and vocal styles, are a cross cultural convergence that blends black American strands of jazz, gospel and blues with *boleros, sons, mambo, danzon, guajira* (a country lament known as the "Cuban blues"), *criolla, descarga* (a fusion of jazz style improvisation with Afro Cuban rhythms), *guayabero* (a "passion fruit" style of singing which talks of everyday life with lyrics filled with sexual innuendo) (see Gold and Williamson)

---

3   The term derives from a Hawaiian expression meaning "something that gives goose bumps" (Harrington: G4).

Cooder's passion for locating, experiencing, reviving and preserving the musical traditions and sounds of diverse cultures appears to be part of a calling, his lifelong quest.

> When I was a little kid, I can remember records that I used to hear on the radio. It's the sounds of the instruments and the idea that people were together and something was happening. But I felt that I was missing it because I couldn't get there. In order to have the experience, to play a certain way and feel a certain way, you have to go make it up. The sad thing for me is... I've spent all my time either trying to find the instruments that make the sound, whatever they were, then trying to locate individuals who are somewhere; and they're dwindling and generally tend to be someplace else now. And if that's the case you have to go where they are. (Harrington 2003: G4)

From Barriers to Bridges

> It's all music. There's notes and you play and sing and it's wonderful and you love it regardless of where it comes from.
>
> David Lindley (Grula: 45)

> You connect with the sound, not the idea.
>
> Ry Cooder (Scherman: 75)

The scope and significance of many of these cross cultural collaborations extends beyond the music itself and the special communication process between the artists who joined together from worlds apart. Religious, social, political, cultural, geographical, and historical dimensions frame the musical encounters.

Another common thread could be found in a context of controversy. Civil unrest and political instability were part of the backdrop, conditions and circumstances surrounding most of the projects. Much of the Brazilian pop and dance music compiled by David Byrne was viewed as "dangerous" by the military regime that ruled the South American country during the 1960s and early 1970s. Many of the artists represented on the compilations were forced into exile as a result of their musical expressions. Their lyrics, rhythms, and electric guitars encouraged and inspired a generation, much to the dismay of the government.

Although Peter Gabriel's soundtrack work for *The Last Temptation of Christ* was largely unaffected, director Martin Scorsese's adaptation generated considerable controversy over its religious portrayals. Lindley and Kaiser arrived in Madagascar to work on *A World Out of Time* amidst a dramatic five-month general strike which had crippled the nation's government and economy. During their two-week stay, there were thousands of demonstrators daily in the streets.

Fidel Castro's long shadow and a U.S. ban on travel cast complications over Ry Cooder's Buena Vista Social Club sessions. Cooder's initial 1996 visit resulted in a $100,000 fine (later reduced to $25,000) because he failed to apply for a license.

Cooder believed cultural exchanges were exempt from such permits. In January 2000, when Cooder applied for permission to return to Cuba to record follow up albums with Ferrer, Galban and others, federal authorities denied his request. A second trip by Cooder would have subjected him to higher fines and possible criminal penalties. As a last resort, Cooder appealed directly to the White House, and as one of his final acts in office, President Bill Clinton granted Cooder and his American band members (drummer Jim Keltner and Cooder's son, Joachim) one-year exemption from the travel ban. Increased post-9/11 prohibitions prevented several of Cooder's Cuban cohorts from touring in the U.S. and attending the Grammy Award ceremonies.

Paul Simon's *Graceland* may have been popular, and praised for its musical merits and for disseminating new music, but Simon drew considerable criticism from many circles for touring South Africa and using the apartheid country's musicians. Many viewed it as yet another example of white American exploitation of black musical expressions. During a segment in Simon's biographical documentary, *Born at the Right Time, New York Times* music critic, Jon Pareles went as far as to suggest Simon might be compared to a "carpetbagger."

> He waltzes into town. He takes the most catchy thing he can find. He brings it back and it's his hit. It's a complicated thing. I'm not saying it's bad; I'm saying it's blatant. On the one hand, ideas belong to everybody. On the other hand, music is a sign of a culture. If you take the sign and sort of leave the culture behind, it sometimes leaves a hollow feeling. (Steinberg and Lacy 1993)

"I don't think politically or culturally first, I think musically," was Simon's response to his critics. (Steinberg and Lacy 1993).[4]

Controversies aside, the American musicians involved in these musical expeditions cast themselves as discoverers and musical missionaries. The recordings which resulted from the various projects have contributed significantly, albeit on a relatively small scale, to an American awakening to World Music, its traditions and artists, and their various vocal, instrumental, and dance styles and expressions.

Miriam Makeba, Ladysmith Black Mambazo, and South African rhythms received considerable exposure from the *Graceland* album and its multi-media marketing synergy that included a tour, concert video, and a cable television special, *Graceland: The African Concert* (1987), an award winning musical documentary (see Chapter 7). David Byrne's tropical trek resulted in the "Brazil Classics" series of compilations for the Luaka Bop label. Following the Madagascar project, Shanachie released records by several artists "discovered" by Lindley and Kaiser during their travels, among them, Rossy, D'Gary, and Dama. Although not all of

---

4 The editing in the documentary magnified the conflict. Pareles' comments were followed by a testy exchange between Simon and an audience member who raised similar issues during a question and answer session at Howard University.

the unknown artists were signed to record deals, the Madagascar and Norway projects marked the first opportunity for many of the musicians to be recorded.

The "Introduction" in the *World Music: The Rough Guide* volume attributes the greater global sound consciousness to these American musical missionaries. "If you just heard Youssou N'Dour on the radio, Ladysmith Black Mambazo on a Paul Simon record, or Margaret Menezes supporting David Byrne. This is the guide that tells you where to go from there" (Broughton 1994).

The missionary analogy becomes more appropriate and salient when considering that before the Kaiser-Lindley Madagascar sessions in 1991, there had never been a release of Malagasy music, traditional or popular, in North America. Only a few difficult to find recordings were available in Europe, England, Japan and the Soviet Union.

The product "packaging" of the records in many cases also appears designed to fulfill a goal of creating a broader cultural awareness beyond the music itself. Shanachie's booklets for the Madagascar and Norway collections are particularly impressive documents. Both *World Out of Time* volumes and *The Sweet Sunny North* each contain 20 to 30 pages of liner notes are informative archival artifacts with a box set spirit. Each is an insightful "geomusicultural" document filled with information about the region, its geography, wildlife, people, customs, language, culture, and history, as well as a song-by-song guide to the artists, American cross-references, musical traditions, lyric translations, terminology, photographs, instruments, techniques, and anecdotal accounts of the recording sessions. The disc and document together are an informative artifact that resembles an issue of *National Geographic* or a Discovery Channel documentary feature.

Cooder's comprehensive Buena Vista Social Club project was transcendent; its scope a touchstone among the various cross cultural collaborations. In addition to the record's 50-page booklet with song-by-song narrative, lyrics, and session photos, the vista of complementary chronicles included a worldwide tour, a documentary by German filmmaker Wim Wenders (1999) and a companion book of photos, interviews, musician biographies and film stills compiled by Wenders and his wife Donata (2000). Cooder had been working on the score to Wenders' film, *The End of the Violence* (1997), when he decided to send the director a demo tape with a significant sampling of music he had recorded with his Cuban compadres in Havana. Cooder's previous cross cultural "obscuriences" haunted him with fears that the music he had uncovered would disappear without documentation or ever being heard.

> Every time those records would get made, I'd sit there and I'd think "they're missing all of it" and it bothered me a lot, And of course the film taught everybody what was in the music that they wouldn't have seen, wouldn't have known. Most folks don't hear things like they see them. (Harrington 2003: G5)

Buena Vista Social Club sparked international interest in Cuban music. The revival and reception equaled, if not surpassed, the response to the South

African sounds presented by Simon in *Graceland,* ten years earlier. A critical and commercial success, the record earned a Grammy and sold 8 million copies, which is more than Cooder's eleven solo albums combined. Wenders' accompanying film was one of the highest-grossing documentaries and an Academy Award winner. And like the Simon, Lindley and Kaiser cultural collaborations, individual recordings from the discovered/rediscovered musicians followed. The *Buena Vista Social Club* spawned and sponsored solo records by Ibrahim Ferrer, Ruben Gonzalez, Manuel Mirabal, Omaro Portuondo and an anthology featuring the Afro Cuban All Stars. *Washington Post* music critic Richard Harrington characterized the cumulative impact of *Buena Vista Social Club* as "the biggest phenomenon in the history of world music" (G1).

Rhythms, Roots and Reverence

Among the common threads linking all of these world music imports are rhythms, roots and reverence. Byrne, Gabriel, Diamond, Shear, Richards, Simon, Cooder, Kaiser and Lindley, clearly demonstrate a deep respect not only for the music, but the cultures they explored. There is a sense of spirituality that is apparent beyond the beats; it resonates as a significant subtext in their world recordings.

While working on the soundtrack for *The Last Temptation of Christ*, Peter Gabriel was inspired by director Martin Scorsese's commitment to the spiritual content and message of Nikos Kazantzakis' controversial novel that he was adapting to the screen. In Madagascar, Lindley and Kaiser believed their project was "blessed by the Malagasy Ancestral Spirits." Ancestral worship is a unique veneration central to the daily lives of the Malagasy people. They believe that their Ancestors govern the living from their vantage point in eternity. The American visitors reverently attributed many of the strange, unexplained occurrences during their recording sessions to "a special communication from the Malagasy Spirit World," which included spirit possession of their instruments on occasion.

The session between Cooder and Bhatt, which took place on a Persian rug by the altar of a Catholic church in the presence of Franciscan monks, was also rooted in the mystic. As a theme to frame his cross cultural collaboration with Bhatt, Cooder chose a parable by the 13th century mystic poet, Jelaluddin Rumi. His "Mathnawi" is a poem about a frog and a mouse who meet on a river bank to converse in a language unhindered by the rules of grammar. The parable was an appropriate metaphor not only for Cooder and Bhatt, but for Neil Diamond, Gabriel, Simon, Byrne, Lindley, Kaiser and their cross cultural collaborators. The merging of these musicians from very different and distant corners of the world unfolded with no boundaries into spontaneous, spiritual, and natural expressions.

These various cross cultural sessions represent musical, as well as spiritual quests which mate modern and ancient music traditions; unify an enormous geographic spread; and bridge cultures. The artists who have pursued these projects are accomplished musicians and composers, as well as knowledgeable

98 *B-SIDES, UNDERCURRENTS AND OVERTONES*

musicologists with a passionate interest, love, and respect for music and its roots. Their reverence for these holy musical unions was expressed as early as 1970 by Neil Diamond in his lyrical liner notes in *Tap Root Manuscript:*

> When rhythm and blues lost its sensuality for me I fell in love with a woman named gospel. We met secretly in the churches of Harlem, and made love at revival meetings in Mississippi. And loving her as I did, I found a great yearning to know her roots. And I found them. And they were in Africa. And they left me breathless. (1970)

Cross Cultural Continuity: Lost in Translation?

> I don't say I'm going around with a magic wand. As one old friend of mine, Jim Dickinson, once said, 'Neglect will kill music.'
>
> Ry Cooder (Marchese 2007)

Artists from Diamond and Simon to Lindley, Kaiser, Cooder and in between, have assumed rewarding roles as B-side explorers and discoverers, visionaries and missionaries. Their expeditions in world music have uncovered, converted and transformed the B-side genre into an A-side crossover, if only temporarily. Despite the initial impact, exposures, critical acclaim and commercial successes, awards and recognition, the collective, enduring mark of these projects is as a significant musical parenthesis more than a major movement. Following the A-side flirtation, most of these world music missionaries and their efforts returned to their peripheral places on the B-Side.

The advanced age of many of the world musical discoveries alone has been a factor hindering continuity of the cultural cause. Two Cooder collaborators recently died, Ibrahim Ferrer in 2005, and Ali Farka Toure in 2006. At the same time, the music media and marketplace collective taste and interests appear to have shifted from world music in its purest forms toward a more accessible pop global sound. Border crossovers such as Ricky Martin, Marc Anthony and Shakira represent the new vista. While Byrne, Gabriel, and Simon are frequently bundled into an 1980s World wrapper, and Cooder and Buena Vista merit an occasional recognizable reference, the more distant, obscure works of Kaiser and Lindley are missing from the media map.

Even the more noteworthy cross cultural collaborations continue to be lost in translation. In the Fall 2001, *Time* magazine published a special issue, "Music Goes Global." The "pop" rather than "pure" world music preference and point of view pervaded the essays. The edition included a "Making Tracks" insert which highlighted "moments when cultures combined to make fresh new music" (McLaughlin). The multifarious musical manifestations of *Graceland* and *Buena Vista Social Club* were mere mentions, but presumably no more meritorious marks on the time line than the smaller scale single duets such as Rolling Stone Mick Jagger with reggae star Peter Tosh on "(You Gotta Walk and) Don't Look Back" in 1978; and in 2001, the blending of Algerian *rai* by Sting and Cheb Mami on "Desert Rose," a song that was used in a Jaguar car commercial.

What is more striking than that simplification is the generational divide and resentful tone presented in David Thigpen's (2001) essay on Cuban music, "Hidden Havana." The subtitle pronounces "The Buena Vista Social Club is yesterday," while Thigpen's text refers to the Buena Vista Social Club as "the geezer vocal group that popularized pre-revolution balladry everywhere except Cuba" (21). Twenty-eight year old Equis Alfonso, a Havana hip hop/*son* fusion artist and member of the group Sintesis, further demystifies the elder ensemble. "People think because of Ry Cooder and Buena Vista that Cuban music became better known. That may be true, but it set us back 40 years. Now we are fighting against the mythological vision of the old Cuba, the Cuba of the Tropicana Club and old cars. All the musicians today have to fight to find a market" (21).

Cooder has grown accustomed to the "Oh who are you to go down there?" scoffing. He dismisses the whispers that he is a dilettante, citing the fallout benefits of his musical excursions. "There are more Cuban musicians working in music than ever before, and what's wrong with that?" said Cooder (Marchese 2007).

Despite the detractors and "carpetbagger" criticism, the over arching intentions of the musical expeditions of Simon, Cooder, Lindley, Kaiser and company are more intrinsically exploratory and expressive than they are exploitative. These world music missionaries have drawn resourcefully and reverently from global genres on the B-side, removing barriers and building bridges. The resulting cross cultural collaborations have contributed to a greater awareness of musical diversity on the A-side, and demonstrated connections between world musicians and their forms, styles, and traditions and American music and culture.

Selected Discography

Afro-Cuban All Stars. *A Toda Cuba Le Gusta* (World Circuit/Nonesuch, 1997).
Ali Farka Toure with Ry Cooder. *Talking Timbuktu* (Rykodisc, 1994).
A World Out of Time: Henry Kaiser and David Lindley in Madagascar (Shanachie, 1992).
A World Out of Time, Vol. 2 (Shanachie, 1993).
A World Out of Time, Vol 3. Music of Madagascar (Shanachie, 1996).
Brazil Classics, Vol 1: Beleza Tropical (Luaka Bop, 1990).
———. *Beleza Tropical Vol 2: Novo! Mais! Melor!* (Luaka Bop, 1998).
———. *Vol. 2. O Samba* (Luaka Bop, 1990).
———. *Vol. 3. Forro' Etc.* (Luaka Bop, 1991).
———. *Vol 4. The Best of Tom Ze': Massive Hits* (Luaka Bop, 1990).
Buena Vista Social Club with Ry Cooder. *Buena Vista Social Club* (World Circuit/Nonesuch, 2003).
Byrne, David. *Rei Momo* (Luaka Bop, 1989).
Cooder, Ry and V.M. Bhatt. *A Meeting by the River* (Water Lily Acoustics, 1993).

100   *B-SIDES, UNDERCURRENTS AND OVERTONES*

—— and Manuel Galban. *Mambo Sinuendo* (Nonesuc/Perro Verde, 2002).

D'Gary. *Malagasy Guitar/Music From Madagascar* (Shanachie, 1993).

Diamond, Neil. *Tap Root Manuscript* (Uni Records, 1970).

Ferrer, Ibrahim. *Buena Vista Social Club Presents Ibrahim Ferrer* (World Circuit/ Nonesuch, 1999).

——. *Buenos Hermanos* (World Circuit/Nonesuch, 2003).

Gabriel, Peter. *Passion Sources* (Geffen Records, 1989).

Gonzalez, Ruben. *Introducing.Ruben Gonzalez* (World Circuit/Nonesuch, 1997).

Jolly Boys, The. *Pop 'N' Mento* (First Warning/Rough Trade, 1989).

——. *Sunshine 'N' Water* (First Warning/Rykodisc, 1991).

——. *Beer Joint and Tailoring* (First Warning, 1991).

Majumadar, Ronu, with Ry Cooder and Jon Hassell. *Hollow Bamboo* (Water Lily Acoustics, 2000).

Mirabel, Manuel "Guajiro". *Buena Vista Social Club Presents Manuel "Guajiro" Mirabel* (World Circuit/Nonesuch, 2005).

Portundo, Omaro. *Buena Vista Social Club Presents Omaro Portundo* (World Circuit/Nonesuch, 2000).

Rossy. *One Eye on the Future One Eye on the Past* (Shanachie, 1993).

Simon, Paul. *Graceland* (Warner Bros., 1986).

——. *The Rhythm of the Saints* (Warner Bros., 1990).

The Sweet Sunny North: Henry Kaiser and David Lindley in Norway (Shanachie, 1994).

The Sweet Sunny North, Vol. 2 Henry Kaiser and David Lindley in Norway (Shanachie, 1996).

Wingless Angels. *Wingless Angels* (Mindless Records, 1996).

Chapter 7

The Vital Visual Voice of the Videotape Editor: Seamlessly Sculpting *Graceland: The African Concert*

For years it has been the client coming into the editing room and telling the editor what they want, and all the editor does is operate the machines. Editing has evolved to where people aren't surprised anymore when they run into an editor who has some really great ideas; they actually expect creative input. Most people have little knowledge of what post production is all about.

Director John Fortenberry[1]

Between the late 1960s and late 1970s, big screen rock music spectacles such as *Monterey Pop* (1969), *Woodstock* (1970), *Gimme Shelter* (1970) and *The Last Waltz* (1978) established the "rockumentary" and concert film as a cornerstone of cultural experience. The form has steadily progressed, from *Pink Floyd's The Wall* (1982) and the Talking Heads' *Stop Making* Sense (1984) to contemporary biographical concert oddyseys, notably *No Direction Home: Bob Dylan* (2005), *Neil Young: Heart of Gold* (2006) and the Rolling Stones' *Shine A Light* (2008). Music performance productions thrive in the expanding technospace of the multimedia market, including cable, home video, Internet and downloads. While the performers, their performances and directorial efforts of notable rockumentarians such as D.A. Pennebaker, Michael Wadleigh, Albert and David Maysles, Martin Scorsese and Jonathan Demme, are conveniently, and deservedly recognized, there are many unsung contributors behind the scenes contributing to the construction of these music-film-video productions.

Of the many voices in television's collaborative chorus, one of the most anonymous is that of the videotape editor. Since the mid-1950s, when videotape revolutionized television production, producers and directors have had the luxury of shooting out of sequence, using the best take, and fixing flaws in editing. Whereas the film editor is commonly recognized as having significant creative skills and input, videotape editors have traditionally evolved as technicians or engineers.

---

1 Fortenberry was the Senior Editor at Broadway Video between 1982-1990. His comments throughout this text are from formal interviews (February, May, June 1988), on site observations at Broadway Video, and continual casual conversations, in person, via phone and e-mail from 1980 to present. Endless thanks to John for his graciousness, time, insights and faithful friendship.

102 B-SIDES, UNDERCURRENTS AND OVERTONES

The cumbersome earliest editing equipment with the two-inch format required an engineer to do the edits. Most were not concerned with the creative aspects as much as they were with technical operations.

Over the years the role of the videotape editor has evolved from strictly mechanical tasks to include creative involvement. More than a machine operator on an assembly line, the editor can be a skilled technician as well as craftsperson with his/her own personal style and vision.

In the collaborative expression of television, it is difficult to single out one individual or stage of production as being a more valuable role or link in the creative chain. Much depends on the successful interaction, negotiation and compromise between the individuals within the art world as a project passes through each phase of production. While the successive stages are interrelated, they all have their own distinct structures, operations and specialists at the forefront and behind the scenes. During the initial stage of production, the writer takes on special significance, just as the director, producer and performer are prominent during the production phase. During post-production, it is the editor who is essential.

While the videotape editor's work is often virtually invisible, it is no less vital. In the cluttered collaboration of the creative chain, the editor is a sculptor who provides the project punctuation mark, shaping, refining and polishing the work in progress toward its completed composition. The editor is commonly among the last to sign the collective signature of a production before it is submitted to producers, network executives, and eventually received by the audience. Just as the editor's name is a blurred B-side on the roll of credits, post production possesses the B-side trait of being an overlooked environment of the television and video creative stages, particularly in the body of literature on television's creative process.[2]

Going to Graceland, Africa

Before becoming a director, with film and television credits that include *A Night at the Roxbury*, *Jury Duty*, *Arrested Development*, *Rescue Me*, and *Everybody*

---

2   Among the relevant models, concepts and theoretical frameworks are production studies which focus on the industry itself (Cantor); key creative personnel such as producers and directors (Ravage; Newcomb and Alley); interaction and decision making within the multi-link chains of the media arts (Ryan and Peterson; Ettema and Whitney; Peterson); assembly line, craft and entrepreneurship (Peterson and Berger); convention, formula, specialists and activities within an "art world" (Becker); audience image, conflict, negotiation (Cantor; Gans); puzzle formulation and puzzle solution (Getzels and Csikszentmihalyi).

A more theoretical-oriented version of this chapter, "The Videotape Editor as Sculptor: Paul Simon's *Graceland in Africa, A Post-Production Case Study*," synthesizes elements of these frameworks and models into a hybrid model applied to Fortenberry's roles, activities and environment as a videotape editor. The case study was part of a special issue "Close Studies of Television: Encoding Research" edited by Bernard Timberg and David Barker for the *Journal of Film and Video*, Volume 41, Number 2, Summer 1989: 42-57.

Loves Raymond, John Fortenberry paid his dues working behind the scenes on what might be considered "the B-side of production."[3] Fortenberry began his apprenticeship in the early 1980s as a videotape editor for legendary comedy producer and *Saturday Night Live* creator Lorne Michaels' New York production company, Broadway Video, located in the historic songwriting factory, the Brill Building.[4] During that period, Fortenberry was involved in various roles besides editing, including producing home video, technical directing for various musical and comedy specials for network and cable, and directing.[5]

In 1987, singer-songwriter Paul Simon hired Fortenberry to be technical director for his *Graceland: The African Concert*, a tour that would be shaped into a 90-minute music special for Showtime cable. While Fortenberry contributed significantly during the preproduction and production stages of the project, it was his experience and skill as an editor during post-production which, according to producer Cheri Fortis and other members of the production crew, "saved the project." For his editing efforts, Fortenberry was nominated for an ACE award for cable excellence and a BAFTA.[6]

The concert, showcasing music from Simon's *Graceland* (1986) record, and South African performers Hugh Masekela, Miriam Makeba and the 10-man a cappella choir, Ladysmith Black Mambazo, was shot in Rufaro Stadium in Harare, Zimbabwe, February 1987, and scheduled to be aired the following May.[7] The shoot was imposing by typical production standards—a $1.4 million budget,

---

3 Among Fortenberry's other notable television credits are *The Reaper*, *Psych*, *It's Always Sunny in Philadelphia*, *Bernie Mac*, *Greg the Bunny*, *Just Shoot Me*, *The Ben Stiller Show* and *The Kids in the Hall*. For a complete listing, see IMDb.

4 Broadway Video was established by Michaels in 1980. The state-of-the-art facility is not as expansive as other New York City production houses. Broadway Video was established as an elite editing boutique which caters largely to high class clientele. Their projects include a wide range of productions, from agency work, such as commercials, to network and cable television productions. Formal interviews conducted by the author with Michaels (November 1984, April 1985) provide further context.

5 Fortenberry's range of credits with Broadway Video include producing, directing, technical directing and editing productions for cable, broadcast, syndication and home video in a variety of genres: compilations (*The Best of Saturday Night Live* (Aykroyd, Chase, et al)); comedy specials for Spalding Gray, Robert Klein, Whoopi Goldberg, Gilbert Gottfried, Sandra Bernhardt, Dennis Miller; music specials, documentaries and concerts (Bette Midler, Randy Newman, Paul Simon, Harry Belafonte); cartoon commemorations (*Looney Tunes 50th Anniversary*); sports (*Spirit of Excellence, 1984 Summer Olympics*); (ESPN), reviewer reels (Broadway shows), openings (New York Yankees on WPIX), and a Clio Award winning promo series for Nickelodeon network.

6 BAFTA is the British Academy of Film and Television Arts. Fortenberry and the original editor Ruth Foster received the nominations for editing.

7 For a good overview of Simon's *Graceland* tour and its political context, see David Fricke (1987).

104   *B-SIDES, UNDERCURRENTS AND OVERTONES*

nine cameras and taping two separate concerts on consecutive days, resulting in a total of 65 hours of footage, a "monster to edit."

Having been hired as technical director, Fortenberry was not scheduled to edit the show. However, early in the post-production stages, the assigned editor left the project after ten days.[8] Panicked producers Fortis and Ian Hoblyn realized that Fortenberry was their logical, and perhaps only choice to replace the departed editor if the project was to be completed on time. From a creative point of view, it was beneficial to have Fortenberry edit the footage instead of bringing in someone from the outside. The producers were familiar with Fortenberry's requisite skills and experience, and he had been involved with the project from the conception stage. Because of these factors, he did not have to depend on others to structure his style and performance as an editor.

During preproduction, Fortenberry worked closely with Paul Simon and director Michael Lindsay-Hogg, audio specialist Stacey Foster, and other production crew members in establishing the technical and aesthetic framework for the concert special. Simon, who conceived the presentation, did not want to feature himself as the star. He envisioned a structure that resembled a variety show, and adapted the elements and spirit of the township jazz revues with which Masekela and Makeba first toured South Africa in the 1950s. Fortenberry and the production crew followed the *Graceland* tour for four performances in Europe in order to familiarize themselves with the show, then spent several days in Zimbabwe at Harare Stadium and in the townships, shooting second-unit footage of African scenes (landscapes, people, markets) which would be integrated into the concert footage.

As the show's "sculptor," it was important to Fortenberry to know the available images on tape that he would be shaping and piecing together into a program. He felt his role as technical director enhanced his creative approach as an editor:

> Technical directing is good for the editor: you're that much more familiar with what's on tape. You do a lot of your cutting during the shoot and it saves you from walking into an editing room with the entire concert. As an editor, I feel that if you want a creative effort from me, I'd have to take the time to view every inch of footage, otherwise, you can't make suggestions about what you don't know. It's vital to know what you've got to work with before you start building.

Technical directing might be viewed as an assembly line function with its structured and routinized tasks for the operator, who switches on commands from the director. Because the concert's nine camera set up made it an overwhelming task for the director alone to call the cuts, Fortenberery had an unusual amount of creative input as technical director of *Graceland: The African Concert.*

---

8   The original editor, Ruth Foster, provided the most basic rough cut of the footage before leaving the project supposedly due to another commitment. Many of the crew members suggested the editor either couldn't, or didn't want to, handle the enormous amount of footage.

He switched much of the show by himself, without Lindsay-Hogg's direction. "T.D. is more technical than creative," said Fortenberry. "But you can take a more creative role in decision making, like moving a camera in a different position."

The assistant director (A.D.) is also crucial to a music production, particularly for timing purposes. Frequently managing multiple stopwatches, the A.D. breaks down the music and lyric sheets to a measure, indicates when a particular instrument solo begins, the length of an "intro" before the singing, and when the lyrics start. In the control room during the production, the A.D. will then prepare the director and/or switcher several measures before they are to cut to the appropriate shot.

The Editor and Director: Rough Cuts

Along with the producer, the director is key in coordinating and overseeing activities in a television production art world. A major part of the editor's role is to work closely with the director, and in performance pieces such as concerts, the artist as well. The standard procedure is for the director to choose an editor (or a particular production house) for the project. Depending on the schedule, the director will either structure the material for the editor, or in some cases, allow the editor some freedom in shaping the footage. "The director will never give it all to you," said Fortenberry. "Normally the first rough cut. But if you understand the project and where it's going, the director may allow you more creative space."

During post production, the director's involvement varies. Some are willing to work long hours with the editors even if not required to do so. According to Fortenberry, the general tendency is for directors to "hang around more" with videotape editing because the process is more efficient than film. Film editors tend to work more independently because many film directors are content to view the rough cuts rather than sit through the tedious, time-consuming editing process.

The post-production process for *Graceland: The African Concert* was simplified since Fortenberry and Lindsay-Hogg collaborated during the production. Whereas film editors are often brought in to observe location shoots, that procedure is not as common with videotape editors. There are some directors who recognize the value of having the editor present during the various stages of production, and either allow for that in the budget or invite the editor to the set. Familiarity with the project is a key consideration as it fosters a shared sense of purpose and common standards of evaluation toward the art form. "In being there for preproduction, you talk about the project and understand the spirit of the piece and the director's intentions," said Fortenberry. "That makes it so much easier to create a piece in editing rather than have them bring all the footage and say, 'Here...'"

There was a high level of trust between Fortenberry and Lindsay-Hogg. Both were comfortable working in the music genre. Much of Fortenberry's editing had been in musical pieces,[9] and Lindsay-Hogg's directorial credits include *Ready, Steady, Go!*, the popular British version of *American Bandstand*, which featured the Rolling Stones as the house band; The Beatles film, *Let it Be* (1970), and Simon and Garfunkel's *Concert in Central Park* (HBO, 1982). While it wasn't Lindsay-Hogg's style to work closely with the editor in post-production, he was also aware of Fortenberry's extensive familiarity with the footage and the goals of the project. Much of their initial interaction involved talking through the entire program, as well as each song, with Simon. "Music is tougher to work with than comedy or drama, but there are fewer surprises," said Fortenberry. "You know what you're covering and it becomes more clinical. It may be a bulk, but at least you know what it is. There aren't unknowns, like and ad-lib, a flubbed line, or missed block."

Post-production: Early Considerations

The creative objectives of the project were to showcase Simon and the other performers, and the *Graceland* and South African music, and to frame the concert within the African location. Within this context, there were several considerations both musically and visually: How would the songs be presented? Which songs would be cut? Which performances of the songs would be used, day one or two? What would the running order be? How would the second-unit footage be integrated into the concert? Since each concert ran two-an-a-half hours, there was considerable cutting to do in order to stay within the 90-minute time frame.

Considering that standard concert shoots are five camera productions, the nine cameras used for Simon's performances provided extensive coverage. "The selection process is more complicated with 65 hours of footage," said Fortenberry. "But it also gives you more options." Fortenberry's priorities with the footage were to highlight the performers, select the best angles, and use the most appropriate transition between shots.

The editor must not only consider the conventions of the genre s/he is working within, but the available techniques and her/his skill and competence in using them. Together these come to define one's personal style. Although the cut is the most basic visual transition, Fortenberry considers it the primary technique in his style:

> To me, editing is something that shouldn't be noticed—it's seamless. Editing for editing's sake; making a good cut at the right place, as opposed to digital effects that manipulate the image, squeeze it and make it swirl around on the screen. That has its time and place, for example, music video. But for me, the effect has to have a purpose.

---

9 Fortenberry has edited music videos for Michael Franks, Jackson Browne, Carly Simon, Tom Waits, Bob Dylan, the Stray Cats, and Nile Rogers.

Graceland: The African Concert reflects Fortenberry's editing personality. During the entire 90 minutes, only two "effects" were used and those were dissolves. The dissolve is also considered a simple effect which can be used without excessive stylizing. While it is used often with musical performances, Fortenberry felt the technique did not fit Simon's African concerts:

> The dissolve works with a particular kind of song—traditional love songs; the soft overlapping images work nicer. None of Paul's songs were really slow here. In concert situations, even the dissolve needs a purpose, for example a change of location. But as long as you're working in the stage area, the crowd, it doesn't make sense to dissolve. It's a concert and you don't want to take away from the performer and get caught up in yourself.

Performer Problems and Preferences

With virtually every performer and production there are usually some special, if not unusual, considerations during the shoot which carry over into post-production. Paul Simon proved to be no exception. Physically, Simon is short. His height became a proportional problem during the concert, particularly when juxtaposed with taller performers such as Miriam Makeba or guitarist Ray Phiri. To avoid awkward shot framing, the camera run on the front lip of the stage was lowered two feet, which accomplished several things. First, it helped conceal the relative differences in height between Simon and the other performers. Second, it kept the cameras out of Simon's line of sight to the audience. Third, on wide shots of the stage from the crowd, the cameras were less visible. Finally, the lower angle provided better shot composition between the foreground and background subjects. In contrast, a camera set at stage level would have picked up musicians' feet or mike stands on the stage's second riser in the background. Shooting from the lower angle showed faces behind Simon rather than feet. The lower angle also allowed other elements in the shots to be emphasized. For example, during "Boy in the Bubble," a song which features the accordion, one shot frames Simon in the lower right of the picture with the accordion being played behind him in the upper left. The shot does not reveal the musician, only his hands on the accordion keys while Simon sings.

In addition to Simon's height being a factor in production, he prefers the appearance of his left side to his right. Fortenberry's production experiences revealed that most performers are concerned with how they look.[10] Simon did not actually express the preference to the crew, but having directed the Central Park concert, Lindsay-Hogg knew Simon was going to be much happier if they stayed

---

10   Fortenberry cited several examples of "special" requests by performers. During Bette Midler's *Art or Bust*, she requested that a shot be removed because it made her arms look fat.

108 B-SIDES, UNDERCURRENTS AND OVERTONES

with the close-ups from the left, and used medium to long shots from his right. The final editing choices and shot selections reflected both of these considerations.

Simon Says: Music and Visuals, Conflict and Compromise

The editorial decisions for *Graceland: The African Concert* were "backwards" by standard production routines, as they were not based on the visuals or camera coverage as much as they were on the audio and performances. There were 27 songs performed at each concert, including three each by Masekela, Makeba and Ladysmith. Nineteen songs would be used in the special. Following the second Zimbabwe concert, Simon suggested which songs and which day's performance should be used. He insisted that two songs of each of his fellow performers be included, which meant that their "weakest" number would be eliminated. From there, the selection process became clinical, with time, performance and promotion of the *Graceland* music key factors. A committee of Fortenberry, Lindsay-Hogg, producers Fortis and Hoblyn, and Simon's audio mixer, Roy Halee, tried to reach some consensus. Because there were considerations to make both aurally and visually, there were considerable differences. Simon (through Halee) had veto power aurally, Lindsay-Hogg visually, but everyone involved made compromises along the way. Fortenberry described the negotiations:

> Some decisions were easy. We couldn't have lost a *Graceland* song for an old one. Paul did "The Boxer," we didn't want it. How many times do we have to hear that? Paul vetoed our decision on which of Miriam's songs to use. We didn't like "Soweto Blues"; it bordered on being a sleeper. It was slow, six minutes long. We preferred a shorter song. But Paul knew that the song and its message meant a lot to her and he's sensitive to other artists' concerns. Simon also fought for his, "Mother and Child Reunion," which everyone felt did not work visually. The song was eliminated after the third rundown. It all comes down to committee and the director is the one to say, "Paul, this just doesn't work." And then Paul either says, "You're right," or "You're fired."

Fortenberry, too, compromised on a song he wanted included, a traditional-into-African version of "Amazing Grace" sung by Simon and Ladysmith. While the performance did not officially make it to the third rundown, Fortenberry inserted the song under the closing credits on his own, and everyone liked it well enough to leave it in.

Some of the creative differences over the selection of songs lingered into the overdubbing. Overdubbing is a standard procedure with live outdoor concerts, and, according to Fortenberry, "a headache to editors." By using the technique, the "live" performance becomes an illusion as the singing is reduced to a "lip sync." The outdoor setting makes it difficult to achieve a quality sound mix. The artist and band routinely return to a studio sometime after the performance to record songs while viewing the concert footage on a monitor. Simon has been known to do extensive post-production audio for all his performances. Nearly 90 percent of *The Concert in Central Park* was overdubbed, apparently because Art Garfunkel's vocals were so off-key during the shows.

Even though Simon's overdubs were not as extensive with the *Graceland* special, the procedure became a major complication in the editing process. Before some of the decisions on songs were finalized, audio supervisor Halee returned to Los Angeles (where Simon and the group were touring) to begin re-cutting some songs with the band. "He decided he liked some songs from one day [of the Zimbabwe shows] better, but he didn't tell any of the video people," explained Fortenberry. "So, here we are in new York cutting visuals to one song from the first show, and Roy's in L.A. doing overdubs and mixes of the same song, but from day two's performance. They are completely out of sync with each other, just as we were."

The conflict with Halee resulted in significant delays in the editing, and an increase in post-production costs. The additional time required to rework the songs was one of the biggest contributing factors to the project's substantial budget. Fortenberry viewed the situation with Halee as a unique problem in his experience. While creative differences are not unusual, economic imperatives alone dictate that communication breakdowns during production stages be kept to a minimum in order to stay within budget.

Blend, Borrow and Steal

Once the selections were made, Fortenberry began molding the individual materials into a cohesive whole. During this stage, puzzle formulation and solution become vital to the editor's work. Fortenberry began the sculpting process by "building a base" for each song, with an option to "steal" footage from the performance from the day not selected. Thus, Fortenberry could combine footage from one day with audio from the other, or vice versa. "Stealing" is a common, but difficult, editorial trick which requires precision in matching the audio track with the video:

> On some shots, if I would have stayed on Paul ten frames more, he would have gone out of sync because the tempos were different. Chances were slim that he'd sing the exact same way both days. So, I could steal maybe a few seconds—a cutaway to a guitarist or background vocal.

The technique also helps the editor solve logistical problems. For example, Ladysmith's final song during the actual concert was eliminated during the selection process. To make it appear that "Hello My Baby" (performed as their second song during the concert) was the group's final number, Fortenberry rearranged pieces from both days, inserting footage of Ladysmith bowing, the audience applauding and the group walking off stage.

Using footage from different performances required close attention to continuity. While the production benefited from similar weather conditions both days and Simon's efforts to keep both shows as alike as possible, there were some changes. For example, during one performance, Simon put on sunglasses, whereas the next day he did not wear the glasses in the same spot. Fortenberry also had to look for details which were less noticeable, such as excessive sweating by the performers.

The light level and shadows were also a factor, particularly in determining the running order of the songs during the edit. Both concerts were shot in the late afternoon, from 3:30 to 6:30. There was a noticeable change from the show's opening to the end, but only enough to affect the last five songs. Fortenberry explained:

> You're limited in changes by the physical look of things. In the middle of the show, I could move things better than later on. Actually, we could have gotten away with it because of the African skies. The rolling clouds changed the light level so often that I think the audience would have been pretty accepting of a song being darker here, lighter there.

Another editorial consideration relevant to the show's running order and effectiveness was the pace. Much of the pace of *Graceland: The African Concert* was determined by the specific songs selected, their length and their tempo:

> We did the first cut, linked them together and played the entire piece, thinking and talking about it. Then you start from major points—running order and pace. What songs slow it down? And make notes from general to specific, and go back and work on it. And you don't have too much time to do that. We only tried three or four running orders, each time refining what specifics we wanted and the second unit footage.

Simon helped the pace by frequently interchanging performers. Nonetheless, Fortenberry was not pleased with the show's length; he felt the special would have worked better as a 60-minute program. "A 90-minute concert is a long time. You really have to appreciate the artist and their work not to lose interest or get claustrophobic," said Fortenberry.

Second-unit Footage: Puzzle Piece Placement

The second-unit footage provided a visual means of escape from the concert. Though it helped to add an aesthetic dimension to the concert, the footage also made the decision-making process more complex, as it presented Fortenberry with another set of puzzle pieces to place. Before the Zimbabwe performance, Fortenberry and a local camera crew shot 35mm footage in the townships. The intent was to capture the essence of the setting—the African people, their customs, lifestyles, dress and the physical surroundings such as streets, landscapes, buildings and markets. The images were impressive. The creative task was to determine how the shots should be integrated into the show. Should the material be used only for the opening montage? For credits? Should it be worked into the songs, and if so, should the lyrics be relevant to the visuals?

Just as the sculptor molds and shapes materials, the editor rearranges footage in a similar fashion, playing with pieces to a puzzle. Fortenberry continually experimented with the images, joining them together with various songs seeking aesthetic arrangements. "What we found was that it was difficult to set a precedent of having footage literally convey what a song was about," said Fortenberry. "So we didn't want to establish the songs as narrative. You don't want to force the footage into a song; it calls too much attention to itself and takes away from the performer."

The second unit footage was used primarily as an opening montage, under the closing credits and during the 15 to 20-second instrumental lead-ins to songs. The footage emphasized the African location rather than the songs themselves. The opening segment establishes the setting as the camera tilts down from vast skies and rolling hills to a long line of villagers running toward town. Following "Township Jive," the opening montage and credits feature an African song and various images (many of which would appear again during the show): a silhouette of a hitchhiker, colorfully dressed women balancing laundry baskets on their heads as they walk, people riding bicycles, trains, traffic, street corners, a church and a waterfall. As the camera zooms out from the waterfall, Simon introduces the performance over three more shots: "Today's concert will be about the music of South Africa and the music from the *Graceland* album."

The use of the footage as lead-ins to songs was considerably less. Only three to five shots appeared before cutting back to the stage for the beginning of the lyrics. When a new performer appeared on stage, Simon's introduction replaced the second-unit footage before the song. In most cases, the images were not lyrically relevant. There were exceptions: a sweeping pan of the vast, cloudy skies preceded "Under African Skies," and Masekela's "Stimela" included an opening shot of workers riding the train (Stimela) to South African mines, and news footage of mine workers throughout the song.

Fortenberry avoided attempts at narrative structure or music video stylization. However, his careful selection and placement of images provided the songs with a sense of rhythmic rather than lyrical relevance. Most of the images used were filled with movement: traffic, children rolling empty tires, people bouncing, dancing, walking and bicycling. Fortenberry controlled the direction of the movement through careful placement of shots. If the subject in one shot moved screen left to screen right, the following shot moved screen right to screen left. In other sequences, the movement in consecutive shots was in the same direction. Rather than a chaotic collage, this structure contributed a sense of flow and rhythm which complemented the music visually. Fortenberry matched several images with the tempo of the music so well it appeared they were staged specifically for the songs. A shot of six boys dancing on a wall, for instance, appears in sync with the opening of "Boy in the Bubble," and the silhouette image of a youth bouncing up and down while playing soccer precisely matches the chords in "Graceland."

Another factor in Fortenberry's selection and placement of the footage was ideological. The *Graceland* tour itself was the center of controversy as many antiapartheid activists claimed Simon's performances violated the U.N. cultural boycott against South Africa (see Fricke 1987). Although Fortenberry claims the intent was not to make a political statement with the show, it appeared difficult to avoid political signification with the second-unit and concert footage, considering how the strife it contained is a part of everyday life in Zimbabwe.

Although Simon's *Graceland* songs are not overtly political, shots of soldiers, a billboard of Mugabe ("Let us all rally behind our authentic and consistent leader, Cde. RG Mugabe") and tanks in traffic appeared during the lead-in to "Boy in the Bubble." Juxtaposed, the images were even more politically suggestive, as was the placement of another shot of soldiers as Simon introduces "the music of South Africa" in the show's opening.

Ideology was perhaps most overt in the music of Masekela and Makeba, both political exiles for more than 20 years. "Because of his political views, he's not allowed back in his homeland," says Simon in his introduction of Masekela. As Masekela begins his opening verse about bringing home Nelson Mandela to Soweto, a shot holds on his raised fist. Masekla's other song, "Stimela," is about the trains that carry workers to the mines. Fortenberry used black and white stock footage shot by the BBC, and the consensus was that it worked nicely with the song. The black and white images are a stark contrast to the colorful, lively second-unit footage, and they emphasize Masekela's lyrics about the miners working long hours for virtually no wages.

Makeba's segments deliver a similar message. Before beginning "Soweto Blues," she says, "I hope and wish someday we will invite Paul Simon to Johannesburg in a free South Africa." As the song begins, a shot appears of a youth leaning against a sign next to a soldier with a dog on a chain. Not only does the image fit the tone of Makeba's song (written by Masekela), it is the only footage used for the entire song. Whereas most songs used from three to five shots, this lone image makes the shot even more dramatic and powerful. The "free South Africa" message of unity is also conveyed during the closing song, the African national anthem, "N'Kosi Sikelei Africa," by combining second-unit footage of a rainbow by a waterfall with concert shots emphasizing the crowd joining hands and singing together.

The producers later discovered the second-unit footage was very popular. "Showtime said, 'We wish you would have had more African footage,'" said Fortenberry. "I feel that when they say that, you used just the right amount."

Warming Up (to) the Crowd

Another key visual element which Fortenberry had to incorporate into the show was the crowd. Virtually every filmed and/or taped concert performance features crowd coverage; it is a staple of the genre. As an editor, Fortenberry suggests the crowd shots often tend to distract from the performer. For the *Graceland* special, he tried to use the fan footage to provide context. "Being in the middle of Africa, you can't present a concert that looks like it could be in Pittsburgh," said Fortenberry. "People want to see something you might not see in the States." While the dress and appearance of the people set the crowd apart from audiences in the United States, perhaps the most revealing difference was in several cutaways to military personnel. "You never see the army at a James Taylor concert," said Fortenberry. "And we were very selective in what was shown from a racial context, careful to avoid all-white, or all-black crowd shots."

A sense of crowd spontaneity is largely an editorial trick of the trade. Audiences are seldom shot during a performance because it requires giving up a camera. "It's important to cover the artist as meticulously as possible," said Fortenberry. "To break a camera to a wide or medium crowd shot, or to find those two people dancing great, or the guy with the funny hat, just takes too long." Fortenberry also acknowledged there is luck involved in capturing that "great moment" in the crowd. Due to some unusual cultural circumstances, at one point during the concert the crew did not have to choose between shooting Simon or the crowd. During his performance of the popular hit, "You Can Call Me Al," the crowd spontaneously formed a huge conga line. Fortenberry explains:

> Everybody went crazy, dancing around. They had heard the song on the radio and were familiar with it. They started yelling, "More, more, more," after the song. Paul turned to [guitarist] Ray Phiri, they have an exchange, Paul nods, turns around and starts playing "Call Me Al" again. We weren't prepared for that in the control room and wondered what was going on, but we shot it anyway.

The crew discovered that in Africa when the crowd yells "More!" it means they want an instant encore of the same song. The response occurred both days, so the crew had the luxury of four different versions to work with. "It was a real bonus," said Fortenberry. "We felt we had the first performance, so when the second began and the crowd formed the huge conga line, we were pretty free to shoot them. The four takes gave us a lot of options."

The strategy employed in getting crowd footage was to turn all nine cameras on the audience during the warm-up performance. "It's an ideal time to get as many shots as you can," explained Fortenberry. "People were 'up,' dancing, clapping, anticipating Paul and the show. The shots you get at warm-ups are consistently good."[11]

Using warm-up footage did not necessarily simplify the editing task. If anything, its use demanded closer attention to details of synchronization and continuity. Fortenberry estimates that at least 60 percent of the crowd shots in the final cut were warm-up footage. While the music of the Boyoboyo Boys Band (an African group who played the warm-up) was similar to the music of Simon's concert, their beat was considerably faster. "Most of the time the crowd's reactions matched pretty well with Paul's," said Fortenberry. "Often it was just a cutaway of two claps in a beat, it becomes obvious the person is clapping to some other rhythm." Fortenberry also had to balance the difference in crowds since the attendance was a little thinner the second day. In order to create the appearance of a packed house, reverse shots from the first day were inserted into the final edit.

The Final Phase: It's Showtime

The editing schedule became more grueling as the concert was being refined into its finished form. By the final weeks before Showtime's deadline, Fortenberry did offline edits from 10:00 am until 8:00 pm, then would "conform" previously completed songs from 8:00 pm until 4:00 am. He returned to resume editing at 10:00 am. On the average, Fortenberry spent 10 to 12 hours doing a song off-line, and three to four hours conforming a song.[12]

During the final stages of editing, Fortenberry's primary interaction was with Lindsay-Hogg, Simon and Showtime's personnel, all of whom would either approve or disapprove of how Fortenberry had shaped the work. Fortenberry also met with graphic artist Sharon Haskell to select appropriate graphics and design for the opening titles and closing credits. The style they chose was a simple, no frills type that was consistent with the show's editing style.

A creative problem any artist struggles with is determining when a project is finished—when the last brush stroke is applied, the last sentence written, the last line drawn. For the editor, deadlines and budgets often dictate when the project

---

11   Fortenberry said the crowd did not respond or act differently because the show was being taped for television. "In the States they do, but not in Africa." The only procedure was to present a general waiver or release, which the audience acknowledged that the concert was being shot and their image might appear on television.

12   "Off-line" is similar to the workprint in film, which is chopped to pieces and marked. Quality is not a concern as the off-line is the initial stage of editing and is used to make decisions. The format is ¾-inch and cheaper (in most cases, an average of $500 per week). "Conforming" is the next stage which is broadcast quality, usually performed on 1-inch tape. The cost can be as high as $400 per hour. "That's why decisions are made during off-line," said Fortenberry. "You can't be sitting there indecisively with conforming; a cut will cost you $200." The advance to digital technology has streamlined the process.

THE VITAL VISUAL VOICE OF THE VIDEOTAPE EDITOR 115

is considered "complete." According to Fortenberry, such deadlines are helpful because the tendency in editing is to keep cutting and reworking to try to make the piece better:

> You learn by experience about when you're over cutting something. By the second, third and fourth cuts, you have to ask, "Are we really making this better, or satisfying the urge to do different things?" In looking at the different versions, it gets tough to say, "I liked it much better before," after you've taken so much time to make changes.

Budgets are also a factor. Producers and networks commonly view the editing room as a "money pit" and are afraid of the "overkill factor." "No one ever goes into the editing room for a few hours and 'quick fixes,'" said Fortenberry. "You sit down for a quick fix and you're in there for 10 hours because you find something else." There are no actual limits set as to how many versions are cut. Fortenberry cited *Randy Newman at the Odeon* (1980), a cable concert special he edited at Broadway Video, as a prime example of overcutting; they did 19 versions of the show. Fortenberry assembled four different versions of *Graceland: The African Concert*:

> We knew all along what we wanted for each song. I'd do a cut, Mike [Lindsay-Hogg] would look at it, we'd discuss it and work with it. To me, the director should be creative, but also encourage others to have ideas and act as a sieve for those ideas. Then he can be the final judge whether it's a good idea or not and tell the editor.

While Simon had "artistic approval"[13] for the project, he was relatively uninvolved during post-production, which was unusual considering his reputation as a perfectionist.[14] Simon did, however, ask that they change a shot because a guitar pick was visible sticking out of his pocket. Simon viewed several of the early rough cuts and made suggestions which Fortenberry and Lindsay-Hogg tried to either accommodate, talk him out of, or negotiate. Their gauge for making changes often was determined by how many times Simon made a particular suggestion:

> What Mike and I judged things on a lot was that if Paul, or anyone, said something twice. If we really felt different from Paul's suggestion on something, maybe we wouldn't change it because we believed it was "right" and belonged where it was. Then at the second screening, if Paul noticed it, then we felt we had to confront the change.

---

13   The term is used in the industry referring to "power" or "creative control."

14   Fortenberry characterized Simon as "very bright," with a good visual sense. Film and video are familiar territory to Simon. He starred in *One Trick Pony* (1980), and had numerous concert specials, as well as *The Paul Simon Special* (NBC, 1978), an Emmy Award winning comedy-variety special which humorously looked at television's production process; and frequently appeared in comic sketches on *Saturday Night Live* and *The New Show*.

116   *B-SIDES, UNDERCURRENTS AND OVERTONES*

Or, you can take the chance of lying, saying, it's the only shot you have—but you always get caught on that one.

Simon saw the project three times throughout post-production. According to Fortenberry, he was not satisfied with the final product:

> I don't think his dissatisfaction was so much what we did with it, as it was the show itself. The African shows were very early in his tour—maybe the sixth to eighth concerts— and he felt the staging and performances were weak and had progressed since then. By the time we showed him the rough cut, he'd been refining the show on his tour.

The final link in the *Graceland* project's decision chain was Showtime. The cable network's involvement during post-production was not like a film studio screening dailies. Representatives only viewed the final rough cut, at which time they compared notes and discussed any changes with Lindsay-Hogg and Fortenberry. Fortenberry has edited projects for the three major networks and most of the cable outlets. He finds little difference between them. "They're not strictly business; they understand the creative side," said Fortenberry. "And while they do tend to focus on ratings and target audiences, they also want what makes good television, and programs that a certain number of people will watch and think are good."

Much of the negotiating with Showtime was done before preproduction even started. The key content decisions usually come down to who has "artistic approval," in this case, Paul Simon. Fortenberry said:

> Much depends on who's pulling the weight. Even though Showtime didn't really like Miriam having six minutes with "Soweto Blues," feeling that it pulled the show down a bit, they're not going to tell Paul Simon, "Take it out." He pulls the weight. It's made very clear beforehand that *he* is making the show and unless there's something immediately objectionable, they'll air the show they get.

Quiet Construction within the Chorus

Though a singular example, John Fortenberry's quiet, creative contributions to *Graceland: The African Concert* illuminate the B-side nature, functions and value of the editor and the post production process and environment in shaping the music and visual symbiosis and structure of the rock concert film.

As a concert special, *Graceland: The African Concert* aligns more with the conventions of the rockumentary than with episodic television or variety show presentations. Because of the time constraints that a weekly show faces, there is considerably less reworking and polishing during post-production, whereas editing is a major creative aspect of a concert special. Fortenberry's opportunities for creative input and his freedom within the art world of the *Graceland* project indicate how the role of the editor has developed over the years. Having been involved with the project during every stage—preproduction and planning, shooting second-unit footage, the concert production itself, and post-production—Fortenberry may have contributed more to the special than any other individual. Even though Simon, director Lindsay-Hogg, producers, and network personnel oversaw the editor's work to some degree, they expected creative input and ideas from Fortenberry. While Fortenberry adhered to the various structures, conventions and forms of the concert genre, his skills, experience and familiarity and comfort with the materials and the musical form itself contributed to the degree of autonomy he was allowed in shaping the footage into an art work. The editor's interactions with the various artists and production specialists within the art world help establish him as a skilled specialist more than as an engineer or assembly-line operator working within specified sets of procedures, or as an artisan who relies on others to structure creative tasks.

The value of the editor's work extends beyond how the structure of a show is achieved to the composition itself. *Graceland: The African Concert*'s visual structure and codes are largely a result of Fortenberry's efforts as an editor. His personal editing style was evident in the transitions between shots and the careful selection and placement of images. His creative contributions were not limited to the opening and closing, but were displayed throughout the entire 90-minute show: constructing of the opening montage and closing credits, matching concert footage with audio tracks, inserting second-unit images throughout the show to provide a context, emphasizing the African setting, and at times, offering a political comment, selecting BBC news footage and rearranging the crowd shots. These were all vital audio and visual decisions, most initiated by Fortenberry himself. Such choices helped define the structure, tone, rhythm, form and aesthetic dimensions of *Graceland: The African Concert*.

Fortenberry's crossover to the role of technical director for the concert also magnifies the merits of editing as a learning tool. Beginning the production ladder as an editor is rather unusual. A more common industry progression is to begin as a writer or production assistant and gradually advance to directing.[15] Fortenberry discovered that his eight-year editing experience provided an ideal initiation, and shaped his vision and approach to directing:

> Directors come from everywhere, and bring that particular skill or vision. The actor directing will have a sense of character and performance; the writer may be more sensitive to story; cinematographers have a better eye for shots and images. I think

---

15 Fortenberry's career ambition was directing. He became an editor because it was "a position that was available at the time." He also benefited from Broadway Video in that they were one of the first production houses to stress the creative role of the editor. Michaels hired an excellent engineering staff so that the editors would not have to worry about the mechanics and machine maintenance and could concentrate on creative tasks. Fortenberry became Senior Editor in 1982, and has worked primarily as a director and producer since the early 1990s.

anyone would benefit coming from a technical background. Editing is a great way to learn the entire production process. I think it's easier to learn about production this way, going from the end to the means. Now when I go to shoot as director, I know instantly what's going to come together, and in my mind it's much easier to shoot out of sequence or arrange shots because I know what's going to work and what you can do with the footage in the edit. The logistics of directing come naturally out of my experience and thinking as an editor.

Fortenberry compares the editor's anonymity and B-side stature and method of quiet construction with decisions other artists make:

Editing footage is very much like being a sculptor—chipping away, patching things, shaping and molding something into a piece. It's seamless. Anonymous. Hopefully, you leave no fingerprints. No trace. In your mind you may haggle over a single frame, look at it many times until you decide how it works. It may sound silly and no one would ever think it, but for a one hour show, you can spend 15 minutes wondering if a cut should be on frame one or frame two. But you do, and because you take such care with each piece and each cut, it makes a great show. No one may know it, but your signature is definitely there.

Chapter 8
Rock Around the Cop:
Bochco's Broadway Blue Print as
Television Musical Muse and Martyr

On the 10 June 2001 edition of CBS's cultural magazine show, *Sunday Morning*, media critic John Leonard invoked the television title *Cop Rock* in the lead to his review of the film *Moulin Rouge*.[1] The citation was a curious connection, or resurrection, considering that the Steven Bochco produced police drama/musical lasted a mere half season, 11 one-hour episodes on ABC in 1990 (September 26-December 26). In contrast, director Baz Luhrman's anachronistic romantic musical spectacle—a three-ring Cirque du Soleil, rock popera, garage collage of farce and folly—received considerable recognition, including an Academy Award nomination for Best Film.

Bochco's experimental *Fame* meets *Hill Street Blues* medley was a formula for failure. The fusion was better suited for stage rather than the small screen. Television audiences were not ready for crooning cops, suspect serenades, junkies jammin,' and judge and jury jingles from week to week in a dramatic series. Audiences, ABC affiliates, advertisers, and critics responses to Bochco's police project ranged from "ambitious, innovative, risky, and audacious to baffling, off-putting and irritatingly odd" (Carter 1990: 25).

Hindsight and context reveal that despite its critical and commercial failure, *Cop Rock* represents a plausible progression for the police genre during the inaugural MTV era of the 1980s into the 1990s and beyond. Bochco borrowed, blended and blew up formulaic fragments from the genre, including conventions from two of the decade's touchstone series—his own *Hill Street Blues* and Michael Mann's stylish "MTV Cops" *Miami Vice*. Bochco also paid homage to Dennis Potter's farcical British televison productions, *Pennies From Heaven* (1978), and more specifically, *The Singing Detective* (1986).

Cop Rock might also be viewed as a musical muse and martyr that foreshadowed the further exploration and integration of music into dramatic and comic narratives.

---

1 Parts of this chapter have appeared in "*Cop Rock* Revisited: Unsung Series and Musical Hinge in Cross Genre Evolution," *Journal of Popular Film and Television*, Vol. 32, No 2 (*Summer 2004*): 64-73; and "*Cop Rock* Reconsidered: Formula, Failure, Fragments and Foreshadowing in Musical Genre" in J. Emmett Winn and Susan Brinson (eds), *Transmitting the Past: Historical and Cultural Perspectives on Broadcasting* (Tuscaloosa, AL: University of Alabama Press, 2005).

120   *B-SIDES, UNDERCURRENTS AND OVERTONES*

Thus, it may not be critical hyperbole to suggest, as Leonard does, that *Cop Rock*'s lyrical legacy can be linked to the Napster approach to postmodern pop/rock period pieces in film such as *Moulin Rouge*, *A Knight's Tale*, and Lars Von Trier's *Dancer in the Dark*, starring Iceland chanteuse Bjork. In television, Bochco's series served as a stepping stone or hinge between Potter's *The Singing Detective* and comedies and musical dramedies, particularly *Ally McBeal*, and other musical episodes of series including *The Drew Carey Show*, *Chicago Hope*, *Buffy The Vampire Slayer* and the short lived *Viva Laughlin*. Retrospection reveals that as a B-side—the flip side as failure—*Cop Rock* quietly cultivated creativity in television soundtracks and contributed dramatic musical license to various productions and cross genre formal and aesthetic advances.

Beginning a Blue Streak

> I think what is amazing about my career is that I've never had any specific goals and ambitions. I like the *process*. I like the work. I have no idea what I'll do next.
>
> Steven Bochco (Christensen 1988: 82)

Television series, like any cultural product, are subject to numerous individual, collaborative, organizational, sociocultural, and economic conditions and circumstances which collectively foster or hinder their inception, development, distribution and success or failure. Production ethnographies, authorship studies, and literature on innovation suggest that within television, the development of an unconventional form, such as *Cop Rock*, may be determined by variables such as a producer's or production company's track record and relationship with a network; a producer's ability to operate "outside" the normal organizational channels; the competitive environment between networks and their positions in the ratings; and programming executives willing to take risks and allow a show time to cultivate an audience (see Ettema and Whitney 1982).

In 1987, Steven Bochco left NBC, the network which had nurtured much of his success as a writer-producer. After turning down an offer to be president of CBS Entertainment, Bochco signed an unprecedented 10 year, 10-series, $50 million guaranteed contract with the ABC network. The deal was ideal and unusual by any creator's standards, as it represented both financial and artistic freedom. If one of Bochco's ideas was rejected or a show ran fewer than the standard 13 episode run before renewal, Bochco was still paid, and paid well. Cancellation compensation was $1.5 million. More staggering to industry observers was the stipulation that Bochco would own the rights to his shows.

To ABC, whose prime-time schedule at the time lacked prestigious and successful programs, Bochco was an investment in high ratings, hits and respectability. Bochco was proven product, a writer-producer with an impressive track record, particularly for police and detective series. His creative cop credits date back to the 1960s as a writer for NBC series *The Bold Ones* and *The Name of the Game.* His 1970s work includes *Columbo, McMillan and Wife, Richie Brockelman, Private Eye*, and the CBS series *Delvecchio* starring Judd Hirsch, and *Paris* featuring James Earl Jones. In the 1980s, Bochco established himself as one of television's top creators of drama with the ground breaking shows for NBC, *Hill Street Blues* (1981-1987) and *L.A. Law* (1986-1994). Both series introduced a new candor to prime-time drama and pioneered what would become central elements of Bochco's stylistic signature: large ensemble casts featuring 10-15 relatively unknown actors and actresses playing complex characters; serial storytelling with multiple plotlines that weave in and out of an episode and take weeks to resolve; absurdist humor; fast-paced scene changes; and a gritty cinematic realism.

Collaborator David Milch was among many who characterizes Bocho as a "Wunderkind," adding that the adulation from his acclaimed shows [*Hill Street* and *L.A. Law*] perhaps tempted Bochco "to think that he could do anything" (Christensen: 81). Some of Bochco's post-*Hill Street* projects and his inaugural ABC endeavors reinforce Milch's notions of Bochco's indulgence in creative whimsy. For example, *Bay City Blues* (1983, NBC), a minor league baseball drama with a big league budget, rivaled Fred Silverman's *Supertrain* (1979, ABC) as one of the biggest financial fiascos in broadcast television history. Production costs included set design consisting of building a stadium exclusively for the show, and hiring crowds at $85 per person per day. The investment did not pay off as the series lasted four episodes.

One of the notable programming trends that emerged in the 1987-1988 prime-time schedule was the comedy/drama hybrid labeled "dramedies," represented in series such as the one-hour *Moonlighting* (ABC), and half-hour series *The Days and Nights of Molly Dodd* (NBC), *Frank's Place* (CBS), *The Wonder Years* (ABC), and *The "Slap" Maxwell Story* (ABC). Bochco's contribution to this subgenre, *Hooperman* (ABC), featured John Ritter as a San Francisco detective. According to Bochco, the show "just popped out of my face…the whole thing came to me in five minutes" (Christensen: 76). In 1989, when *Hooperman* ended its two season run, Bochco paid tribute to his father, a child prodigy violinist, with *Doogie Howser, M.D.*, another half-hour dramedy series about a 16-year-old physician.

The Soap Copera: Hill Street, Broadway and the BBC

> It would not make sense to invite comparisons with a breakthrough program like *Hill Street* unless you find a compellingly different way to reach people And music reaches people; it reaches them underneath their flak jackets.
>
> Steven Bochco (Carter: 34)

During the 1980s, conventions of the police/crime genre on network television were largely redefined by the cluttered, gritty realism of Bochco's *Hill Street Blues'* (NBC, 1981-1987) and the pulsating pastels of Mann's *Miami Vice's* (NBC,

1984-1989). According to broadcast programming lore, the idea for *Miami Vice* originated from a note—"MTV Cops"—scribbled by NBC entertainment President Brandon Tartikoff. Mann used Jan Hammer's theme and score, along with popular songs performed by original artists, to create a striking soundtrack which linked music to story the same way composer Henri Mancini did in the 1950s with *Peter Gunn*.[2]

Bochco and Mann took somewhat divergent paths of progress with the sequels to their successes. Mann chose the retro route with *Crime Story* (NBC, 1986-1988), a cop and mobster *Untouchables* update set in Chicago in 1963. The only hint of *Miami Vice* in the show was in the opening theme, featuring a revamped version of Del Shannon's 1961 hit, "Runaway." With his next project, Bochco looked beyond the commercial viability and creative convenience of duplicating *Hill Street Blues* in its entirety.[3] He was particularly interested in advancing the use of music beyond the norms of soundtrack. Bochco's vision was vaudevillian; he was inspired by both Broadway and British productions, specifically the work and vision of Dennis Potter, whose characters frequently break into song, miming the words from old recordings. "I think [*The*] *Singing Detective* is possibly the best seven hours of television I've ever seen. Period; without qualification," states Bochco. "It gave us permission, at least internally. Creatively, it gave me permission to do *Cop Rock*" (Shebar 1992).

In addition to Bochco's admiration for Potter's productions, he considered a suggestion to adapt *Hill Street Blues* to Broadway as a musical. Though the theatrical project did not materialize, the seeds of song for a small screen "soap copera" had been sown. "Why not reverse it [the idea of a police musical], I thought; bring it to this medium [television]," said Bochco (Carter: 33) Mike Post, one of television's most prolific composer-arrangers, cautioned Bochco about the costs and creative risks of producing a weekly television musical. Despite the words of discouragement from his friend and collaborator, Bochco proceeded, and even convinced Post to be the show's musical producer despite his reservations.

Post's concerns about the elaborate nature of such a production appeared well founded. Every stage of the process, from pre production to post production, presented unusual problems that required special planning and puzzle solving. Casting weekly guest roles had to be based on performers' abilities not only to act, but to sing and dance as well. Complicated rehearsals required an eight-day-per-episode shooting schedule, one more than standard for an hour-long show.

---

2 Because the songs were performed by the original artists, *Miami Vice*'s producers spent an average of $50,000 per episode for music licensing rights.

3 Perhaps the closest Bochco comes to producing a *Hill Street Blues* sequel is with *NYPD Blue*, which premiered on ABC in 1993, complete with content controversy. Conservative groups targeted the show, objecting to its sex, profanity, and violence. Initially, 57 of 225 ABC affiliates did not air the show. As *NYPD Blue*'s ratings, critical acclaim, and advertising revenues increased, so did the number of station programmers who abandoned Reverend Donald Wildmon's conservative cause for Bochco's *Blue* bandwagon.

The editing process was also demanding as it required mixing music and dialogue tracks. The cumulative result was a budget for *Cop Rock* that exceeded the average cost for a one-hour show by nearly 40%, translating into approximately $1.3 million a week to produce.

The fragmented formula for the series required two creative staffs, one for the script and one for the songwriting, music and choreography. Bochco envisioned five original songs per episode, with no cover versions and no lip-syncing. Projected over a season of 22 episodes, that meant 110 songs would have to be to be composed, performed, and choreographed within conventional dramatic scenes. The songs were central to the narrative, serving essential dialogue purposes of providing information, advancing the plot, and revealing character and emotion. Popular singer-songwriter Randy Newman composed and performed *Cop Rock*'s main title theme, "Under the Gun," and wrote the pilot episode's five songs. However, the cost of keeping a company of songwriters of Newman's caliber on a weekly song-on-demand basis was not feasible. In subsequent weeks, six to eight lesser known songwriters were assembled under Post's musical direction. The group included Amanda McBroom, who wrote the song "The Rose," and Donnie Markowitz, who won an Oscar for the song "I Had the Time of My Life" in the film *Dirty Dancing*. Bochco hoped to eventually enlist other popular artists such as Paul Simon and Billy Joel as special guest composers for episodes. Another long term musical goal was to compile the show's best songs into a *Cop Rock* soundtrack. "My anxiety with *Cop Rock* wasn't whether it would be a hit, but whether we could actually do the damn thing and get it on the air every week," said Bochco of the production process (Tucker 1996: 65).

The "*Hill Street Blues* on Broadway via the BBC" blueprint became *Cop Rock* on September 26, 1990 at 10 p.m. (EDT) on ABC. True to its novel design, and framed by Bochco's signature style of storytelling, characterization and production values, *Cop Rock*'s premiere fused familiar conventions of the police/detective genre with traditional elements of the musical. From the opening scene—a cluttered, nocturnal collage of hovering helicopter search lights, plainclothes officers, and swarming S.W.A.T. teams in a frenzied, break-the-door-down descent upon a crack house—the nervous camera, shadowy, low lighting, gritty realism and urban setting is vintage Bochco, with a hint of the reality camcorder cop series *Cops* (Fox).

Cop Rock's unflinching violence, unsettling plot twists, frank dialogue, realism and intensity rise above the levels of other television dramas. A car chase involving cops and a red-light-running van squealing and swerving through streets and alleys appears like standard stock from cop formulas seen in *C.H.I.P.S* or *T.J. Hooker* until the pursuit climaxes with a graphic shootout near a playground and a slain officer, which establishes the "cop killer revenge" theme. During an interrogation in "the box", a determined detective tortures a suspect by forcing him to drink hot coffee after each question until he urinates in his pants. As the storyline develops, the same renegade detective shoots a bound suspect point blank and becomes a heroic avenger to the squad. The lone dissenter is the captain, who, like *Hill Street*'s head Frank Furillo, represents the busy precinct's moral center.

In addition to Bocho's usual masterful exploration of the gray areas of the law through cops who often resemble criminals, there is characteristic contrast in partners: male/female, young/old, black/white, clean/corrupt. Sprinkled in for comic relief are a few off beat characters such as a pistol-packing police chief who duels with a mechanical gunslinger in his office closet for spontaneous rounds of target practice.

The familiar dramatic narratives shift into diverse song and dance intervals that substitute for action and dialogue. Following a drug bust, a group of apprehended suspects who are being escorted into squad cars begin rapping a response in a handcuffed chorus taunting the arresting officers, "In these streets, *we* got the power." A junkie mother croons a lullaby on a bus stop bench before selling her baby. A police line-up becomes a threatening chorus line. A cop's eulogy is transformed into a spiritual. Some of the production numbers border on spectacle: homeless people emerge from under a bridge into the streets to perform an extensively choreographed musical number reminiscent of the "Be a Pepper" long-form television commercials for Dr. Pepper or the pop star Pepsi ads showcased during the Grammy Awards during the 1980s. The mayor does her best Helen Reddy roar about graft and corruption from atop her office desk. A jury delivers its "guilty" verdict in a rousing gospel choir fashion, with the entire court room swaying and clapping to the beat. Other performances seem better suited for animated Disney tales. A forensics specialist sings a forlorn love ballad in his dim lit den. The good captain listens to his wife's lyrical lament about "watching my dreams and wishes drown in dirty dishes." Still others are farcical. An agitated Yuppie watching his BMW being impounded after being busted for buying cocaine in a seedy parking lot, wails a pseudo-soulful "I want my Beemer back."

Singin' the Blues

Despite a heavy promotional campaign, which included trailers in movie theaters (an uncommon marketing strategy for television series at the time), *Cop Rock* could not sustain sufficient audience numbers beyond the initial episode's curious crowd. Nor was there a groundswell of support from critics. Though many commended Bochco for his creative courage, they also got carried away with cute in their columns, using playful pity in paraphrased epithets pronouncing the police project "Flop Rock" and "Cop Wreck." The critical consensus concluded that Bochco's police force needed to be de-*Famed*; the shotgun marriage of musical fantasy and inner city mayhem just did not work. Though programming executives at ABC pledged patience, they were not encouraged by the initial ratings response to the series. "When you try something as different as *Cop Rock*, you have to be prepared as a programmer for the fact that it is just not going to work," said ABC Entertainment President Robert Iger (Roush 1990: 3D). The struggling third place network was committed to developing shows that "created different experiences" for viewers. From 1989-1990, in addition to *Cop Rock,* ABC boldly introduced *Twin Peaks*, the David Lynch/Mark Frost surreal "sap opera" set in a timber town in the Pacific Northwest; *Elvis*, a bio-drama of Elvis Presley's early years; *The Young Riders*, a revisionist Western about Pony Express recruits; and *America's Funniest Home Videos*, a contemporary *Candid Camera* and programming precursor to the reality show trend.

Cop Rock exceeded ABC's ambitious agenda for "different" programming in excessive, not to mention, expensive, form and fashion. However, in this case, deviant distinction meant demise. "Viewers do seek a comfort level in programs and the music can create some discomfort and probably has," said Iger of *Cop Rock*, sounding like a programming doctor diagnosing an ailment, or perhaps more appropriately, a coroner at an autopsy (Roush 1990: 3D). *Cop Rock* went from an off-Broadway audition to off-television as the series was canceled in December after eleven episodes.[4]

Iger's assessment of the audience's uneasiness may be understated. Bochco himself was likely aware from the show's conception stage that he might be committing telecide with his small screen "soap copera." Fusing fragments of Tin Pan Alley, Disney, Broadway, and MTV with a realistic police drama was a drastically different, if not discomforting, experience for viewers. The musical medley both challenged and violated standard expectations inherent in the genre. The singing was incompatible with character and continuity, and too often interrupted the narrative flow. Minus the music, *Cop Rock*'s storylines and characters combined to create a quality drama comparable to any on television, including Bochco's best. Yet, the musical interludes became intrusions that fostered apprehension and misplaced anticipation of the next song rather than plot twists or character arcs. The singing sequences demanded that viewers suspend disbelief and balance intense emotionalism with farce and absurdity of characters who appeared to have trained with Debbie Allen at a dance academy rather than at a police academy. *Cop Rock*'s colliding conventions were so incongruous that the show could not even manage "acquired taste" status beyond the initial curiosity attraction of the pilot episode. In subsequent weeks when viewers were presumably better prepared for the show's musical elements, the distraction did not diminish; the show's ratings dwindled. In the end, Bochco's creative vision was undermined

---

4 *Cop Rock*'s swift demise did not deter Bochco from his risk taking approach as a creator of television drama. His ensuing project in 1992 was *Capitol Critters*, an animated series set at the White House, featuring vermin—rats, mice and roaches—as its central characters. The series' run was shorter than *Cop Rock*'s, lasting a mere four episodes. In 1995, Bochco's *Murder One* (ABC) deviated from conventional law dramas by following one case for the entire 22 episode season. The timing of the series suggests the concept may have been inspired, in part, by the exhaustive coverage of the O.J. Simpson case. In 2007, FX's legal series, *Damages*, starring Glenn Close, adapted Bochco's *Murder One* blueprint.

126 *B-SIDES, UNDERCURRENTS AND OVERTONES*

as much as anything by the venue itself. Even with music video established for nearly a decade by MTV in the American cultural experience by the time *Cop Rock* premiered in 1990, the musical in its more traditional form did not translate well to the confines of television sets in living rooms. *Cop Rock* was better suited for a theatrical stage and setting where audiences *expect* characters to sing their lines, a point which Bochco himself concedes.

> In retrospect, I think the show embarrassed viewers—it made them uncomfortable to see characters bursting into song in a TV drama. When we tested the pilot for groups of people, it always went over great. Now I realize it was because we had a group of people together, as you would in a Broadway theater. But watching it in your living room, it came off more like Uncle Joe, loaded at Thanksgiving, with a lamp shade on his head and singing 'Sweet Sue.' (Tucker 1996: 65)

Musical Interludes: Scenes, Soundtracks and Small Screen Spectacle

In the early 1990s, creators of crime-time television series did not take a musical cue from Bochco's chorus of cops. Instead, producers preferred camcorder cops. Low budget, reality-based dramatic crime re-creations and missing person crusades emerged as a programming trend in *Cop Rock*'s immediate wake. The video verité variations included *Unsolved Mysteries* (NBC)—hosted by a trio of ex-television cops Robert Stack, Raymond Burr, and Karl Malden—*Top Cops* (CBS), *Cops* (Fox), *FBI: The Untold Stories* (ABC), *Secret Service* (NBC), *True Detectives* (CBS), and *Stories of the Highway Patrol* (Syndicated).

Music continued to be come widely integrated into other comic and dramatic presentations during the same period, though not on the scale of *Cop Rock*. *Northern Exposure* (1990-1995, CBS), and to a lesser degree, its obscure kindred spirit, *Due South* (1994-1996, CBS), uses of music were arguably the most eclectic, obscure, captivating, reflective synthesis of soundtrack and storyline on television. David Chase's *Northern Exposure* averaged twelve songs per episode, an unusually high number for a television series at the time, exceeding the more musically celebrated *Miami Vice*. While much of the series soundtrack was channeled through the local radio station KBHR (K-Bear) and the jukebox at Holling's bar in the fictional Cicely, Alaska, the song selections employed during each episode's closing three minutes provided particularly poignant moments. A scene depicting a coffin containing the frozen remains of a stranger catapulting through the sky toward its final resting place in a lake as "we tripped the light fantastic" from Procol Harum's "A Whiter Shade of Pale" provides a lyrical complement. In another, Fleetwood Mac genius Lindsey Buckingham's "D.W. Suite" (an homage to crazy via the late Beach Boy Dennis Wilson) accompanies images of the local men stripping off their thermals and jogging in the town's annual nude streak through the snowscapes to mark the spring thaw. The scenes are emblematic of the meditative codas to the narratives involving Cicely's colorful characters, their relationships and rural rituals. By 2000, *Northern Exposure*'s episode-ending musical montage evolved into a conventional punctuation practice for television's one-hour series.

Pop star cameos also became commonplace, especially during competitive ratings sweeps periods. Soundtrack synergy also emerged, just as Bochco had envisioned with *Cop Rock*. One hour dramatic series, particularly those with key teen demographic appeal such as *Melrose Place* (Fox) and *Party of Five* (Fox), spawned accompanying music collections of songs featured in the shows. By the late 1990s, soundtracks were well established as standard synergy across genres on networks and cable. Shows ranging from *Dawson's Creek* (WB), *Gilmore Girls* (WB) and *Providence* (NBC), to *Friends* (NBC) and *Scrubs* (NBC), to *The X-Files* (Fox) and *The Sopranos* (HBO) were among the expanding catalog of television music. By the early 2000s, the music mandate and its demographic vista were further magnified by teen dramas *The O.C.* and *One Tree Hill* (WB), as well as adult series such as *Grey's Anatomy* (ABC), and *Six Feet Under* (HBO).

An increasing number of series began to devote at least one of its 22 episodes in a season to a special musical production, often presented in some fantasy form or dream narrative. Recent examples include *That 70s Show* (Fox), which marked its 100th show in 2001 with a musical episode featuring The Who. On *Scrubs* (NBC), a comedy which utilizes numerous unconventional production techniques, including *Wonder Years*-style voiceover commentary, a group of young interns transform Sacred Heart Hospital into song and dance scenes from *West Side Story*. Perhaps the most stunning stage-like presentation can be found in *Buffy the Vampire Slayer*'s (UPN) musical episode, "Once More With Feeling," a surreal, small screen spectacle featuring original singing performances by the cast. Promoted as a "special television event," the episode was nominated for an Emmy Award, and complete versions of all the songs are compiled in an original soundtrack recording.

Elaborate mini-production numbers have become a distinguishing trait of *The Drew Carey Show* (ABC). The blue collar comedy's opening title tunes—the Vogues' "Five O'Clock World" for two years, and in subsequent seasons, a cover version of Ian Hunter's "Cleveland Rocks"—have been accompanied by large cast choreography. Flamboyant productions over a number of seasons include a *Full Monty* strip routine, a rowdy dance-off outside a midnight showing of *The Rocky Horror Picture Show*, and a musical fantasy sequence with Carey explaining his escape from a mental institution to Leo Sayer's "Long Tall Glasses." In 1999, the series commemorated its 100th episode with an ambitious "Brotherhood of Man" production adapted from *How to Succeed in Business Without Really Trying*. Its 2001 season premiere, "Drew Carey's Back to School Rock and Roll Comedy Hour," features Sugar Ray, Uncle Kracker, Motörhead, Joe Walsh, Peter Frampton, SHeDAISY, and Smash Mouth at the Cleveland cast's watering hole, the Warsaw Tavern (see Chapter 9).

128   *B-SIDES, UNDERCURRENTS AND OVERTONES*

Cop Rock Crossovers: Music and Medicine, Lyrics and Lawyers

I'm singing because it's easier than talking. It's like a mask; it's one step from reality.

Dr. Jeffrey Geiger, *Chicago Hope* (1997)

Every time she speaks it sounds like a song to me.

Client to Ally McBeal, *Ally McBeal* (2002)

A 1997 musical episode of the medical drama, *Chicago Hope* (CBS), created by Bochco protege David E. Kelley, simultaneously mirrors *Cop Rock* and magnifies some of its generic miscalculations.[5] Elements such as setting, soundtrack and the subconscious combine to make the presentation more accessible as a musical.

The storyline centers around neurosurgeon Dr. Aaron Shutt, who is stricken with a life threatening brain aneurism. The script establishes music as the central narrative thread when the cantankerous Shutt collapses in pain to the floor of a convenience store while trying to unplug an annoying old-timey, tin roll piano locked in an unrelenting "Red Red Robin" loop. Shutt's perilous condition not only grounds the story with an inner logic that lacked in *Cop Rock*'s episodes, it provides permission for a surreal, soul searching sing along involving friends, family and colleagues. As Shutt is gurneyed down the halls of the the emergency room, the disabled doctor is in delirious drift. His cloudy colleagues hovering over him appear as lounge lizards lip syncing Dean Martin's "Ain't That A Kick in the Head." The setting smoothly shifts from emergency room into a nightclub with the singing doctors dressed in tuxedos, leaning against a bar. Various medical personnel check charts and push morphine drips in criss cross choreography through the scene. The visual transition is one of several seamless segues. In another, as the anesthetized Shutt drifts off into oblivion, the camera pans from the operating room into a recording studio where the staff rehearses, once again with lyrical tongue-in-cheek, "Well I think I'm going out of my head/Over you."

Melody and movement mix well with all things medical. The set, props and iconography supply a more natural backdrop for a musical production than the streets, tenements, alleys, guns, speeding cars and low-watt interrogation rooms of a police drama. A hospital's interiors intrinsically resemble a stage set, from the emergency room entrance to the colorful checkered floors of linoleum to the long hallways leading to luminous operating rooms. Studio-like props abound: carts and charts, tubes and operating tables, X-rays and exit signs, monitors and machines. Characters appear in costume wearing scrubs, gowns, lab coats, and masks, accented with accessories such as stethoscopes and syringes.

Within this setting, the singing is less intrusive; music is a staple of surgery, recovery and bedside manner. Diverse production numbers become an ethereal

---

5   Bochco mentored Kelley as a writer on *L.A. Law.* The two also worked closely together on *Doogie Howser, M.D.*

narrative for Shutt as he confronts his mid-career crisis, clashes with colleagues, and life choices and changes. The performances are playful, among them a roller skating nurse's flirtatious Melanie classic, "Brand New Key;" the hard line chief surgeon's soft and supportive gender reversal of Helen Reddy's "You and Me Against the World;" and the surgical staff in a coordinated Elvisian coif and costume chorus of Frankie Valli and the Four Seasons, "Walk Like A Man." An elaborate, full cast song and dance routine to Frank Sinatra's "Luck Be A Lady" fuses fear and fate into benediction moments before Shutt's delicate surgery. When a complication suddenly arises during the procedure, a multiple monitor montage chronicles Shutt's life in music video fashion with Jimi Hendrix's electric version of "All Along the Watchtower" playing. The song and dance details delightfully and faithfully mirror Dennis Potter's *The Singing Detective*, and to a lesser degree, self-reflexive elements of *Cop Rock*. The homage is undeniable as the brain surgeon brought in to operate on Shutt is named "Denise Potter."

The episode illustrates subtleties between singing and soundtrack. Whereas *Cop Rock* opts exclusively for authenticity with the cast performing original compositions, *Chicago Hope* goes the safer route with its medical staff lip syncing familiar songs. Other than Shutt's off-key Sinatra, the only character who actually sings is Dr. Jeffrey Geiger (Mandy Patinkin), whose numbers include a shivering falsetto cover of the Jackson Five's "I'll Be There," and a vaudevillian "Red Red Robin" which echoes Shutt's convenience store collapse. The production and casting nuance is that Patinkin, in addition to being a Tony award-winning actor, is an established recording artist who specializes in show tunes.[6] Though both dramas deal with life and death situations, *Chicago Hope*'s costume karaoke approach signals a more fanciful presentation. *Cop Rock*'s characters singing original, unfamiliar tunes may be a slight contrast to lip sync and cover versions. Yet the method amplifies the incongruity between the music and narrative's dramatic realism. As always, there are exceptions. In the *Buffy the Vampire Slayer* musical, the characters sing original songs. The disparity again lies in the setting. The horror/fantasy realm of *Buffy*'s dark underworld is theatrical, thus conducive to creepy choruses, singing spirits, and dancing demons. For television series, especially those merging music with narratives, location may not be everything, but it certainly does make a difference.

Incorporating musical elements into a storyline of a single episode is obviously less complicated than sustaining singing from week to week as the basis for an entire series. *Cop Rock* clearly demonstrates that the pitfalls outweigh the possibilities when producing a weekly musical. A single episode or special production contains novel appeal for audiences, creators and casts. Audiences are willing to tolerate, if not welcome, a refreshing diversion from the weekly, often weak, formulaic

---

6 When Shutt confronts his long-time colleague Geiger—"Hey, why is that your real voice? Stop with the singing! I have never liked your singing. Never!"—it becomes subtext, a reference to critical reviews that have widely characterized Patinkin's falsetto as an "acquired taste."

130   *B-SIDES, UNDERCURRENTS AND OVERTONES*

storylines. Likewise, writers, producers and performers have a rare opportunity to temporarily deviate from the norm and construct a creatively convenient, "anything goes" atmosphere, often in the form of flashbacks, fantasies, or dream sequences for their characters and storylines. In addition, the special episodes usually benefit from extensive promotion as "viewing events," which better prepares the audience and modifies conventional expectations.

Cop Rock's telecidal mission magnifies the "one episode musical" as the safe standard, the genre and audience allotment for a series. It is highly unlikely that *Chicago Hope* would have succeeded had it been designed solely as a musical series. Conversely, it is safe to speculate that *Cop Rock* might have lasted longer minus the music. And Bochco likely could have arranged a musical extravaganza with *Hill Street Blues*, *L.A. Law*, or *NYPD Blue*, as long as it was limited to a single episode.

There is one network program which provides a series, rather than single episode frame of reference for music and narratives. The same season the *Chicago Hope* musical aired, its creator Kelley expanded elements of the experimental hospital episode into *Ally McBeal* (Fox), a flighty, one-hour legal dramedy which closely approximates *Cop Rock*'s musical ambitions. Obscure singer Vonda Shepard is cast as an accompanist on the show. She not only performs the opening theme, "Searchin' My Soul," which became a hit single, but is cast in dual roles, as a maestro and meandering muse. Shepard's piano-driven, bluesy cover song serenades thread scenes with moods and motifs; provide glimpses of leading lady Ally's thoughts and emotions; and serve as nightclub karaoke classics for lawyers looking for love and libation at the local lounge.

Beyond Shepard, music is manifest in many variations throughout the show. "You get the feeling sometimes the song comes first, and David [Kelley] writes the story and script around it," says producer Steve Robin (Carter 2002: E2). Swinging stall door song and dance numbers are common in the law firms's unisex bathroom. Ally's therapist, played by Tracey Ullman, encourages clients to have a personal "theme song." The cavalcade of musical cameos includes Sting, Elton John, Mariah Carey, Tina Turner, Al Green, Gladys Knight, Gloria Gaynor, the Barrys—White and Manilow—and teen baritone Josh Groban. Jon Bon Jovi's appearance led to a nine-episode acting stint. Conversely, Robert Downey Jr.'s role resulted in several musical moments for him, including a "Every Breath You Take" duet with Sting, and an impressive rendition of Joni Mitchell's "River." Other cast members' rock star and neon-Broadway fantasies routinely surface in minor, self-indulgent subplots which evolve no farther than the nightclub stage with Shepard's piano accompaniment in scenes which often conclude episodes.

In its five seasons (1997-2002), *Ally McBeal* generated more than 400 songs or musical performances. On the surface, that total is striking, especially for a show not billed exclusively as a musical presentation. Yet, projections of Bochco's aims with *Cop Rock* (five or six songs per episode, multiplied by the standard 22 episode block for a series, meaning 100-120 songs per season) would have exceeded 400, and set a precedent for music and drama. *Ally McBeal* also fulfills Bochco's vision for musical guests, composers, and soundtrack synergy. The series's songs were compiled into four soundtracks featuring Vonda Shepard: *Songs From Ally McBeal* (1998), *Heart and Soul: New Songs from Ally McBeal* (1999), *A Very Ally Christmas* (2001), and *Ally McBeal: For Once in My Life* (2001).

Ally McBeal may lose a hypothetical hindsight battle of the bands by the numbers, but its five seasons dominate *Cop Rock*'s mere eleven episodes. The reasons are obvious. Whether single episode or series, producer Kelley places music in a different dramatic context than Bochco.[7] The settings and situations on *Ally McBeal* were safer, often surreal, and sometimes silly. Places make musical performances permissible and plausible. This primary distinction is deftly demonstrated in the opening musical montage of *Ally McBeal*'s series finale in May 2002. As episode fragments frantically flash before a wistful Ally in Wonderland—an urban Dorothy swirling in her inner tornado—cries out, "But what about the music?" The record-scratch sound effect abruptly interrupts, and a voice over clarifies, "It's a fantasy!" For punctuation, the law firm's familiar bathroom stall door opens, and Barry Manilow appears, singing "Even now..."

Permission and Possibility, Homage and Hinge

> When we first did *Hill Street*, people didn't get it at all. Then they kind of accepted what we were doing. And once they accepted it, it really did kind of change the rules of dramatic television. I think we can potentially do the same [with *Cop Rock*]; I think we can expand what's possible.
>
> Steven Bochco (Carter: 34)

Eighteen years after its final episode, *Cop Rock* lingers in obscurity as a televersion of the B-film, albeit without a B-movie budget. Its scant eleven episodes are barely enough to block a "cult classic" court, cop, or comedy mock marathon in cable's kitschy late night landscape. In July 2002, one of those rare *Cop Rock* citations materialized from the files of failure. This one was predictably less complementary than John Leonard's literate linking of *Cop Rock* with *Moulin Rouge* on *Sunday Morning*. In its July 20-26, 2002 issue, *TV Guide* presented a list of "The 50 Worst Shows of All Time." *Cop Rock* ranked number eight.

The deriding distinction is typical of *Cop Rock*'s legacy. Predictably, the predominant view is that *Cop Rock* is more laughable than legitimate. Attributing some sense of impact, influence, or inspiration to such a critical and commercial failure is a premise likely to be regarded as ridiculous and easily rejected on any level. Even minuscule mentions such as those by Leonard should not be misconstrued as literate lobbying for *Cop Rock*'s lofty place in broadcast programming history. Any acclaim for the show from critical corners risks revealing one of the potential

---

7 Kelley may have benefitted from having another legal series in prime-time on another night, *The Practice* (ABC), where he could use serious storylines.

132 B-SIDES, UNDERCURRENTS AND OVERTONES

perils of the auteur approach, that is, emphasizing the creator over the work itself, an evaluative blind spot which can elevate an undeserving production to a level of redeeming aesthetic quality.

Likewise, it is a comparable critical convenience to emphasize only successful texts—those leading in the ratings, charts, box office sales, and critical kudos— and neglect or ignore the failures, overlooking any value they may contain. *Cop Rock* demonstrates how fragments of failure are capable of floating and finding themselves in other forms and fashions. Just as the short-lived series' significance should not, and likely never will be, overstated, its value should not be dismissed, especially when placing the production within the context of genre evolution and cross-genre contributions.

The individual works that comprise any genre represent stepping stones or links in its evolution. Whether the steps are big, small, or stumbling, the series of inventions and conventions embodied in narratives unfold and develop, defining and redefining a genre over a period of time. Following *Hill Street*'s and *Miami Vice*'s important aesthetic advances within the police/crime genre's evolution in the 1980s, *Cop Rock*'s inventive steps further explored and expanded the parameters of the genre's familiar conventions. "If you look at a 30-year curve, television has gotten much better, and you can't stop its progress, "says Bochco. "We're moving forward, like it or not. Take a long look at television and you realize it just continually becomes smarter, broader in its appeal, more sophisticated" (Tucker 1996:65).

More markedly, *Cop Rock* signaled a subtle shift on the television time line that extends beyond its own genre. By importing *The Singing Detective* and integrating its elements within the police/crime programming progression via *Cop Rock*, Bochco accomplished more than mere homage to Dennis Potter. *Cop Rock* represents a hinge, a pivotal point on the door of possibility. Just as *The Singing Detective* gave Bochco "permission" to create *Cop Rock*, Bochco, in turn passed along similar lyrical license to other producers to explore the further variations of music and narratives, whether situation comedy, dramedy, police, law, hospital, horror or family dramas.

By the 2002 television season, the police/crime genre was so prevalent that the network prime-time schedule appeared to be wrapped in the yellow "Police Line" tape that outlines a crime scene. From Dick Wolf's *Law and Order* franchise on NBC, which includes *Special Victims* and *Criminal Intent* units; to Jerry Bruckheimer's highly rated *CSI* (CBS) series, its Miami and New York clones, and all precincts, perpetrators and procedural points in between, prime time has become a crime wave, a place crawling with copycat cops, corpses, coroners, and forensics experts. Though none of the characters in television's crime spree and nightly police lineup sing or dance, music continued to be central as soundtrack and more closely integrated with narratives. In 2006, a storyline for a *Cold Case* (CBS) unsolved crime was constructed around the lyrics of nine Bruce Springsteen songs, with a subsequent episode based on the music of U2 (see Weiner 2006).

Michael Mann and *Miami Vice* were the most frequently praised predecesssors of the musical movement, particularly soundtracks. While there may have been limited evidence of *Cop Rock* at the scenes of the late 1990s/early 2000s crime wave in television's dramas, traces of Bochco's musical blueprint continued to reveal themselves in other popular prime-time productions. The hospital comedy *Scrubs* increasingly synthesized medicine with music via soundtrack, guest cameos, performance and production numbers, including adaptation of *West Side Story* scenes, and an original song and dance spectacular, "My Musical" (18 January 2007). In an episode of the family drama, *7th Heaven* (WB), the father, Eric Camden, undergoes heart bypass surgery. While under anesthesia, Camden hallucinates that he is Elvis Presley. Costumed variously in black leather, gold lame, and a spangled Vegas jumpsuit, Camden delivers Elversions of "All Shook Up," "Don't Be Cruel," "Teddy Bear," and "Rock-A-Hula Baby."

These musical moments are deja view; they are distant duets that nod to Ally McBeal, her karaoke cast and queen Vonda Shepard, and Buffy's singing spirits. Eric Camden mirrors Aaron Shutt in Chicago Hope's operating room. The evolution of these musical interludes can be traced to Bochco's blueprint in 1990 with *Cop Rock*. Then, a few homage(nous) steps farther to 1986 with *The Singing Detective*.

Though *Cop Rock* will routinely be recognized among the "Worst Shows of All Time," it nonetheless remains an unsung series. *Cop Rock*'s consequence is as a hinge, a preface of permission and possibility for music and narrative in television. In 2005, producer Peter Bowker listed *Cop Rock* among an odd assortment of inspirational sources—*Six Feet Under*, *Buffy the Vampire Slayer*, *Pennies From Heaven* and West End and Hollywood musicals—for his BBC America series, *Viva Blackpool*, a quirky karaoke musical murder mystery. Bowker's approach to *Blackpool* echoed Bochco: "I thought it would be interesting to see how far you can push (musicals) on a television screen, really, because obviously the sheer scale of the thing is smaller. But because of that the whole thing can burst out of the screen" (Bianco 2005: 4A). CBS scheduled an American television adaptation of *Viva Blackpool*, renamed *Viva Laughlin*, and starring Hugh Jackman and Melanie Griffith, for its 2007 schedule. The series lasted a mere two episodes before being cancelled, (dis)qualifying as a viable series to supplant *Cop Rock* on "worst" lists. The *Viva* versions provide strands of evidence for *Cop Rock*'s case. *Cop Rock*'s fusion and fragments may not resonate, rather its residue and relevance ripple as a reminder beneath the surface of small screen scenes and soundtracks. It is there from the B-Side, the false notes of the flip side as failure, that *Cop Rock* whispers, winks and whistles a faintly familiar television tune.

Chapter 9

Must Sing TV:
Pop Rock Sitcom Cameo Obscuras

When network television programming executives announced their Fall 2006 prime-time lineups, there were several musical notes of interest in series slated for the schedule. In a synergistic marketing move to promote the release of his album, *Continuum*, John Mayer was booked to perform two songs on the two-part season premiere of *C.S.I.* (CBS). In a scene set in a Las Vegas nightclub, Mayer sings "Waiting for the World to Change" and "Slow Dancing in a Burning Room." The storyline for the episode featured 1960s Partridge Family member turned 16th minute celebrity Danny Bonaduce, playing an ex-rock star who is murdered. Later in the highly-rated crime procedural's season, The Who's Roger Daltrey is cast as a menacing mobster in an episode titled "Living Legend." Several other music artists appeared in dramatic series. Steve Earle continued his minor role as "Walon," a recovering addict on HBO's *The Wire*. Dave Matthews played a piano prodigy "Patrick" with an unusual neurological condition on *House* (Fox). Jewel Kilcher, as herself, is stranded with car trouble in the lighthearted *Northern Exposure* facsimile *Men in Trees* (ABC), set in the folksinger's native Alaska.[1]

There were also a number of comedy cameos. Aerosmith's Steven Tyler appears as Charlie's disruptive Malibu neighbor in the situation comedy *Two and a Half Men* (CBS). On the animated front, Dusty Hill and ZZ Top were central characters in a *King of the Hill* (Fox) episode, "Hank Gets Dusted," while the White Stripes, Jack and Meg White, were among the traditional parade of animated celebrity cameos cast for *The Simpsons* 18th season. In one of the most anticipated shows of the new season, Mick Jagger and his lux Manhattan apartment were the basis for ABC's bumbling burglar half-hour comedy series, *The Knights of Prosperity* (originally titled *Let's Rob Mick Jagger*).

The musical guest stars, from the Stripes to the Stones, were mere markers for what had become a more subtle strand of random rock formations in television, particularly in the situation comedy genre. From the mid-1990s on, an unlikely cast of singer-songwriters continued to accumulate quirky cameo credits. Among these boomer bit players were Yoko Ono, Bob Dylan, Elvis Costello, Tom Petty, John Hiatt and Warren Zevon. Fragments of the trend were compiled in VH-1 cable music network's "greatest" series, *The Greatest: 25 Greatest Rock Star Cameos*, which aired in May 2003.

---

1 The storyline may have been a sly sub-reference to Kilcher's biographical accounts of living in a car before her singing career.

TV Land of Ozzies: From Nelson to Osbourne and Beyond

The unusual undercurrent dotted television's musical programming history in between music family fare that spans Ricky Nelson on *Ozzie and Harriet* in the late 1950s to *The Beatles* Saturday morning cartoon (1965-1969, ABC) and *The Monkees* madcap series (1966-1968, NBC) in the mid-1960s, to *The Partridge Family* in the early 1970s and *Saturday Night Live* beginning mid-decade, through MTV's arrival in 1981 to *The Osbournes* in the 1990s and beyond. The collection of pop rock sitcom cameo obscuras forms a B-side bracket and alternative programming chronicle.

During television's infancy in the 1950s, variety shows such as *The Ed Sullivan Show*, were the most common and natural setting for musical performers. By the mid-1960s, as rock music and television continued to evolve as commercial and cultural forms, there were numerous multi-media moments of mutuality and convergence beyond live performances in the variety show format. With much of programming still being broadcast in black and white, musical groups could be seen and heard, performing songs, both vocal and instrumental, in a variety of program formats, including prime-time dramas, situation comedies and animated series. Even daytime soap operas integrated music, as The Lovin' Spoonful and the Castaways, playing their garage hit, "Liar, Liar," appeared in episodes of *Never Too Young*.

Music performances were presented as a natural part of storylines, with scenes structured around settings such as nightclubs, band rehearsals, stages, teen dances, battle of the bands' competitions, discotheques and outdoor parties. Episode titles were frequently linked to the musical theme. Predictably, instrumentals were used for scene transitions, background music and over credits, though frequently the musical performances were not credited. For example, Davie Allan and the Arrows appeared in scenes in *Get Smart* and *The Invaders* but their surf instrumentals were nor credited. On rare occasions, band members had speaking lines that accented the teen-targeted hip dialogue of the scripts. The popular duo Boyce and Hart managed to have lines in each of the three shows they appeared in—*I Dream of Jeannie* (which also featured producer Phil Spector), *Bewitched* and *The Flying Nun*.

The range of "name" bands with cameos was just as varied as the types of shows they were cast in. Little known groups such as the Enemys, Crocodiles, Daily Flash, Opus 1, Sundowners, and Lewis and Clarke Expedition appeared in *Burke's Law*, *The Beverly Hillbillies*, *The Joey Bishop Show*, *The Girl From U.N.C.L.E.*, *Perry Mason*, *The Flying Nun*, and *I Dream of Jeannie*. The mid-level group, the Spats, followed their *American Bandstand* appearance and album release, *Cooking With the Spats* (1965), with a performance in an episode of *My Mother the Car*. Every Mother's Son had the opportunity to play their sole hit, "Come On Down to My Boat Baby" during a fight scene in *The Man From U.N.C.L.E.*

While the song, scene and series seem somewhat incompatible on the small screen surface, there were other peculiar cameos. The Strawberry Alarm Clock appeared in a psychedelic freak out scene in the tame environment of *The Danny*

Thomas Hour. The Buffalo Springfield performed "Bluebird" and their protest song "For What It's Worth," in the background of two night club scenes in *Mannix*. Despite the detective series' limited teen appeal and a primarily older adult target demographic, the show's routine inclusion of bands in scene backgrounds was surprising.

Cameos in cartoon and comic series of the era translated into a novelty nature. In a *Batman* episode, Paul Revere and the Raiders, whose uniforms fit the series costumed characters well, support an arch-villain with a campaign song, "Vote for Penguin," sung to the tune of "Yankee Doodle Dandy." In *The Munsters*, the Standells cover the Beatles's hit "I Want to Hold Your Hand" and "Do the Ringo" in the family's living room while son Eddie spins their album on the turntable. *The Flintstones* spoof the popular 1960s teen dance show, *Shindig*, with an episode titled "Shinrock A-Go-Go." The animated Stone Age adaptation features *Shindig* host Jimmy O'Neil, the Wipe Outs, and the Beau Brummels, who perform one of their hits, "Laugh Laugh," appearing in a nightclub and on Wilma's television screen. The *Shindig* house band, The Shindogs, appear in an episode of *The Patty Duke Show.*

Bands not only appeared as themselves but frequently played fictional groups. The Wellingtons, who perform the theme song to *Gilligan's Island*, appear in an episode of the show as "The Mosquitos"—Bingo, Bango, Bongo and Irving. The Seeds, performing their hit "Pushin' Too Hard," appear as "The Warts" in *The Mothers in Law* episode "How Not to Manage a Rock Group." The Standells, who appear as themselves in the medical series *Ben Casey*, also portray a band called the "Love Bugs" in *The Bing Crosby Show.* The Strawberry Alarm Clock play the Dungeons in the pilot episode of *The Best Years*, a series that never materialized.

In B-Side fashion, particles of music minutae are sprinkled throughout the 1960s cameo obscurities. Ex-Leaves member Bobby Arlin's band, Hook, is in a scene at a drug commune in an episode of detective series *Ironside*. In a *Flintstones* episode, the Fantastic Baggys, the backing band for "Jimmy Darrock" (James Darren), was the popular songwriting team P.F. Sloan and Steve Barri. Sloan composed the 1960s anthem, "Eve of Destruction," popularized by Barry Maguire. Among their other notable collaborative credits are writing and producing for the Grass Roots.

Lowell George's pre-Little Feat band, The Factory, performs in episodes of *Gomer Pyle, U.S.M.C.* and *F-Troop.* In *F-Troop*, the band, mistakenly cited as the Factory Rock Quartet in various sources, including *TV Guide*, appears as "The Bed Bugs" and perform "Camptown Races" and various instrumental tunes.[2] In the same episode, the The F-Troopers form their own group, The Termites— "We eat our way into your hearts." With no regard for the time frame that the series

---

2 "Rock Artist TV Cameos," 27 January 2003, is an excellent source that is part of the cool archive "The Rock Video 60's Project," retrieved 2 June 2005 from http://members. aol.com/Rockvideo2/TVCameo.html.

is set in, Wrangler Jane delivers renditions of contemporary tunes "Lemon Tree" and "Mr. Tambourine Man."[3]

Some stars used their series to showcase their own bands. Don Grady, who played Robbie Douglas in *My Three Sons*, was involved with 1960s bands Yellow Balloon, Windupwatchband and Palace Guard. His band, the Greefs, rehearse in the Douglas living room and play at a teen club in a *My Three Sons* episode "Falling Star." In *The Andy Griffith Show/Mayberry R.F.D.*, Sound Committee performs in a teen party living room scene. Their instrumental, "Opie's Theme," and the episode title, "Opie's Group," reinforced speculation that the band was Ron Howard's.

The Peppermint Trolley Co. was notable beyond their appearances in *Mannix* and *The Beverly Hillbillies*, and mistaken identity with the Strawberry Alarm Clock. The band was signed to perform the theme song for *The Brady Bunch* family comedy which was set to premiere in 1969. When the band broke up before the recording session, studio musicians completed the theme song. The Peppermint Trolley Co. still received the credit. The band also recorded the theme song for another late 1960s/early 1970s series, the comedy anthology *Love American Style*, as did the Cowsills.

That '70s (No) Show

The pop rock sitcom cameo connection dramatically subsided during the 1970s. Samplings were sparse: Marcia, Marcia promises to book Monkee Davy Jones for the prom on *The Brady Bunch*; Alice Cooper in song and sketch on *The Muppets*; and the Doobie Brothers help bust record bootleggers in a cleverly titled two-part episode, "Doobie or Not Doobie," on the African-American sitcom *What's Happening!*, based on the film *Cooley High*. The undercurrent would not start to sprinkle television's schedules again until the late 1980s. During an era commonly characterized as "the Second Golden Age of Comedy," situation comedies dominated television's Top Ten ratings during the 1970s. The quality of writing, production and performance matured into comedies that were smarter, more sophisticated and serious. The environments of touchstone series such as *All in the Family* and *The Mary Tyler Moore Show* were not well suited for pop rock guest stars, nor was there demographic appeal in other presentations such as *The Carol Burnett Show* variety hour.[4] In 1975, with protest anthems of the previous decade diminished by disco's dominance, NBC's late-night satire, *Saturday Night Live* arrived and quickly became an irreverent refuge and prestigious popular music performance platform for television. By the end of the decade, as many of

---

3   Rhino Records compiled Lowell George and The Factory on *Lightning Rod Man* (1993).

4   A Sammy Davis Jr. cameo on *All in the Family* suggested a subtle shift to mainstream "entertainers."

the popular series aged and ran their courses, the situation comedy genre slumped significantly. In 1981, with the arrival of the cable music network MTV, music video and its multi-media marketing synergy became the performance priorities for artists and their record companies.

Petty Programming Prologue

During the initial stages of its quest to become the fourth broadcast network, the fledgling Fox's only prime-time block of programming in the mid-1980s was on Sunday night. Fox's quirky comedy lineup included the edgy family sitcom *Married With Children*, versatile British comedienne Tracey Ullman's sketch comedy, *The Tracey Ullman Show*, which featured *Life in Hell* cartoonist Matt Groening's animated shorts about an offbeat family known as "The Simpsons," and the unconventional *It's Garry Shandling's Show*. Shandling played himself, a standup comic and star of a TV show, telecast from his ficticious Sherman Oaks, California condominium. Borrowing from the late 1950s Burns and Allen technique of "breaking the fourth wall," Shandling frequently addressed the audience, commenting on plots, updating stories or telling jokes.

During a 1987 episode of the show, there is a knock at Garry's door. He answers. It is his neighbor, rock star Tom Petty (as himself), returning Shandling's hedge clippers that he borrowed. "Thanks 'Gare', the hedges never looked better," says neighbor Tom. Petty was cast as a semi-regular in the series. He frequently dropped by Shandling's condo, whether Christmas caroling or singing with the neighborhood quartet. In his most memorable visit, Petty serenades expectant mother Jackie with an acoustic living room rendition of his song "The Waiting" after negotiating with Garry to trim the hedges while Petty was away on tour.

Petty's droll presence was a preview that marked the understated beginning of the backside bracket of pop rock sitcom cameos that continued as an undercurrent in television for the next twenty years. Mirroring the initial 1960s cluster, the contemporary cameos embody an array of artists, primarily playing themselves, cast in musical related scenes in a wide variety of half-hour situation comedies.

Act Naturally

Television, specifically the situation comedy, and rock and roll, particularly its old school baby boom artists, seem an incongruous union on the surface. The casting compatibility is often curious at best, with many of the cameos conveying a pervading sense of randomness that undermined believability even within a comic context. As peculiar as the scene is with Petty returning Shandling's hedge clippers, there is some quirky credibility that the two were neighbors. Just as it is plausible that Greg's law firm has to handle some of k.d. lang's legal matters on *Dharma and Greg*. Other rock cameos were less convincing, the casting conspicuous. For example, in an episode of NBC's Thursday night "Must See TV" hit *Friends*, Pretenders front woman Chrissie Hynde plays "Stephanie Schiffer," a singer booked at Central Park. Phoebe, an aspiring folkie whose notable tune is "Smelly Cat," is threatened. She pettily points out that Stephanie "knows all the chords but her guitar doesn't have a strap." Though the scene plays well comically and Hynde appears as a character, not herself, there is suspended skepticism. The show's incestuous cast of terminal twenty somethings, its cheery Rembrandt's theme song "I'll Be There For You," and its audience constituency do not match the spiky, post punk rock Pretender profile.[5] In contrast, Darius Rucker's cameo when the gang goes to a Hootie and the Blowfish concert in another episode is much more credible. Another odd match is Warren Zevon, who guests alongside Rick Springfield in a dating flirtation episode of the soft edged situation comedy *Suddenly Susan*, starring Brooke Shields. Zevon's morose, literary songwriting and his excitable boy persona were more suited for HBO's funeral home series *Six Feet Under* (see Chapter 11).

For the many striking cameos, there were those that were less intrusive. Perhaps the most unaffected portrayals are those from Cyndi Lauper, who appeared in several episodes of the New York City sitcom *Mad About You* over a number seasons between 1993 and 1999. Lauper earned an Emmy Award for her recurring role as Ira's ex-wife Marianne Lugasso. Lauper possesses an inherent dramatic presence, her colorful caricature established early on in the MTV era with her "Girls Just Want to Have Fun" video, and reinforced with a brief stint with the World Wrestling Federation. Lauper also appeared as "Miss Petuto" on Nickelodeon's teen comedy *That's So Raven*. Like Lauper, Lyle Lovett (*Mad About You*; *Dharma and Greg*), Queen Latifah (*Fresh Prince of Bel Air*) and Joe Walsh (*The Drew Carey Show*) are among a small troupe of musicians who had recurring roles as characters on situation comedies, often over a number of seasons.

Yoko Ono also delivers a natural, albeit a more predictably understated comic presence, in the central storyline of a 1995 episode of the comedy *Mad About You.* In the episode, "Yoko Said," Paul Buchman, a documentary filmmaker, and his wife Jamie are interested in chronicling Yoko's series of film happenings for the Explorer Channel. Beatles references sustain the humor from the time the Buchmans arrive at the Dakota for their meeting with Yoko, who suggests that Paul film the wind instead. Immediately following the anxious Buchman pronouncement to each other—"Don't talk about the Beatles"—Yoko enters to "I want to hold your hand" on the soundtrack. Then there is Yoko's expression to the Buchmans "that you broke up the..." and an obligatory John joke as Paul wonders when he would have thought of putting Ringo out front. The closing credits re-create the iconic John and Yoko "Bed In" with the Buchmans. Yoko flashes the peace sign and says "Give Peace a Chance," followed by Paul delivering his signature line from the series, "That's all we're saying."

---

5   Hynde's appearance was reminiscent of actor Sean Penn's edgy cameo in the series.

Beyond Yoko's instant recognition, the most mainstream musical guests could be seen on *Will and Grace*. The series, a contemporary mingling of *The Odd Couple*, *I Love Lucy* and *Three's Company*, routinely featured artists who fit seamlessly, if not stereotypically, into the show's sassy storylines and gay characters. The pop parade of stars playing themselves included Jack's idol Cher, Will's heroes Barry Manilow and Elton John, Hall and Oates, Jennifer Lopez, Janet Jackson and Britney Spears. Madonna and Harry Connick Jr. appeared in character roles, with Connick's becoming a regular role as Grace's love interest.

Backstage Musicals

Many of these television productions borrowed from traditional Hollywood and Broadway musicals, as well as Richard Lester's behind the scenes approach to the Beatles rehearsals and concerts in *A Hard Day's Night*, integrating the guest appearance, their music and performance as a natural part of the narratives, thus making them more conceivable. Common settings and themes included backstage at concerts (Ted Nugent, *That 70s Show*; Jermaine Jackson, *The Facts of Life*; Barry Manilow, *Will and Grace*), recording studios and jam sessions (Stevie Wonder, *The Cosby Show*; k.d. lang, Bob Dylan, *Dharma and Greg*); dance halls (Boy George and Culture Club, *The A Team*), battle of the bands in a Cleveland tavern (Joe Walsh, *The Drew Carey Show*), garage rehearsals (Los Lobos, *Greetings from Tucson*), in a church telethon (James Brown and Lloyd Price, *Amen*), Las Vegas wedding (Jennifer Lopez, *Will and Grace*), a serenade (Kenny Loggins, *Dharma and Greg*); a benefit performance in a living room (Alanis Morissette, *Curb Your Enthusiasm*); fantasies (Barry White, *Ally McBeal*); business dealings (Snoop Dogg, *Just Shoot Me*); and chance celebrity encounters (Cher, *Will and Grace*; John Hiatt, Bret Michaels of Poison, *Yes, Dear*).

The musical performances in the recent set of cameos tended to be more abbreviated than those during the 1960s. Similar to soundtrack strategy, placement of the musical moment was designed to enhance the comic and dramatic situation. Because the cameos were ratings ploys and highly promoted hooks that would likely attract new viewers who were not regular fans of the show, but specifically tuned in for the cameo, audiences had to wait for the star moment in the storytelling. Most of the cameos tended to occur in the second half of the thirty-minute sitcom format. The cameos were often important to the comic/dramatic climax and frequently used in conjunction with the closing credits.

Not all the appearances were mere punch lines. Los Lobos' patio performance of John Lennon's "Beautiful Boy" provided poignant punctuation to a tender Christmas episode of the ethnic sitcom *Greetings from Tucson*.[6] In the storyline, the Mexican-American family patriarch, Joaquin, is sharing the moral of the "you can't always get everything you want for Christmas" story with his son David.

---

6   Los Lobos played the show's opening title and closing credits theme.

Joaquin recalls how as a boy, he wanted the *Double Fantasy* album, but his father refused, saying that "John Lennon is a hippie and a waste of time." Joaquin is moved when David fulfills his long lost wish and gets him the *Double Fantasy* album for Christmas, until he discovers that the record in the sleeve is broken.

Calculated Cameos

By both television and music industry modes of operation, most of the cameos were more calculated than they were accidental or arbitrary. By the 1990s, synergy was well established as the marketing standard across the mass media industries. From the music industry vantage point, the timeless adage that "any publicity is good publicity" applied. The television appearances were often a commercial convenience that coincided with the guest star's new record release. From a television programming perspective, cameos are considered "stunt casting," a strategy employed by producers and the networks to attract viewership and provide a spike in the weekly ratings.

The axiom "timing is everything" is also relevant. The stunt casting technique is commonly employed during peak and priority programming periods—season premieres in the fall, season and series finales in May, or during one of the quarterly "sweeps" months. Sweeps, the comprehensive ratings of all time periods, are conducted in November, February, May and July. These special guest episodes are not scheduling surprises; they are usually preceded by extensive network promotion. Predictably, a significant number of the pop rock cameos took place during sweeps episodes.

The novel nature and ratings gimmickry inherent in stunt casting are often overshadowed by the prestige that accompanies a cameo. Booking a rock star carries cachet for a show and its producer among its competitors. However, the cameo-at-all-costs approach without regard to the story, cast chemistry and show compatibility, can contribute to an awkward appearance and critical backlash. One such example is the 2004 season premiere of *Two and A Half Men*, which features Elvis Costello, and actors Sean Penn and Harry Dean Stanton as part of Charlie's Malibu male support group. Costello's attempt to write lyrics based on Penn's thoughts dead end at "grocery list," while Stanton knocks down Scotch. The response to the triangular stunt casting was not overwhelming. *Variety*'s Brian Lowry wrote that the scene was "forced, 'Hey look who we could get!' fashion" (2004). The episode is listed among the leading candidates for *Two and a Half Men*'s "Jump the Shark" programming peak, its dubious defining moment.

"Play Lady Play": Dylan does Dharma

Arguably one of the most "prestigious cameos" was Bob Dylan's guest spot on *Dharma and Greg*. In the episode, "Play Lady Play," forever flower child Dharma, whose husband is a straight laced attorney, has an audition as a drummer for a band. Bob Dylan happens to be the band leader of an outfit that includes Joe Henry and T-Bone Burnett. After suggesting different beats, including meringue and polkas, Dharma drums a little and says, "That's kind of too funky for your style, eh?" "Not at all," says a wry Dylan, doing his best to restrain laughing at Dharma's off beats. Following a brief jam, Dylan demurs when Dharma asks if she "can play with you guys? You want me to play some more?" Oblivious to the polite rejection, the free spirit shrugs, tells them that she's in a band, then asks for help loading up her stuff. "Yeah, sure," says Dylan, a willing roadie.

To casual fans and hard core Dylanphiles, the appearance was both welcome and curious. While the series possessed a standard sitcom sensibility, it also maintained a free spirited, 1960s vibe through Dharma and her parents' characters, a stark comic contrast to Greg's conformity. In addition to "Play Lady Play," the series consistently adapted rock song titles for its episodes, among them "Papa Was Almost a Rolling Stone," "Mother and Daughter Reunion," "Lawyers, Beer and Money," "Shower the People You Love with Love," "Let's Get Fiscal," "Talkin' 'Bout My Re g-g-generation," "Instant Dharma" and "Fairway to Heaven." *That 70s Show* borrowed the title technique; all of its 2003 episodes were named after Who songs, while its 2002 season featured Led Zeppelin titles.

The Dylan cameo evolved out of producer Chuck Lorre's fondness for musician cameos. Lorre's recruiting record included Lyle Lovett, k.d lang and Kenny Loggins for *Dharma and Greg*, and Elvis Costello and Steven Tyler for *Two and Half Men*. When Lorre learned that one of the show's writers, Eddie Gorodetsky, was an acquaintance of Dylan's, he followed up on the contact.[7] Dylan requested tapes of *Dharma and Greg* episodes before committing. He agreed to appear one month later (The Bridge 1999). Ironically, the *Dharma and Greg* cameo was a playful "coming out" for Dylan. The sitcom scene marked an inauguration of an occasionally demystifying multi-media procession. In between two remarkable records, *Love and Theft* (2001) and *Modern Times* (2006), Dylan's series of projects included the disjointed film *Masked and Anonymous* (2003), a 2004 Victoria's Secret ad cameo with "Love Sick" on the soundtrack and an exclusive in-store CD compilation, his autobiography *Chronicles, Volume 1* (2004), the Martin Scorsese documentary *No Direction Home* (2005), a host gig on the XM satellite show "Theme Time Radio Hour," and commercials for Apple iTunes in 2006, and Cadillac Escalade/XM Radio in 2007.[8]

Other cameos also evolved out of personal and professional connections. Men at Work front man Colin Hay's appearance as a wandering troubadour in a *Scrubs* episode is loosely linked to his connections with Chad Fischer of Lazlo Bane, whose "Superman" is the show's theme song, and the series' lead actor Zach Braff. Braff

---

7   Gorodetsky became a producer for Dylan's XM satellite Radio show.

8   Both ads prompted widespread responses, among the more humorous—"Bob Dylan can still drive?"—retrieved 19 February 2008 from http:www.thedailyswarm.com/watch/bob-dylan-cadillac-comercial/.

144   B-SIDES, UNDERCURRENTS AND OVERTONES

became an indie music arbiter with the film *Garden State* and brought his hipster soundtrack sensibility to *Scrubs* Sacred Heart Hospital setting (see Chapter 10).[9]

So You Want To Be a Sitcom Star

> I finally realized every rock star's dream—hating being famous.
>> Homer Simpson, "That 90's Show" *The Simpsons* (27 January 2008)

The rock cameos play well as reflectors of a cultural preoccupation, if not obsession, with fame and celebrity. The pursuit of such fantasies are the premise for episodes of the blue collar *Yes, Dear* ("A List Before Dying") and animated *The Simpsons* ("How I Spent My Strummer Vacation"), both of which aired during sweeps periods and featured multiple cameos. In *Yes, Dear*, Jimmy Hughes, a security guard at a Hollywood film studio lot, decides to update his childhood list of dreams following a near death experience. Through their personal and professional contacts, and some comic conniving and serendipity, Jimmy's wife and friends assist in crossing off the celebrity-slanted items on his list. Jimmy dances with a super model, the twist being it is Fabio; he fights with ex-hockey great Gordie Howe; he drives in a stock car with Dale Earnhardt, Jr. Another dream of Jimmy's is to write a song that would be recorded by a famous musician. Jimmy's best friend recruits John Hiatt, who happened to be shooting a music video on one of the studio lots, for an unplugged living room rendition of the tune Jimmy had been working on, "Things I Think About at Work." Jimmy's security box meditation is a rap worthy rhyming stream of (un)consciousness dominated by food and celebrity name dropping: free bagels and locks, different colored socks, vanilla coke that really rocks, donuts on stage five, Captain Kirk, Abe Vigoda is still alive, donuts left on stage five, the movie *Memento*, Joe Gibbs and the Washington Redskins, Pierce Brosnan as a jerk, Mister T versus Russell Crow in a fight, Mr. Britney Spears.

The punch line occurs as Jimmy, his dream list fulfilled, watches television with his wife. Hiatt appears on the small screen, premiering his new music video, "The Things I Think About at Work," a montage that includes images of Jimmy, Hiatt, Fabio, Howe, Earnhardt. Jimmy's wife turns to him seeking reassurance that he copyrighted his song. Hiatt's convincing rendition generated considerable curiosity among his fans on Internet forums, with many wondering about the origins and availability of the song.

In a similar scenario on *The Simpsons*, Homer, in pursuit of his elusive dream, encounters an all-star cast at "The Rolling Stones Rock and Roll Fantasy Camp." "Experience the rock and roll lifestyle without the lawsuits and STDs," boasts camp counselor Keith Richards. His Glimmer Twin Mick Jagger demonstrates his signature cock strut, while Tom Petty leads a lyrics workshop, Brian Setzer, whom

---

9   Braff had seen Hay play at the Largo in Hollywood and recommended his music to producers.

MUST SING TV 145

Homer calls "Seltzer," teaches guitar, Lenny Kravitz operates the Thread Shed, Elvis Costello manages the Instrument Shack, and Richards leads an "escape to the limo" obstacle course. Kenny Loggins appears briefly, only to be shamefully exiled by Kravitz for a crotch stuffing violation.

The episode is rich, with the writers and artists not missing a biographical beat, from Richards' obvious chain smoking to the costuming detail of his head band and silver bracelet. When Costello's glasses get knocked off, he panics, "My image!" Jagger and Richards are portrayed as an old married couple nagging each other. As the weekend winds down, the Stones lament a return to their normal lives of putting up storm windows and mowing the lawn. Following an epic chaotic concert climax, Petty's muted "The Last DJ" on Homer's car radio fades into closing credits.

Anima(tion) Rising: Cartoon Cameos

In addition to daytime children's programming fare such as *The Muppets* and *Sesame Street*, animated series such as *The Simpsons* were the most fashionable comedy sub genre for pop rock guests. These cameos became so routine on *The Simpsons* that they appeared to be a generic convention of the show. In addition to the lineup from Rock Fantasy Camp episode, the diverse roster and their roles includes Johnny Cash (coyote spirit guide), Michael Jackson (mental institution patient Leon Kompowsky), Tom Jones (kidnapped singer), The Ramones (perform "Happy Birthday"), Paul and Linda McCartney (establish Lisa's vegetarianism), Barry White, Bette Midler and the Red Hot Chili Peppers (campaign to save Krusty the Klown's "kancelled" TV show), Metallica (hijacked to school by Bart after their tour bus breaks down), Aerosmith (perform "Walk This Way" with Moe the bartender), Smashing Pumpkins, Cypress Hill, Peter Frampton, Sonic Youth (in lineup for Homerpalooza music festival), the White Stripes (animated adaptation of their video "The Hardest Button to Button"), The Who (concert to unite Olde and New Springfield town feud), Weird Al Yankovic (concert lineup with Homer's band Sadgasm parodying their hit "Brain Freeze"), Blink 182 (playing live in Bart's dream apartment), U2 (concert interrupted by Homer's campaign for Sanitation Comissioner), Kid Rock (Spring Break concert with Joe C.), Cyndi Lauper (sings "The Star Spangled Banner" to the tune of "Girls Just Want to Have Fun"), Elton John (marriage saving concert), Jackson Browne (transforms his song "Rosie" into "Marjorie"), R.E.M. (perform in Homer's new garage bar and join the family for Thanksgiving dinner of tofu and gluten), the mockumentary parodists Spinal Tap (killed in a bus accident), and Kurt Cobain's "cousin" Marvin.

In addition to *The Simpsons*, Matt Groening's other cartoon series, *Futurama*, along with *King of the Hill*, *Family Guy* and *South Park*, are among broadcast and cable prime-time and late-night animated series that routinely featured pop rock cameos. With a hint of homage to the Beatles cartoon series of the mid-1960s, portrayals of rock stars as animated figures, in this case with their own voices delivering their lines, was inherently humorous. The writers take creative and comic advantage of their cartoon world's animated setting and characters, borrowing musical and biographical bits, as well as historical moments, then bending them into often bizarre scenes that border on the absurd. In a *Futurama* Godzilla parody, Beck is robotized and the brothers Hanson, the only 1990s boy band that wrote their own material and could play instruments, are crushed as they sing the chorus to their hit "Mmm Bop." On *Family Guy*, Peter hires Michael McDonald to sing back up for everything the guys say. The peculiar plotline, only plausible in a cartoon universe, is an accurate subreference to the distinctive Doobie Brother's extensive credits that he has accumulated as a background vocalist beyond his solo and band recordings as backup singer. In *The Simpsons*' "That '90s Show," a *Back to the Future* homage episode and cautionary tale about rock stardom, the origin of "grunge" ("Guitar Rock Utilizing Nihilist Grunge Energy") is traced to Homer's 1990s band Sadgasm. As they perform at an outdoor campus concert, with Homer in full Cobain costume (striped t-shirt over long sleeves, hole in jeans) Marvin Cobain is in the crowd and calls his cousin from a nearby pay phone, "Hey Kurt, about that sound you were looking for…" The rest is rock history.

There are a few recurring roles. *South Park* employed the late Isaac Hayes' voice as "Chef."[10] Similarly, the producers of *King of the Hill* recruited Tom Petty to lazily speak the lines for "Lucky," a corn chip factory worker who is awarded $53,000 in a settlement after slipping on urine in a Wal Mart. The series also casts Jazz musician Chuck Mangione as the Mega Lo Mart spokesperson. As a quirky running gag, Mangione's character trumpets "Taps" then segues into his hit "Feels So Good," the store theme song. In one episode, he is engulfed in a fireball from a propane explosion. In the strangest storyline involving Mangione, Dale suspects that it is Mangione, not an infestation of pests, that may be the source of after-hour mischief at Mega Lo Mart. During a late night stakeout, Dale, Hank and the guys are chased around the store by people they can't identify. Dale sets a trap, expecting to catch Mangione. Instead, he nabs two employees who are pretending to be Mangione. The mystery is solved, until Dale learns later that it actually was Mangione who caused the trouble.[11]

Though not animated, a parallel universe that became the hip locale for pop rock cameos was Nickelodeon network's *The Adventures of Pete and Pete*. The latter day *Wonder Years* chronicles life in Wellsville via the Wriggley family, with two brothers, both named "Pete." In numbers proportional to the *The Simpsons*' Springfield guests, the surreal series set in Wellsville attracted a steady stream

---

10   Hayes left the show in March 2006, apparently offended by the classic Tom Cruise episode that satires Scientology. *South Park* creators Matt Stone and Trey Parker were puzzled since the show routinely ridiculed various religions.

11   According to "Frequently asked questions" about the series, creators Mike Judge and Greg Daniels, when searching for a B-list celebrity spokesperson for Mega Lo Mart, may have been inspired to choose Mangione when they heard "Feels So Good" used by the Coen brothers in the film *Fargo*.

of musicians in its three seasons (1993-1996). Artists along the burgeoning alternative axis were foremost: Luscious Jackson (as themselves), Kate Pierson of the B-52s (mysterious blind millionaire), Sonic Youth drummer Richard Edson (janitor), Gordon Gano of the Violent Femmes (teacher), ex-New York Doll David Johannsen/Buster Poindexter (cop), L.L. Cool J (teacher), Marshall Crenshaw (meter man), Suzzy Roche (Inspector 34's traffic cop love interest), Velocity Girl's Sarah Shannon (grocery clerk who smuggles an outdated tapioca pudding label), Bongwater singer Ann Magnuson (postal carrier), Iggy Pop (Nona's father), ex-Golden Palomino Syd Straw (math teacher), Blondie's Debbie Harry (neighbor), Blake Babies front woman Julian Hatfield (cafeteria worker) and R.E.M.'s Michael Stipe (Captain Scrummy pedaling frozen fish from his bicycle on the beach).

Acting their Age

Collectively and as individual episodes, the unusual union of the pop rock star and situation comedy is an undercurrent that represents a convergence of cultural and commercial considerations. The context embodies the prevalent occupation and preoccupation with celebrity and fulfilling rock star fantasies; promotional and programming strategies; personal and professional connections and cachet within the television and music industries; and the all-access, on-demand expectations of the viewing audience.

The pop/rock cameos have accumulated into an important, albeit obscure, collection that provides a curious complementary chronicle within television programming history. These singular appearances have inconspicuously progressed into a catalog and nature analogous with the bootleg recordings. Similar to the underground circulation of rare recorded performances, the unique television cameos are thinly distributed on the Internet from You Tube to various fan, music and television web sites. The guests are also cited as promotional pawn highlights of television series season DVD compilations.

The musician motivation for showing up in situation comedies remains somewhat elusive, particularly with the Baby Boom bit players.[12] Were the television cameos an act of desperation, a post-midlife crisis of relevance or mere publicity ploys instigated by management or record labels and enabled by television network programmers? Perhaps they were nothing more than a "Why not?" whim, a fun gig or favor to a friend, a rare opportunity, an item to cross off their own "Bucket List" or "Do Before Dying."

The historical happenstance of television programming, particularly the situation comedy, provides further cameo context. As a genre, the situation comedy

---

12 Britney Spears' appearances in *How I Met Your Mother* (CBS, 2008) in the immediate wake of her excessive, self destructive behavior appears to be a painfully obvious case of damage control, denial, image makeover and career reinvention.

148   *B-SIDES, UNDERCURRENTS AND OVERTONES*

gradually evolved into a B-side television format, its quality, volume, popularity and magnitude diminished singificantly. Cost-efficient reality shows, spectacle or "event" television, and crime procedural series dominated programming during the 1990s and into the 2000s. Situation comedies were no longer a priority to network programmers and producers. The sitcom decline accelerated mid-1990s, as NBC's Thursday night mythical "Must See TV" era began to wind down. Following *Seinfeld*'s exodus in 1998, *Friends* and *Will and Grace* sustained as uneven, aging hits until 2004 and 2006 respectively. Representation from the genre grew sparse among the top rated shows in the weekly Nielsen ratings. During the Fall 2007 television season, CBS's *Two and Half Men* was the only situation comedy that consistently reached the Top Twenty.[13]

The recent undercurrent of pop rock comic cameo obscuras may not be entirely a post-MTV anti-music video manifestation, nor necessarily a rock respite to reality shows which dominated the broadcast and cable schedules, beginning with MTV's *The Real World* in 1992 and continuing through the *American Idol* phenomenon which began a decade later. Neither high nor hip culture, the situation comedy ironically represented a more dignified television outlet for the baby boom generation of musicians than youth-targeted music video and narcissistic cable pop-rock-related reality shows such as *Tommy Lee Goes to College*, Bret Michaels' poisonous dating show *Rock of Love*, Gene Simmons' *Family Jewels*, and *House of Carters*, featuring Backsteet Boy Nick, brother Aaron and siblings. The situation comedy provided a B-Side refuge for baby boom rockers, a place in television where they could age gracefully, gleefully and occasionally, grungefully. A place where they could act their age.

Select Episode Guide

The following episode guide provides a compilation of pop rock cameos in television comedy, particularly the situation comedy, from 1960 to present. With a few exceptions, such as one-hour genre straddlers *The A Team* and *Ally McBeal*, appearances in dramatic series and day time soap operas which may have been discussed in the text are not included. The list is divided into two brackets: 1960-1970 and 1980-present. Information for the entries includes: the artist/band (listed alphabetically), television series, network (in parenthesis), episode title (if available), air date (if available)). Episodes which aired in November, February or May were during network television's "sweeps," which measure comprehensive ratings of all time periods. The plentiful pop portrayals in *The Adventures of Pete and Pete* and *The Simpsons* are listed separately.

---

13   The Fall ratings may have been skewed by a looming writer's strike. There were cynics in the critic ranks who suggested that based on the quality of comedy in television, the writer's strike had been going on for quite some time before its official beginning 5 November 2007.

MUST SING TV

1960-1970[14]

Davie Allan and the Arrows. *Get Smart.* (NBC) "Kiss of Death" (31 December 1966).

Beau Brummels. *The Flintstones.* (ABC) "Shinrock A-Go-Go" (2 December 1965).

Boyce and Hart. *The Flying Nun.* (ABC) "When Generations Gap" (20 March 1970).

——. *Bewitched.* (ABC) "Serena Stops the Show" (19 February 1970).

——. *I Dream of Jeannie.* (NBC) "Jeanie and the Hip Hippie" (17 October 1967).

Crocodiles. *The Joey Bishop Show.* (NBC) "Joey, Jack Jones and Genie" (11 April 1964).

Enemys. *The Beverly Hillbillies.* (CBS) "Hoe Down A-Go-Go" (24 November 1965).

Factory. *Gomer Pyle, U.S.M.C.* (CBS) "Lost, The Colonel's Daughter" (22 March 1967).

——. *F-Troop.* (ABC) "That's Showbiz" (9 February 1967).

Fantastic Baggys. *The Flintstones.* (ABC) "Surfin' Fred" (12 March 1965).

Greefs. *My Three Sons.* (CBS) "Falling Star" (15 December 1966).

Lewis and Clarke Expedition. *I Dream of Jeannie.* (NBC) "Jeannie, My Guru" (30 December 1968).

Paul Revere and the Raiders. *Batman* (ABC) "Hizzoner the Penguin" (2 November 1966).

Seeds. *The Mothers in Law.* (NBC) "How Not to Manage a Rock Group" (28 April 1968).

Shindogs. *The Patty Duke Show.* (ABC) "Partying is Such Sweet Sorrow" (29 September 1965).

Sound Committee. *The Andy Griffith Show* (CBS) "Opie's Group" (6 November 1967).

Spats. *My Mother the Car.* (NBC) "My Son, the Ventriliquist" (16 November 1965).

Standells. *The Munsters.* (CBS) "Far Out Munsters" (18 March 1965).

——. *The Bing Crosby Show.* (ABC) "Bugged by the Love Bugs" (18 January 1965).

Strawberry Alarm Clock. *The Danny Thomas Hour.* (NBC) "The Scene" (25 September 1967).

Sundowners. *The Flying Nun.* "A Whole New World" (26 September 1968).

Turtles. *That's Life.* (ABC) (Unknown episode title) (24 September 1968).

Wellingtons. *Gilligan's Island.* (CBS) "Don't Bug the Mosquitos" (9 December 1965).

---

14   See The Rock Video 60's Project: "Rock Artist TV Cameos" (2003).

1980-present

Boy George. *The A-Team* (NBC) "Cowboy George" (11 February 1986).

Brown, James. *Amen.* (NBC) "Deliverance (part 2)" (11 May 1991).

Cher. *Will and Grace.* (NBC) "Gypsies Tramps and Weeds" (16 November 2000).

Costello, Elvis. *Two and a Half Men* (CBS) "Back off Mary Poppins" (20 September 2004).

Doobie Brothers. *What's Happening* (ABC) "Doobie or Not Doobie" (parts 1 and 2) (28 January 1978 and 4 February 1978).

Dylan, Bob. *Dharma and Greg.* (ABC) "Play Lady Play" (12 October 1999).

Hay, Colin. *Scrubs* (NBC). "My Overkill" (26 September 2002).

Hayes, Isaac. (voice of "Chef") *South Park.* (Comedy Central) (1997-2006)

Henley, Don. *Just Shoot Me.* "A & E Biography: Nina Van Horn" (9 May 2000).

Hiatt, John. *Yes, Dear* (CBS) "A List Before Dying" (3 May 2004).

Houston, Whitney. *Silver Spoons.* (NBC) "Head Over Heels" (15 September 1985).

Hynde, Chrissie. *Friends* (NBC) "The One With the Baby on the Bus" (2 November 1995).

Jackson, Jermaine. *The Facts of Life.* (NBC) "Starstruck" (3 February 1982).

Jagger, Mick. *Knights of Prosperity* (ABC) (March 2006).

John, Elton. *South Park.* (Comedy Central) "Chef Aid" (7 October 1998).

lang. k.d. *Dharma and Greg* (ABC) "Hell to the Chief" (9 May 2000).

———. "The Trouble With Troubador" (8 February 2000).

Lauper, Cyndi. *That's So Raven.* (Nickelodeon) (2005).

———. *Mad About You.* (NBC) "The Final Frontier" (24 May 1999).

———. "Stealing Burt's Car" (10 May 1999).

———. "Money Changes Everything" (27 April 1995).

———. "A Pair of Hearts" (18 November 1993).

Loggins, Kenny. *Dharma and Greg* (ABC) "Tie Dying the Knot" (11 November 1999).

Lopez, Jennifer. *Will and Grace.* (NBC) (16 September 2004).

———. *Will and Grace.* (NBC) "I Do. Oh, No You Di-in't" (29 April 2004).

Los Lobos. *Greetings From Tucson* (WB) "Christmas" (December 2002).

Lovett, Lyle. *Dharma and Greg* (ABC) "The Trouble with Troubador" (8 February 2000).

McDonald, Michael. *Family Guy.* (Fox) "Padre de Familia" (18 November 2007).

Madonna. *Will and Grace* (NBC) "Dolls and Dolls" (24 April 2003).

Mangione, Chuck. *King of the Hill* (Fox) "Mega Dale" (12 January 2003).

———. *King of the Hill* (Fox) "Propane Boom" (17 May 1998).

Michaels, Bret (Poison). *Yes, Dear.* (CBS) "Greg's Big Day" (6 November 2000).

Midler, Bette. *Seinfeld.* "The Understudy" (18 May 1995).

Morissette, Alanis. *Curb Your Enthusiasm* (HB0) "The Terrorist Attack" (13 October 2002).

———. *Sex and the City* (HBO) "Boy Girl, Boy Girl…" (25 June 2000).

Nugent, Ted. *That '70s Show.* (Fox) "Backstage Pass" (15 May 2001).

Ono, Yoko. *Mad About You* (NBC) "Yoko Said" (12 November 1995).

Petty, Tom (voice of "Lucky") *King of the Hill* (Fox) (2005 season-present).

———. *It's Garry Shandling's Show* (Fox) "No Baby, No Show" (6 November 1987).

Queen Latifah. *The Fresh Prince of Bel Air* (NBC) "She Ain't Heavy" (4 November 1991).

———. *The Fresh Prince of Bel Air.* (NBC) "Working It Out" (6 May 1991).

Snoop Dogg. *Just Shoot Me.* (NBC) "Finch in the Dogg House" (27 September 2001).

Spears, Britney. *How I Met Your Mother* (CBS) (24 March 2008).

Springfield, Rick. *Suddenly Susan* (NBC) "Bowled Over" (24 May 1999).

Tyler, Steven. *Two and A Half Men.* (CBS) (31 August 2006).

Walsh, Joe. *The Drew Carey Show* (ABC) "Drewstock" (29 January 1997).

White, Barry. *Ally McBeal.* (Fox) "Bygones" (20 May 2002).

———. *Ally McBeal* (Fox) "Those Lips, That Hand" (12 April 1999).

Wonder, Stevie. *The Cosby Show.* "A Touch of Wonder" (20 Februay 1986).

Zevon, Warren. *Suddenly Susan* (NBC) "Bowled Over" (24 May 1999).

———. *Suddenly Susan* (NBC) "The Song Remains Insane" (1 March 1999).

———. *Dream On.* (HBO, Fox) "Music in My Veins" (two parts) (13 and 20 September 1995).

———. *The Larry Sanders Show.* (off camera) (15 September 1993).

Z.Z. Top. *King of the Hill* (Fox) (1 April 2007).

The Adventures of Pete and Pete (Nickelodeon, 1993-1995)

Crenshaw, Marshall. "Hard Day's Pete" (1993).

Edson, Richard. (Sonic Youth) "Valentine Day's Massacre" (1993).

Gano, Gordon. (Violent Femmes) "X=Why?" (1994).

Harry, Debbie. (Blondie) "New Year's Pete" (1993).

Hatfield, Juliana. (Blake Babies) "Don't Tread on Pete" (1993).

Iggy Pop. Multiple episodes (1993-1995).

Johansen, David. (Buster Poindexter). "On Golden Pete" (1994).

LL Cool J. "Sick Day" (1994).

Luscious Jackson. "Dance Fever" (1995).

Magnuson, Ann. (Bongwater) "Crisis in the Love Zone" (1995).

Miracle Legion. (as Polaris) Theme song, "Hard Day's Pete" (1993).

Pierson, Kate. (B-52s) "What We Did on Our Summer Vacation" (1993).

Roche, Suzzy. (The Roches) "Inspector 34" (1994).

Shannon, Sarah. (Velocity Girl) "Sick Day" (1994).

150 *B-SIDES, UNDERCURRENTS AND OVERTONES*

Stipe, Michael. "What We Did on Our Summer Vacation" (1993).
Straw, Syd. (Golden Palominos) "Hard Day's Pete," "Valentine Day's Massacre" (1993);
"X=Why?," "Space, Geeks and Johnny Unitas" (1994);

The Simpsons (Fox, 1991-2008)

Aerosmith. "Flaming Moe's" (21 November 1991).
Blink 182. "Barting Over" (16 February 2003).
Browne, Jackson. "Brake My Wife, Please" (11 May 2003).
Cash, Johnny. (as the coyote) "El Viaje Misterioso de Nuestro Jomer" (5 January 1997).
Cobain, Kurt. ("voice" on phone) "That 90's Show" (27 January 2008).
Costello, Elvis. "How I Spent My Strummer Vacation" (10 November 2002).
Cypress Hill. "Homerpalooza" (19 May 1996).
Elton John. "I'm With Cupid" (14 February 1999).
Frampton, Peter. "Homerpalooza" (19 May 1996).
Jackson, Michael. (as Leon Kompowsky, credited as John Jay Smith) "Stark Raving Dad" (19 September 1991).
Jagger, Mick. "How I Spent My Strummer Vacation" (10 November 2002).
Jones, Tom. "Marge Gets A Job" (5 November 1992).
Kid Rock. "Kill the Alligator and Run" (30 April 2000).
Kravitz, Lenny. "How I Spent My Strummer Vacation" (10 November 2002).
Lauper, Cyndi. "Wild Barts Can't Be Broken" (17 January 1999).
Loggins, Kenny. "How I Spent My Strummer Vacation (10 November 2002).
McCartney, Paul and Linda. "Lisa the Vegetarian" (15 October 1995).
Metallica. "The Mook, the Chef, the Wife and Her Homer" (10 September 2006).
Petty, Tom. "How I Spent My Strummer Vacation" (10 November 2002).
Ramones. "Rosebud" (21 October 1993).
Richards, Keith. "How I Spent My Strummer Vacation" (10 November 2002).
Red Hot Chili Peppers. "Krusty Gets Cancelled" (13 May 1993).
R.E.M. "Homer the Moe" (18 November 2001).
Setzer, Brian. "How I Spent My Strummer Vacation" (10 November 2002).
Smashing Pumpkins. "Homerpalooza" (19 May 1996).
Sonic Youth. "Homerpalooza" (19 May 1996).
Spinal Tap. "The Otto Show" (23 April 1992).
U2. "Trash of the Titans" (26 April 1998).
White, Barry. "Krusty Gets Kancelled" (13 May 1993).
White Stripes. "Jazzy and the Pussycats" (17 September 2006).
Who, The. "A Tale of Two Springfields" (5 November 2000).
Yankovic, Weird Al. "That '90s Show" (27 January 2008).

Chapter 10
Umbilical Musical Chords:
Lineage, Legacy and
Mom and Pop Pedigree[1]

You're a chip off the old block
Why does it come as such a shock
That every road up which you rock
Your dad already did[2]

John Hiatt, "Your Dad Did"

Since the mid 1960s, four decades before singer Billy Ray Cyrus's daughter Miley turned teen phenomenon as Disney diva "Hannah Montana," there have been intermittent clusters of popular music progeny—singers/songwriters and musicians whose parents are/were recording artists. One of the most notable offspring emerged in country western music in 1964, when Hank Williams, Jr. recorded his father's songs for the film biography *Your Cheatin' Heart*. One year later, Frank Sinatra, Jr., a self-described "diligent apprentice" to his dad, released *Young Love For Sale* on father Frank's Reprise label. Frank Jr.'s sister, Nancy, got into the family act in 1966 with her debut record, *Boots*. The album, the first of five she recorded on Reprise, featured "These Boots Are Made For Walkin," a Lee Hazelwood song that reached the top of the charts. The Sinatra siblings' successes were not substantial nor sustaining. The kidnaping of Frank Jr. from his hotel room at Harrah's Lake Tahoe and his being held for $240,000 ransom surpassed the son of Sinatra's musical notoriety.[3] Beyond the benefits of the family name, Nancy Sinatra's three-year arc of stardom was marked by Hazelwood's collaboration as a songwriter and producer, numerous pop covers and arrangements that captured the

---

1   This chapter is a revised and expanded version of "The Kids Are Alright: Legacy and Lineage in 1990s popular music," *Studies in Popular Culture*, vol. 24.1, October 2001: 1-17.

2   "Your Dad Did." Words & Music by John Hiatt © Copyright 1987 Careers-BMG Music Publishing Incorporated, USA. Universal Music Publishing MGB Limited. Used by permission of Music Sales Limited. All Rights Reserved. International Copyright Secured.

3   On the eulogistic *As I Remember It* (1996), Frank Jr. tells his father's story through performances of senior's songs and thoughtful narratives about his father, his songs and their lyricists and composers.

lightweight Top 40 charm of the period, and a hit dad/daughter duet, "Somethin' Stupid."

Around the same time, teeny bopper favorites Dino, Desi, and Billy released *I'm A Fool* (1965), also on the Reprise label. The trio consisted of the sons of Dean Martin, Desi Arnez, and a real estate broker who had sold houses to both the Martin and Arnez seniors. Although two singles from their album—"I'm A Fool" and "Not the Lovin' Kind"—reached the Top Twenty, the group lacked staying power and were soon eclipsed by psychedelia.

The most successful of the early showbiz kids, Gary Lewis, was not of Rat Pack descent, although his father was a close associate of Sinatra's and Martin's. Gary Lewis and the Playboys, led by the drummer son of actor/comedian Jerry Lewis, sold more than 7.5 million records. Following their number one hit, "This Diamond Ring," the group had six consecutive Top Ten singles in 1965 and 1966—"Count Me In," "Save Your Heart for Me," "Everybody Loves A Clown," "She's Just My Style," "Sure Gonna Miss Her," and "Green Grass."

Chips Off the Old Rocks

The next wave of pop progeny that surfaced during the late 1970s and into the 1980s is an eclectic collection of artists with relative degrees of recognition and accomplishment, some whose careers have endured for decades. Some of the more celebrated offspring include the late great Nat King Cole's daughter Natalie, whose *Unforgettable* (1991) earned her a Grammy; Doris Day's son Terry Melcher (see Chapter 1); John Lennon's (and Cynthia Twist's) first son, Julian; Whitney Houston, who is Dionne Warwick's niece and the daughter of soul singer and Elvis and Aretha Franklin backup, Cissy Houston; the Judds, featuring Naomi and daughter Wynonna; Bob and Rita Marley's reggae-rocking son, Ziggy; and country-rocker Carlene Carter, daughter of June Carter and Johnny Cash. Cash's daughter from his first marriage, Roseanne, is also an established country singer-songwriter.

There are a number of lesser known branches of music's family tree from this period. The late Kirsty MacColl, daughter of folk singer-songwriter Ewan MacColl, released five folk-pop records that were popular in the U.K.[4] Pop sensation Wilson-Phillips was a California combination of Chyanna Phillips, whose parents Michelle and the late John Phillips were Mamas and Papas with Denny Doherty and Cass Elliott; and Carnie and Wendy Wilson, whose dad Brian was a brilliant Beach Boy. The group Bloodline was another second-generation hybrid consisting of Miles Davis's son, Erin, Allman Brothers Berry Oakley's son, Berry Jr., and Waylon Krieger, son of Doors guitarist Robby Krieger. Blonde wimp duo Nelson (Ricky Nelson's twin sons, Matthew and Gunnar), black harmony group The Reddings (Otis's sons Dexter and Otis III and cousin

---

4   Kirsty MacColl died in December 2000 in a boating accident in Mexico.

Mark Lockett), Levert (O'Jays leader Eddie Levert's sons Gerald La Vert and Sean), and Womack and Womack (featuring Sam Cooke's daughter, Linda, and Bobby Womack's niece) appropriated their household names. Other bands included Ceremony, fronted by Chastity Bono (Sonny and Cher); hard rockers Bonham, led by drummer Jason Bonham (son of Led Zeppelin's John Bonham); Pretty in Pink, featuring Chaka Khan's daughter, Millini; and pop-funk Rockwell, the pseudonym for Kennedy Gordy, son of Berry Gordy, Jr. Soloist daughters include Nona Gaye (Marvin Gaye), Louise Goffin (Gerry Goffin and Carole King), and Jennie Muldaur (Maria and Geoff). Ringo Starr's son, Zak Starkey, also a drummer, has toured and recorded with his father among others. Mother Frank Zappa's children, Dweezil, Ahmet, and Moon Unit have collective credits that include MTV veejay, avant gardist, guitarist, and singers. Paul Simon and Art Garfunkel's sons, Harper and James, are also active musicians. On the fringes are occasional Fleetwood Mac contributors Becca Bramlett, daughter of Delaney and Bonnie, and Billy Burnette, son of Dorsey Burnette of the Memphis-based Rock and Roll Trio, which featured rockabilly great turned teen idol Johnny Burnette.

New Kids on the Block

During the 1990s "Baby Boom," another spawn of musical lineage and legacy emerged. The notable number of debut releases by second generation artists during the mid to late part of the decade that continues to present marked a collective "coming out" for these potential "heirs of parents." This second wave of pop progeny is equally diverse in musical genre and style, an array that ranges from children of Hank Williams, Jr. (Hank III) to Tony Bennett (Antonio). Predictably, the 1960s and 1970s lineage is prominent: Bob Dylan (Jakob, and Wallflowers), Pete Townshend (Emma), John Lennon and Yoko Ono (Sean), Mama and Papa John Phillips (Bijou), Van Morrison (Shana), Steven Stills (Chris), David Crosby (James Raymond of CPR), Leonard Cohen (Adam), the late Tim Buckley (the late Jeff); the Guess Who and Bachman-Turner-Overdrive founder Randy Bachman (Tal), Crosby Loggins (Kenny Loggins), the late Warren Zevon (Jordan), members of The Band, Robbie Robertson (Sebastian) and Levon Helm The Band (Amy of Ollabelle), Ozzie Osbourne (Kelly), and Steve Earle (Justin Townes).

Husband and wife pairs—though the majority are now ex's—are well represented: Richard and Linda Thompson (Teddy), British folk duo Martin Carthy and Norma Waterson (Eliza), James Taylor and Carly Simon (Sally and Ben), Canadian folksters Sylvia and Ian Tyson (Clay), and Gregg Allman and Cher (Elijah Blue Allman of the band Deadsy) and Nashville's Waylon Jennings and Jessi Colter (Shooter Jennings). Folky Loudon Wainwright has the distinction of fathering singing siblings in marriages to two separate singing sisters, one with Kate McGarrigle (Rufus and Martha), the other with Suzzy Roche (Lucy). Third generation lineage extends from Woody Guthrie to 1960s son Arlo to Arlo's daughter Sarah in the 2000s.

156   *B-SIDES, UNDERCURRENTS AND OVERTONES*

Jazz versions include the children of trumpeter Don Cherry (Eagle Eye and rapper Neneh), John Coltrane (Ravi), tenor saxophonist Dewey Redman (Joshua) and Ellis Marsalis (Branford and Wynton), Nina Simone (Simone, born Lisa Celeste Stroud). World music strands are evident in Afrobeat pioneer Fea Kuti (Fema Kuti), Bossa nova great Joao Gilberto (Bebel Gilberto), Julio Iglesias (Enrique), citar master Ravi Shankar (Norah Jones and Aroushka Shankar) and multi-instrumentalist and soundtrack specialist Ry Cooder (Joachim).[5]

Teach Your Children: Progeny and Prodigy

> With some kids, if their parents are business people, they become stockbrokers. Others choose medicine because mom or dad's a surgeon. I never really thought about anything but music. The fact is, I tried to do everything I could to avoid music, as a career, I mean. But it was always there, and at some point, I just recognized that this was what I had to do.
>
> Crosby Loggins (*We All Go Home*: 2008)

Genealogy, continuity, sociocultural conditions, celebrity culture, and the mythmaking/demystification process, are among the numerous dimensions which provide some context to help frame this bio-musical undercurrent. Heredity and following in familial footsteps may be the most obvious, if not fundamental factor present in this second generation wave of singer-songwriter successors. It is a biological inevitability that some of the skills, aptitudes, gifts, and competencies possessed by these artists are inherited or passed along from swimming in the same gene pool as their parents. Experiences further shape individual interests, identities, and career directions. Many of these artists are products of environments which provided unique possibilities for cultural enrichment and musical nurturing, be it instrumentation, writing, or performance. The opportunities with mom and/or dad and their circle of singing, songwriting friends may transcend mere "taking an interest" in music, but involve an experience of genuinely "living the artist lifestyle" as well. Accessibility to instruments, instruction, studios and touring

---

5   There are numerous singers/songwriters whose parents have noteworthy careers in walks of life other than music. Among those with literary lineage are Lucinda Williams, whose father Miller is poet laureate, and James McMurtry, son of prolific Western novelist Larry McMurtry. Country artist Tim McGraw is the son of former major league pitcher Tug McGraw. To further broaden the kinship context, there are popular music offspring who have established careers outside their parents' vocation, notably actress Liv Tyler, daughter of Aerosmith's Steven Tyler; and Paul and Linda McCartney's daughter, Stella, a fashion designer for the French label Chloe. British newspapers reported that sales at Chloe quadrupled when McCartney joined the company. And Lionel Richie's daughter Nicole is the prototypical celebrity, perhaps more attributable to her sidekick status with Paris Hilton and *The Simple Life* more so than Dad.

become integral components of their childhood development stages, socialization, and routine. Pursuit of their own careers in music seems only natural.

Randy Bachman, founder of Canadian groups the Guess Who and Bachman Turner Overdrive, recalls son Tal as a two-year-old climbing up to the drum kit during band rehearsal breaks, adding that Tal "had this intuitive thing with music and a natural affinity for instruments." "Everything he touched he could figure out how to play within an hour—piano, fiddle, bass, and guitar. It was uncanny," said Bachman (Jennings 1998: 55).

Rufus Wainwright and Joachim Cooder are further examples of progeny who were playing instruments by the age of eight, and touring with their parents before they turned 13. "There wasn't a lot of hardware around when I was a kid, piano was like my computer," says Wainwright (Jennings: 55).

Jakob Dylan uses the analogy of a family business—"working on cars, running a hardware store: How many sons and daughters do exactly what their parents did? I wanted the sound of amps turning on; I wanted to see cable run across my living room. I loved the way the bus felt. It had been there since I was small. The only way to keep it was to do it myself" (Fricke 2000: 48).

In contemporary American popular music, cultural consumers have become conditioned to images of "gifted" children, some prodigious, others pressured pawns of parents projecting dreams. The accelerated allure of fame and fortune have contributed to widespread perceptions of many cases of overbearing parental presence. The disturbing image of six-year-old murder victim Jon Benet Ramsey in full-costume competing in a child pageant was a surreal slice of suburbia, *Little Miss Sunshine* tinted in David Lynch's *Blue Velvet.* All that was missing from the repetitious footage was the Rolling Stones singing about "mother baby, standing in the shadows" eerily echoing on the soundtrack.

Sports routinely provides convenient, yet well-documented, examples of such Great Santinian excess. Tiger Woods' golf god greatness overshadows the carnival exploitation of the four-year old prodigy putting on *The Tonight Show* in front of Johnny Carson. Former University of Southern California quarterback Todd Marinovich's father designed and mandated a birth-to-big-league rigorous regimen for his son that included training, diet, and lifestyle. The professional tennis tour is notorious for its hovering parental presence, particularly the women's division. The irrepressible fathers of several highly ranked players have been issued restraining orders and tournament bans due to their boorish behavior.

The star-making machinery of the music industry is not immune from similar stage parenting, particularly in the postmodern marketplace of cultural production that includes disposable packaging, *American Idol*, and multi media synergy and franchising. Look no further than Ashley and Jessica Simpson's father, Joe Simpson, who quit his day job to become full time manager of his daughter's criss crossing careers. Despite the commercial imperatives, seductive spotlight and prowling producers seeking sensational scoops and celebrity exposes for VH-1 rockumentaries and other cable programming fare, the Mommy Dearest and (dis)like father-(dis)like son nightmare narratives have not been as common

158   *B-SIDES, UNDERCURRENTS AND OVERTONES*

in these musical family circles, where the values of community and creativity may be more deeply ingrained than competition.

Fortunate Scions? The Blessings and Burdens of Biography

"Following in family footsteps" is familiar fodder for our cultural fascination with fame and celebrity. Such narratives and images abound in the all access scrutiny of the era, from "like my father before me" political legacies to sports and entertainment. In 1998, American culture was saturated with a refresher course on America's "royal family" mythology following John F. Kennedy Jr.'s fatal plane crash. "Penny Lane, played by Kate Hudson, daughter of Goldie Hawn" seemed a mandatory mention in reviews of Cameron Crowe's film, *Almost Famous* (2000). The hip trivial pursuers acknowledged Hudson's less famous father, comedian Bill Hudson of *The Hudson Brothers* variety show infamy. Likewise, discussions of Sophia Coppola's directorial debut, *The Virgin Suicides* (2000), were footnoted with father Francis and *Godfather* (1972) references, including trivia citing the scene in the classic film in which baby Sophia was baptized. Film families span actress Angelina Jolie and her father, actor Jon Voigt to Jamie Lee Curtis, daughter of Janet Leigh and Tony Curtis to Kirk Douglas and similarly square jawed son Michael to the Bridges boys, brothers Jeff and Beau and father Lloyd to the new wave that includes Tom Hanks' son Colin and director Ivan Reitman's son Jason.

In professional sports, family trees proliferate, with roots running from baseball's Boones (Bob, sons Aaron and Bret) to basketball's Barrys (Brent, Jon and Drew, the sons of ex-great Rick) to the broadcast booth (the Careys—the late great Harry, his son Skip and his son Chip)[6] to the Bowden bunch in college football (patriarch Bobby and sons Tommy, Jeff and Terry). Perhaps the highest profile professional father and sons are consecutive Super Bowl (2007, 2008) winning quarterbacks, Peyton and Eli Manning, sons of famous football father Archie.

The rock press has been no different in its use of progenitor prefaces in features, interviews, articles and reviews involving the younger artists and their endeavors in the family vocation. Citing parental predecessors and linkages certainly appeals to the collective consumer curiosity. The matter of family facts also represents a simultaneous journalistic obligation, an angle that can be presented as a lead, mere mention, or highlighted as a human interest story. The tendency with "higher profile" cases such as those bearing the names "Lennon," "Dylan" or "Presley" is to want to make ancestry *the* story rather than *part* of the story.

The "son of" or "daughter of" biographical badge is a B-Side that is both blessing and burden. There is a natural assumption that privilege accompanies a prestigious pedigree, that lineage and last name open doors for young artists and

---

6   Appearance and behavior suggest that comedian Drew Carey might also be a long lost Carey son/brother.

potentially shortens the dues paying period that is a record industry rite. Just as the family name can create opportunities, lineage can be a liability, creating pressures, unreasonable expectations, and inevitable comparisons. The cumulative result can deprive young artists of an apprenticeship period.

There are examples among the current wave of pop progeny that illustrate this duality. After dropping out of college, Tal Bachman had the opportunity to briefly join his father's band when their drummer was injured. Then, when his father toured with Ringo Starr's All Starr Band in 1996, Tal recorded a demo in dad's studio. Tal endured numerous record company rejections until his father shopped his demo tape to former Electric Light Orchestra member and producer Jeff Lynne. The connection led to a chain of events that resulted in Bachman's self-titled debut on Columbia Records in 1999. The single, "She's So High," charted in *Billboard's* Top Twenty for weeks.

Joining Bachman on Columbia for his self-titled debut is fellow Canadian Adam Cohen. Before signing the major label deal, Adam benefitted from being affiliated with his father Leonard's Los Angeles based company Stranger Music, not to mention that Leonard Cohen also happened to be under contract with Columbia.

As the offspring of critically acclaimed but commercially marginal musicians, Rufus Wainwright was privy to a non-glamorous side of the record business. "I saw the real side of it. The struggle of putting together a few thousand dollars for the next project," says Wainwright (Hamilton 1998: P3). Yet Wainwright readily acknowledges that his parents gave him instant cachet at the prestigious DreamWorks entertainment empire. Wainwright's father, Loudon, best known for the 1972 novelty hit "Dead Skunk," passed along Rufus's demo tape to producer Van Dyke Parks, who in turn shared it with DreamWorks music executive and long-time producer Lenny Waronker. It was Waronker who signed Rufus's mother, Kate McGarrigle, to Warner Brothers in the 1970s. Dream Works invested nearly $1 million in Wainwright's recording. The company's support was rewarded with *Rufus Wainwright* (1998), a striking debut that earned Wainwright "Best New Artist" recognition in *Rolling Stone* and critical praise for originality from critics, including the preeminent Robert Christgau.

Bachman's, Cohen's and Wainwright's fortunate son scenarios and major label opportunities are not the standard among the wave of second generation artists. Whether out of economic necessity, lack of interest from labels, or a conscious effort to counter perceptions of parental privilege, many of these artists travel the independent route. For example, David Crosby's son, James Raymond, and his band CPR, produced three records in two years that were distributed exclusively via their web-site.

Clay Tyson also relies on Internet connections. Though he is linked to both his parents, Ian's and Sylvia's web-sites, Clay prefers not to exploit the family name. "I don't want to be judged like that," he says. "I'm doing totally different music." Tyson, who admittedly shares his father's stubbornness and disdain for the music industry, prefers the independent route for his avant garde and punk pursuits.

"I used to think a record deal was the end of the rainbow but after my experience [as bassist] with the Look People [a satirical, Frank Zappa-inspired band of the 1980s], I'd rather do it myself and have more control,"says Clay, who financed his album, *Break It Down* (2000), with earnings from a part-time job as a theatrical set painter (Jennings 1998: 55).

While many of these younger artists may have inherited musical proficiency and interest from their parents, many also illustrate that musical tastes and preferences are not necessarily hereditary. Some, such as Chris Stills on his debut, *100 Year Thing* (1998) Atlantic, the same label his father began recording on, deliver like-father, like-son vocals and guitar licks that echo Crosby, Stills, Nash and Young 1960s rock, and Steven Stills' solo and Manassas works. "I don't mind sounding like my old man at all," says Chris. "I don't want to stray too far from that era. Those are the records I still love best" (Zimmer 2000: 290).

Whether rebellion or creative diversion, others have established their own sound signatures that distance themselves from their parents' genres. Emma Townshend's sparse, lilting *Winterland* (1998) more closely resembles Tori Amos than her windmill wielding, instrument-smashing, father's Who performances. Rufus Wainwright's influences—opera, Handel, and Gershwin among them—are far from being rooted in his folks' folk traditions. A melodist varyingly characterized as a "1990s Stephen Foster" or "queer Harry Nilsson," Wainwright's style blends Tin Pan, cabaret, romantic theatricality, orchestral noir and droll lounge. "They [parents] liked the pure, simple line and I went for the baroque," says Wainwright (Binelli 2005: 54). "Rufus actually likes just about every kind of music but folk," says his mother Kate McGarrigle. "I think my dad loves what I do, but I think I'm far enough away from his own genre that it doesn't threaten him," says Wainwright (Offspring 1998: 59).[7]

Elijah Blue Allman has pursued a different musical path since debuting in his mother's band during the 1988 MTV Video Music Awards. His synth-driven industrial goth rock with his band, Deadsy, is not derived from either of his parents' (Cher and Greg Allman) music. The guitar prodigy, who auditioned for Nine Inch Nails, rejects many of the automatic parental presumptions attached to his, and most of his fellow music offspring's careers:

> I don't think my music has anything to do with either of them and any intelligent person will realize that. The funny thing is the press. There have been enough Jakob Dylans and Julian Lennons that it's just a copy of the same old story…grew up, famous parents, went to prep school, left. I got the record deal, frankly, because I got kicked out of my mom's house and I knew I could do it. (Offspring: 62)

---

7 A more curious connection and likeness was apparent when Jakob Dylan and Bruce Springsteen performed together during a 1997 music awards show. The younger Dylan's wincing mannerisms, vocals, and stage presence strikingly suggested a Bruce offspring as much as Dylan genes.

Here Come the Sons

You've got to know your past to face the future.

Sean Lennon (Fricke 1998: 41)

His [Bob Dylan] history doesn't depend on any of the things mine does. His thing is so huge. It's been going on for so long. It's in history books, in your schools. There's countless biographies. In most of the books, there might be one page that mentions the names of his children. That's it. I don't want to be a page in the book.

Jakob Dylan (Fricke 2000: 46)

The longest parental shadows may be those cast by John Lennon and Bob Dylan. Their sons' tasks of claiming their own identities and focusing on their own music rather than their father's legends have been predictably more pronounced than other musical offspring. Even protective parenting and awareness of the burdens of fame that their children would bear could not totally diminish the indelible birth mark. "John and I were very careful about not trying to influence Sean musically or telling him who we were," says Yoko Ono. "Sean came home from school one day and said, 'Daddy, were you a Beatle?' John had never mentioned it to him" (Binelli: 51).

Sean Lennon shied away from major labels, which likely would have meant a multi-record deal, complete with up-front money and tour support. Instead, he opted for the indie route, signing with Grand Royal, a label owned by the Beastie Boys. "It seemed a great way to focus on my music and not the legacy of my father," says Lennon (Kaufman 1998: 31).

Another family factor weighing on the younger Lennon was his half-brother Julian's experience. Sean believes Julian was "exploited and discarded," and ultimately denied a reasonable period of time to develop as an artist. Despite the industry's shorter windows of opportunity for artists, increasing demands for instant hits and commercially viable music that (cash) registers on SoundScan charts, Julian Lennon managed to release four records for the Atlantic label between 1984 and 1991. Seven years passed until his next record, *Photograph Smile* (1998), which coincided with Sean's debut, *Into the Sun*. Though Sean was determined to "seek out situations where I could be just like everyone else," the truth, or *a truth*, of the family matter is that he is not. Some critics call Sean's situation "the hippest form of slumming," pointing out his inheritance not only of the Lennon legacy, but Yoko Ono's presence and song publishing rights from the Beatles catalog not owned by Michael Jackson.

"It's this weird paradox," says Lennon of his inherent dilemma. "I've got all the connections, I've got all the opportunities. But, man, is the world ready to beat you over the head with it, to kick you back in the dirt. The world is really ready to say 'You suck. You're not as good as your parents'" (Fricke, 1998: 128).

Like Sean Lennon, Jakob Dylan has also displayed extreme reluctance to trade on his family connections. Producer Andrew Slater recalls an early Wallflowers rehearsal at the low-budget Fortress Studio: "The shittiest place in L.A.—five dollars an hour. I'm thinking, 'Here's this guy who obviously has access to any piece of gear he wants in any rehearsal space. And he's in this shit hole" (Fricke 2000: 48). Dylan's fellow band members initially only knew him as "Jake." "I was not a last name guy. I didn't care," says Jakob.

For years, Dylan the younger was reluctant, if not refused, to speak of Dylan the elder. With the release of The Wallflowers third record, *Breach* (2000), Jakob reportedly grew more comfortable with his own achievements. As long as *his* music precedes his last name in a story or interview, Jakob showed slightly more willingness to discuss dad. Journalists point out that the young Dylan's conversations, especially those in front of tape recorders, remain cautious. Jakob seldom, if ever, says the name "Bob" or uses the words "my father" or "my dad," only elliptical third person referents: " he," "his," "him" (Fricke 2000: 46).

Joachim Cooder's career is a case in contrast. The percussionist may be the most anonymous of the generation next artists. In that respect, he is like his father Ry, who, despite being one of music's most respected guitar virtuosos and multi-instrumentalists, is averse to the spotlight and stardom. Joachim has not recorded a solo album. Nor does he have a contract with any label, major or independent. Joachim does have a band, Speakeasy, its eight members consisting of two sister singers and six guys who play percussion, drums, accordion, trumpet, violin, lap guitar, and trombone.

The younger Cooder's unique apprenticeship appears to include a more worldly view, with values and virtues that might be considered more nurturing than dues paying. For most of his life, Joachim's education has consisted of traveling with his father outside the musical mainstream, from composing film soundtracks and scores to seeking sessions with musicians in exotic locales such as India, West Africa, and Cuba. Joachim participated in all the sessions as a percussionist. In addition, with each of Ry's film music projects, Joachim's production responsibilities expand. On *Primary Colors* (1998), Joachim wrote four of the instrumental songs for the soundtrack (see Chapters 5, 6).

In a 1999 *Esquire* magazine feature, Alec Wilkinson provides a particularly poignant passage that characterizes the Cooder's father-son relationship, and reveals the "typical parent" presence in musical lineage and legacy. This scene is Wilkinson's account of accompanying Ry Cooder to see Joachim's band perform at a small club in Hollywood:

> Cooder and I arrived at the club early and drank two margaritas. There was a stage at one end of a dance floor and a bar to one side, Cooder said that the place was similar to plenty of clubs he had played during the early days of his career, when he traveled with a guitar and mandolin and played by himself. "I used to love to come to these places early," he said. "Arrive and watch the waitresses set up and lay out napkins. It was a nice, quiet time." Before long, he grew nervous, though. He began to pace. Then he sat down and tried to keep still. He went to talk to the sound man, because he said they

usually only know how to set up microphones for heavy-metal bands and that his son's band was more complicated than that. Joachim arrived, and I heard Cooder tell him,

"The song's too slow."

"Still?"

"Give it a bit of a groove tempo. It'll still feel down, but it won't be so down," he said, the way another kind of father might say, "Quit chasing the ball. Don't swing until you get the pitch you really want." (144)

Growing Pains and the Ties that Bind

Who needs family counseling when you've got a record contact?

(Smith 1998: 39)

My own fame was extremely difficult for my father. We had a horrible relationship for about six months when my first record came out. We were ready to kill each other.

Rufus Wainwright (Binelli: 55)

The wave of pop music offspring embodies continuity as both genetic and mythological building blocks. Perhaps there is no better example of this cultural continuity and kinship than *Three Hanks: Men With Broken Hearts* (1996), an aural artifact of three generations of the Williams lineage and legacy, from Hank Sr., to Hank Jr. to Hank III.

Coverage in the rock and popular presses suggest that these second generation singer-songwriters are keenly aware of their A-side parents and their pasts. While there is no denying the privileges of heredity, in some ways their lineage resembles other "normal" families marked by different degrees of dysfunction, divorce, and death. The disparity, of course, lies in these children's "growing pains" and experiences within celebritized circumstances and the music lifestyle.

"There's a mysterious gravitational pull that seems to bond the children of legendary musicians," observes Mark Binelli in a *Rolling Stone* profile, "The Children of Rock." "Encounter enough of them and it starts to feel like a secret society. They've all grown up with parents who have simultaneously rejected society's rules and reaped its rewards, and they all recognize certain traits in each other" (55).

Chris Stills elaborates. "It's not like some automatic pass into this club. It's kind of like we grew up behind the stage, so we're privy to the smoke and mirrors and the strings holding up the puppets. Most people have their eyes on the puppets. So that knowledge bonds us" (Binelli: 53).

A cross section of interviews suggest that a sense of empowerment transcends the intrinsic entitlements in lineage and legacy for these sons and daughters. They appear to possess the maturity to balance the blessings and burdens of their names, to keep in perspective pressures and privileges, and to distinguish between parent and persona.

164   *B-SIDES, UNDERCURRENTS AND OVERTONES*

While these younger artists perpetuate and reciprocate predominant images of their god-like predecessors—often through striking physical resemblances—they simultaneously demystify by painting parental portraits that render mom and dad as mere mortals. The meditative tone in Sean Lennon's reflections on his father depict such human qualities:

> The main difference is, he wasn't a god. He was a person like you and me, flesh and blood. He was imperfect; he had doubts. And he had days when he felt like shit, days where he felt People forget how easy it is to overglorify that human being, to mythify them. The reality was, he was my dad. Sometimes he would yell at me for no fucking reason, scream and shout, and I would cry hysterically. If there's anything the public doesn't understand it's that he was a human being. That when he died, he left a real family behind. And that I miss him every day. I don't miss John Lennon the persona. I miss my dad. I don't miss the Beatle. I mean, I miss the Beatle—as a fan of that era. But, really, what I miss is the guy who put me on his shoulders and we walked on the beach together. (Fricke 1998: 128)

Criss crossing careers can also result in family discord. Loudon Wainwright III and Kate McGarrigle divorced when Rufus was three years old and sister Martha a new born. Their father-son relationship was fragile from the start since Loudon had spent much of Rufus's childhood on the road. Despite his father's help navigating the music industry, personal wounds reopened as Rufus's star began to rise during the late 1990s. At the same time, Mom and Dad's genre—folk music—was growing more marginalized from the music mainstream and commercial culture. Rufus admits to not handling the sudden spotlight and the press very well. His early interviews resembled therapy sessions that revealed more personally than professionally, with Rufus routinely commenting on being abandoned as a child and his determination to be more famous, cooler and more in touch with the kids than his father. Following a father-son photo shoot for *Rolling Stone* in 2005 and a few drinks afterwards, Rufus told his father that, thanks to him, he finally made it back into *Rolling Stone.* "He never quite forgave me for that comment," says Rufus. "A lot of patching up had to be done after that" (Binelli: 56).

Routine, respectful expressions among the musical offspring balance the tensions, trappings and demystifaction of parental fame and previous generational ideals, conditions and circumstances. Beyond Natalie Cole's posthumous duet with her father on *Unforgettable* (1991), smaller scale parental homage can be found in Jason Bonham's Led Zeppelin tribute *In the Name of My Father* (1997) and Shana Morrison "borrowing" her father Van's "Sweet Thing" to cover on her *Caledonia* (1999) record. She also delivers a soulful rendition of "Irish Heartbeat" with Brian Kennedy on the Van Morrison tribute record *No Prima Donna* (1994). Roseanne Cash's reverence resonates, from her stirring rendition of "I Walk the Line" at the Kennedy Center Awards ceremony honoring her father Johnny, to her graceful reminisce in the essay "Songs My Daddy Sang Me" (1999).

These reverent renditions are in part reciprocal as there is proud parental precedence in songs inspired by their sons or daughters. Perhaps the most notable is John Lennon's "Beautiful Boy," written for Sean. Paul Simon has honored his children with "St. Judy's Comet" and "Father and Daughter," which appeared on the Nickelodeon network's film *The Wild Thornberry*'s soundtrack (2002) and later on Simon's solo *You're the One* (2006). Nona Gaye is the subject of "I Want to Be Where You Are." Rufus Wainwright managed one song from each parent—"Rufus is a Tit Man," a breast feeding tune from Dad Loudon III, and the benedictive "First Born Son," from Mom Kate McGarrigle, while his sister Lucy got dad Loudon's "Daughter."

Redemption and reunion are also dimensions of popular music's lineage. While recovering from his 1995 liver transplant, David Crosby found out the identity of his first son, James Raymond, a pianist. The discovery was a warmly ironic echo of the title of Crosby's first solo record, *If I Could Only Remember My Name* (1971).[8] Crosby, Raymond, and guitarist Jeff Pevar, formed the band CPR (fitting initials for the 1960s survivor Crosby). Before reuniting with long-time partners Steven Stills, Graham Nash and Neil Young for a new record and a *CSNY2K Tour*, Crosby played the small venue circuit and recorded three albums with CPR. The trios' live performances and recording repertoire feature numerous tunes from Crosby's solo, Byrds, Crosby-Nash, and Crosby, Stills, Nash and Young catalogs.

The mutual mentoring evident in CPR is but one demonstration of the reciprocity of family ties. While the familiar name and progenitors' careers have helped expose the young artists, the offspring's music and career coverage fosters an awareness of their parents' music as well, especially among younger audiences. In some cases, career revivals or reinvention result. Billy Ray Cyrus's revitalized career, which included hosting the country music *American Idol* adaptation, *Nashville Star*, coincided with daughter Miley's rapid rise to teen stardom as "Hannah Montana."

Such umbilical links are commonplace in the family cross referencing and at individual artist, record label, and music retail web-sites. There is a cartoon depicting a record store scene which playfully comments upon this "generation gap" and its musical misconceptions. In the drawing, two teenagers are standing in front of a poster for Bob Dylan's album *Time Out of Mind.* Standing to their right behind the counter is the store clerk, a bearded, aging-hippie type. The cartoon's caption reads: *"So when did Jakob Dylan's dad take up music?"* The young customers' Bob blasphemy presumably triggers the pained, wide-eyed expression of confusion and annoyance on the face of the tie-dye throwback.[9]

---

8   Around the same time Crosby was reunited with his son, fellow 1960s folk icon Joni Mitchell also located her long lost daughter in what might be considered another Woodstockian soundtrack moment—"I came upon a child of God..."

9   I saw this cartoon on display on the counter of Wildman Steve's, the local independent record store in Auburn, Alabama. Unfortunately, the cartoon was removed

166 *B-SIDES, UNDERCURRENTS AND OVERTONES*

Just as the majority of pop rock offspring have been cautious discussing their lineage, the parents of these artists have downplayed and distanced, rather than dwelled upon, their children's musical aspirations and influences. James Taylor and ex-wife Carly Simon's reserved responses regarding their children, Sally and Ben, reflect the standard among the pop progeny's proud parents. During an *NBC's Today Show* (December 2000) performance, Taylor bashfully aw shucksed, "Yeah, it's nice that they are interested in the same thing that I do." In a segment on *CBS Sunday Morning* (January 2001), Simon was more mother than muse, gushing about her love for her children rather than focusing on their music. Billy Joel's parental perspective is similarly supportive and simultaneously safely detached from his, and ex-wife supermodel Christie Brinkley's daughter Alexa, a musical theater major at New York University:

> I've tried to leave some room for her to grow and find her own way. She's an excellent songwriter. But when she tells me that I'm an influence on her, I don't necessarily want to be, because with her name, she may have some difficulty being taken seriously. I don't want to impinge on her ability to have a career as a musician, so I'm a little shy about being too involved. (Binelli: 56)

"Weird Floating Islands"

Whether detached or determined to claim their own careers, all of these artists are vicariously linked to each other as pop music progeny. When asked by David Fricke for *Rolling Stone* if he paid attention to other celebrity sons and daughters of pop music, Sean Lennon replied, "From afar...In a way we feel like these weird floating islands" (1998: 128).

It's difficult to speculate if, and how, individually and collectively, these second generation "weird floating islands" will impact popular music. More than likely, most of their career courses will parallel a proportional number of performers without parental precursors. Some careers will sustain, from mainstream to fringe, with a few fortunate sons or daughters perhaps surpassing their parents' achievements. Most will remain musical B-sides to their A-side parental accomplishments. There will likely be some one hit wonders among the group. Others may survive for a few records before being replaced by the next trend in the music market. A number of records will be destined for the discount bins, followed by the formulaic fade, or career reinvention.[10]

---

before I could document the author and/or source. And, in keeping with the character of most aging hippies, store owner Steve Bronson doesn't remember too much.

10   One example of such reinvention is MacKenzie Phillips, who starred in the Disney Channel show *So Weird*. Phillips plays a rock star mom on a comeback tour who is raising her son, Jack, and her best friend's daughter, Annie, who attracts paranormal phenomena.

UMBILICAL MUSICAL CHORDS 167

No matter the career arc, the familiar names themselves will likely linger as bio-byte inscriptions in the rock and roll registry. They will surface and be cited as both familiar and obscure entries from collections and archives to a branch on the "Family Tree" trivia list on some web-site or post-millennium edition of Dave Marsh's *Book of Rock Lists*, to categories and questions on rounds of *Rock and Roll Jeopardy* or as the sensationalist subject of a VH-1 rockumentary.

For those whose careers continue to unfold, critics and curious alike will listen closely for allusions to lineage in lyrics. Dylanologists will wonder if Jakob Dylan's Wallflower composition "I've Been Delivered" is a nod to his father's *Basement Tape* hymn "Nothing Was Delivered;" or "Hand Me Down," with phrases such as "never amounting to much," "won't ever make us proud" and "think you would be enough"[11] is legacy laced; and the solo "The End of the Telescope" contains father-son subtext. Likewise, what biographical bits might be deciphered in "Amity," Carly Simon's duet with daughter Sally Taylor on the film soundtrack to *Anywhere But Here*, the adaptation of Mona Simpson's novel about a mother and daughter who leave Wisconsin for Hollywood?

Though no imaginative promoter has yet to recognize the unique opportunity to organize a corporate sponsored Lilith Fair/Lollapallooza-like, Boomer baby band Bonnaroo festival uniting these musical sons and daughters with their mothers and fathers on stage, MTV launched a "DNA Duel" reality series, *Rock the Cradle*, in April 2008. The *American Idol* adaptation featured pop, rock and rap artists offspring in a sing-off competition. Among the contestants were children of Joe Walsh (Lucy), Eddie Money (Jesse), Twisted Sister's Dee Snider (Jesse Blaze), Bobby Brown (Landon), Al B Sure (Lil B), Olivia Newton-John (Chloe Latanzi), MC Hammer (A'Keiba Burrell), Doobie Brother Tom Johnston (Lara) and Kenny Loggins (Crosby).

Family franchising has not yielded a *Time-Life*-like record compilation packaged as a *Baby Boom (Box) Set*. However, hints of such collections surfaced in 2007, when the retailer Target released *Song for My Father* on its niche label. The exclusive 14-song compilation featured pop/rock offspring (Chapin, Goffin, Taylor, Allman, Wilson, Phillips et al.) covering their parents' tunes.[12]

The Kids are Alright: G-G-G-Generation Next

The pop progeny cycle will likely continue its course in music, the pop charts and marketplace, spanning the fringes to the mainstream. Despite the disposable

---

11   "Hand Me Down." Words and music by Jakob Dylan. Jumbo Brother Music (ASCAP). 2000.

12   The possibility of such a spectacle may not be so implausible when considering the groundswell of hype for a second generation prize fight between Laila Ali and Jacqui Frazier, the event scheduled on Father's Day 2001, three decades after their fathers, Mohammed Ali and Joe Frazier, met in their storied heavyweight championship boxing bouts.

168   B-SIDES, UNDERCURRENTS AND OVERTONES

nature and short attention span theater that is contemporary consumer culture, the size of the offspring collective itself, along with expanding outlets of distribution and exposure, from artist and record label web-sites and Internet locales such as My Space Music, to soundtracks and commercials, increase the likelihood of some endurance among the ranks.

An even younger wave of musical heirs of parents aligns on the horizon. During interviews following the release of his Grammy-nominated record, *You're the One* (2000), Paul Simon, who is married to singer Edie Brickell, mentioned how impressed he is with their daughter's songwriting skills and that recording may be in her future. Rod Stewart's daughter, Ruby, signed a recording contract, although Stewart says he "will make her finish school first or she will be gone forever."[13]

An item about super-producer Glen Ballard circulating in the rock press early in 2001 further foreshadowed, if not dramatically reinforced, the progression of the 1990s family tree trend.[14] Ballard was overseeing the debut record of another pop music B-side of a prominent A-side parent—Lisa Marie Presley (Feature Story: 7). The possibility of a Princess Presley in the profession was instantaneously rife with pop/rock ramifications, keys to the kingdom consequences and curiosity, and perpetual posthumous parallels. Though she was a relative latecomer to the legion of music lineage, Lisa Marie's Presley pedigree, combined with her marital interlude with Prince of Pop Michael Jackson, contained the capacity to mark a zenith in the pop progeny sphere that could potentially eclipse the mythohistories of the sons of Dylan and Lennon. In 2003, another Presley second coming became prophecy fulfilled as Capitol released Lisa Marie's long-awaited debut *To Whom it May Concern.* Her second record, *Now What*, followed two years later.

Beyond the DVD releases of seasons of *The Osbournes* reality show, other instances of singer-songwriter successors appearing alongside their parental predecessors continue to checker the music and media landscape, further embodying the A-Side/B-side metaphor. Images of Ry and Joachim Cooder, side by side in studio sessions and the streets of Havana, are a prevalent thread in Wim Wenders's documentary film *Buena Vista Social Club* (1999). In 2001, retailer Gap's "My First Love" ad campaign paired Carole King and daughter Louise Goffin singing verses from "So Far Away" and "Love Makes the World" to each other. The spot punctuates with Goffin saying, "My first love...? My Mom." The two were also a natural choice to contribute a duet of "Where You Lead I Will Follow" for the soundtrack of the WB network's mother-daughter

---

13   Stewart was responding to one of perky host Katie Couric's "talking points" during a brief interview before his performance on NBC's *Today* summer concert series, April 27, 2001. The lineage line of questioning has become routine, particularly with musical guests on *Today*, where Couric has had similar "children chats" with James Taylor, Paul Simon and Billy Joel.

14   Ballard's credits include albums by Michael Jackson, No Doubt, Alanis Morissette's record breaking *Jagged Little Pill* (1995), and Dave Matthews Band's *Everyday* (2001).

dramedy *Gilmore Girls*. Similarly, James Taylor and son Ben shared a rendition of "America the Beautiful" at the 2005 U.S. Tennis Open. Granting equal time for his mother, Carly Simon, Ben co-wrote "I'll Just Remember You" for her album *Into White* (2006). He and sister Sally join their mother on the record, providing backing vocals for her bittersweet reading of their father James's "You Can Close Your Eyes." Like the Simon-Taylor chorus, other family unions evoked hip Von Trappian *Sound of Music* images. In 2004, Ziggy, Stephen, Julian, Damian and Ky-Mani Marley toured together for the first time while honoring their father at the "Bob Marley: Roots, Rock and Reggae Festival." Joachim Cooder and Roseanne Lindley routinely join their fathers Ry Cooder and David Lindley during European tours, with some of the performances documented on the 2006 independent release *Cooder/Lindley Family Live in Vienna 1995*. In 2008, Edie Brickell joined her step son, Harper Simon (Paul's son from a previous marriage), to record an album with The Heavy Circles. John Hiatt's daughter, Lily, contributes background vocals to several songs on dad's *Same Old Guy* (2008).

Rock of Ages

Another inevitable dimension of the pop progeny progression has begun to manifest itself—a parent's passing. Beyond earlier deaths of legends Nat King Cole, Elvis, and Bob Marley, and the Lennon sons' tragic circumstance of their father's murder, recent rock artist deaths from natural causes have resulted in poignant expressions of musical inheritance and continuity. In 2006, Roseanne Cash's grievous Grammy-nominated *Black Cadillac* was a hauntingly beautiful record following the deaths of her mother, Vivian Cash Distin, her step mother June Carter Cash, and her father Johnny, all within a two-year period. A few years before, Dhani Harrison helped co-produce and performed on his father George's final recording *Brainwashed* (2002) and the tribute *Concert for George* (2003) following the former Beatle's death from a brain tumor in November 2001. Similarly, Jordan Zevon co-produced the multi-artist tribute record *Enjoy Every Sandwich* (2004), which honored his father, Warren, following his death from lung cancer in 2003. On the record, Jordan performs a family heirloom, one of his father's previously unreleased compositions, "Studebaker" (see Chapter 11).

On October 12, 2004 during *Late Show with David Letterman*, Jakob Dylan and Wallflowers were performing "Lawyers, Guns and Money," their cover contribution to the Warren Zevon tribute record. Jordan Zevon joined the band for the song. As Dylan was midway through the second verse about "gambling in Havana," he turned to Zevon behind him and graciously surrendered his lead vocal for the next verse that punctuated with "*Dad* get me out of this."[15] The timing of Dylan the younger's yielding to his fellow son-of-rock-star was not coincidental nor contrived. The moment was not only sweetly honorable, but sublime in its

---

15   Warren Zevon. "Lawyers, Guns and Money," 1978 Zevon Music BMI.

170 *B-SIDES, UNDERCURRENTS AND OVERTONES*

subtlety and as a sliver of summary. The reverent recognition and duality of the word "Dad" keenly conveyed the nuances, linkages and complex convergences of pop music's biological B-sides, the weird floating islands of the progeny undercurrent.

Selected Discography

The discography highlights recordings primarily from the contemporary current of pop progeny, approximately 1985 to present.

Bachman, Tal. *Tal Bachman* (Sony/Columbia, 1999).
Bonham, Jason. *In the Name of My Father: The Zepset Live from Electric Ladyland* (Sony, 1997).
Buckley, Jeff. *Grace* (Sony/Columbia, 1994).
——. *Sketches (for my Drunken Sweetheart)* (Sony/Columbia, 1994).
Carter, Carlene. *Stronger* (Yep Roc Records, 2008).
Cash, Roseanne. *Black Cadillac* (Capitol, 2006).
Carthy, Eliza. *Angels and Cigarettes* (Warner Bros., 2001).
——. *Red Rice* (Topic (UK), 1998).
——. *Eliza Carthy and the Kings of Calicutt* (Topic, 1997).
Chapin, Jen. *Ready* (Hybrid Recordings, 2006).
——. *Linger* (Hybrid Recordings, 2004).
——. *Open Wide* (Purple Chair Music, 2002).
Cherry, Eagle Eye. *Desireless* (Sony 1998).
Cherry, Nenah. *Homebrew* (Virgin, 1992).
——. *Raw Like Sushi* (Virgin, 1989).
Cohen, Adam. *Adam Cohen* (Sony/Columbia, 1998).
Coltrane, Ravi. *From the Round Box* (RCA, 2000).
——. *Moving Pictures* (RCA, 1998).
Cooder/Lindley Family. *Live at the Vienna Opera House.* (www.davidlindley. com, 2006).
CPR. Chain Poets (CPR Music, 2000).
——. *Live at the Wiltern* (Samson, 1999).
——. *Live at Cuesta College* (Samson, 1999).
——. *CPR* (Samson, 1998).
Cyrus, Miley. *Breakout* (Hollywood Records, 2008).
Deadsy (with Elijah Blue Allman). *Deadsy* (Elektra, 1997).
Dylan, Jakob. *Seeing Things* (Sony, 2008)
Earle, Justin Townes. *The Good Life* (Bloodshot Records, 2008).
Gilberto, Bebel. *Tanto Tempo* (Six Degrees, 2000).
Guthrie, Sarah Lee and Johnny Irion. *Exploration* (New West, 2005).
——. *Entirely Live* (Rt 8 Music, 2004).
——. *Songs From the Dam Farm* (Independent Girl, 2002).

———. (Rising Son, 2001).

Heavy Circles, The (Harper Simon). *The Heavy Circles* (Dynamite Child, 2008).

Iglesias, Enrique. *Enrique* (Uni/Interscope, 1999).

Jennings, Shooter. *The Wolf* (Universal South, 2007).

———. *Electric Rodeo* (Universal South, 2006).

———. *Put the O Back in Country* (Universal South, 2005).

Jones, Norah. *Not Too Late* (Blue Note, 2007).

———. *Feels Like Home* (Blue Note, 2004).

———. *Come Away With Me* (Blue Note, 2002).

Joel, Alexa Ray. *Sketches* EP (ARJ Music, 2006).

Kuti, Fema. *Shoki Shok.* (MCA, 2000).

Lennon, Julian. *Photograph Smile* (Fuel 1999).

———. *Help Yourself* (Atlantic 1991).

———. *Mr. Jordan* (Atlantic, 1989).

———. *The Secret Value of Daydreaming* (Atlantic, 1986).

———. *Valotte* (Atlantic, 1984).

Lennon, Sean. *Friendly Fire* (Capitol 2006).

———. *Into the Sun* (Grand Royal, 1998).

Loggins, Crosby and the Light. *We All Go Home* (Premiere Artists, 2007).

Marley, Ziggy (and the Melody Makers). *Time Has Come: The Best of Ziggy Marley and the Melody Makers* (Virgin, 1997).

———. *Fallen is Babylon* (Virgin, 1997).

———. *Free Like We Want 2B* (Virgin, 1995).

———. *Joy and Blues* (Virgin, 1993).

———. *Jahmekya* (Virgin, 1991).

———. *One Bright Day* (Virgin, 1989).

———. *Conscious Party* (Virgin, 1988).

Morrison, Shana. *Caledonia* (Monster, 1999).

——— and Roy Rogers. *Everybody's Angel* (Roshan Records, 2000).

Ollabelle (Amy Helm). *Riverside Battle Songs* (Verve Forecast, 2006).

——— *Ollabelle* (Sony, 2004).

Osbourne, Kelly. *Sleeping in the Nothing* (Sanctuary, 2005).

———. *Changes* (Sanctuary, 2003).

———. *Shut Up* (Sony, 2002).

Phillips, Bijou. *I'd Rather Eat Glass* (Almo Records, 1999).

Presley, Lisa Marie. *Now What* (Capitol Records, 2005).

———. *To Whom It May Concern* (Capitol Records, 2003).

Redman, Joshua (Quartet). *Passage of Time* (WEA/Warner Bros., 2001).

———. *Beyond* (WEA/Warner Bros., 2000).

———. *Timeless Tales (For Changing Times)* (WEA/Warner Bros., 1998).

———. *Freedom in the Groove* (WEA/Warner Bros., 1996).

——— (Quartet). *Spirit of the Moment: Live at the Village Vanguard* (WEA/Warner Bros., 1995).

——— (Quartet). *Moodswing* (WEA/Warner Bros., 1994).

———. *Wish* (WEA/Warner Bros., 1993).

———. *Joshua Redman* (WEA/Warner Bros., 1993).

Roche, Lucy Wainwright. *8 More* (Oneearup, 2008)

———. *8 Songs* (Oneearup, 2007).

Shankar, Aroushka. *Breathing Under Water* (Manhattan Records, 2007).

———. *Rise* (Angel Records, 2005).

Simone. *Simone on Simone* (High Priestess/Koch, 2008).

Stills, Chris. *Chris Stills* (V2, 2006).

———. *100 Year Thing* (Atlantic, 1996).

Taylor, Ben. *Another Run Around the Sun* (Iris, 2005).

——— Band. *Famous Among the Barns* (Iris, 2002).

Taylor, Sally. *Apt. 6-S* (What Are Records, 2000).

———. *Tomboy Bride* (What Are Records, 1998).

Thompson, Teddy. *A Piece of What You Need* (Verve Forecast, 2008).

———. *Up Front and Down Low* (Verve Foreceast, 2007).

———. *Separate Ways* (Verve Forecast, 2006).

———. *Teddy Thompson* (Virgin, 2000).

Townshend, Emma. *Winterland* (WEA/Elektra, 1998).

Tyson, Clay. *Kick It Down* (Borea, 2000).

Various Artists. *A Song for My Father* (180 Music, 2007).

Wainwright, Martha. *I Know You're Married but I've Got Feelings Too* (Zoe/ Rounder, 2008).

———. *Drowned in Sound* (Rounder, 2005).

Wainwright, Rufus. *Release the Stars* (Geffen, 2007).

———. *Want Two* (DreamWorks/Geffen, 2004).

———. *Want One* (DreamWorks, 2003).

———. *Poses* (DreamWorks, 2001).

———. *Rufus Wainwright* (DreamWorks, 1998).

Wallflowers. *Rebel, Sweetheart* (Interscope, 2005).

———. *Breach* (Interscope, 2000).

———. *Bringing Down the Horse* (Uni/Interscope, 1996).

———. *Wallflowers* (Virgin, 1992).

Wilson Phillips (Carnie and Wendy Wilson, Cyanna Phillips). *California* (Sony, 2004).

———. *Shadows and Light* (Capitol, 1992).

———. *Wilson Phillips* (Capitol, 1990).

Williams, Hank III (with Hank Williams and Hank Williams Jr.). *Three Hanks: Men With Broken Hearts* (WEA, 1996).

Zevon, Jordan. *Insides Out* (New West/Ammal Records 2008).

Chapter 11

Die Another Day:
Warren Zevon's Desperado "Deteriorata"

It's a good idea to be able to say good bye to yourself.

Warren Zevon (Fricke 2002)

Did you hear the one about the guy who walks into the doctor's office for a check-up, tells his doctor, "I'm feeling kid of rough." Doctor says, "I'll break it to you, son. Your shit's fucked up. It happens to the best of us."[1] Turns out that guy was singer-songwriter Warren Zevon. He wrote the joke, told the tale, sang the song and in 2002, Zevon became his own punch line.

Few songwriters mutate a routine medical exam into a three-minute Stephen King novella. The frightfully funny, foreboding, frankness of "My Shit's Fucked Up" is a familiar feature in the substantial and sardonic, literary and cinematic, Warren Zevon Songbook, which has quietly accumulated on the peripheries with critical acclaim during the past three decades.[2] The blunt tune is on Zevon's *Life'll Kill Ya* (2000), a gem of a record with songs ranging from wry to reflective. There are odes to David Crosby ("I Was in the House When the House Burned Down,") and Elvis "eating fried chicken with his regicidal friends" ("Porcelain Monkey"); a redemptive cover of Steve Winwood's "Back in the High Life Again;" a graceful grail and holy ride rendering ("Ourselves to Know") and a concluding prayerful plea about aging, health and stupidity ("Don't Let Us Get Sick"). On the cover, Zevon's tilted head, slight smile, black turtleneck pose exude a Burt Bacharach aura. However, lurking inside the record's booklet are images of a creepy skeletal marching mass and a faint, floating shadowy shroud of Zevon. The somber sensibility continued on his next record, *My Ride's Here* (2001), though the title is slightly more subtle. The "ride" is an allusion to a hearse; the record's cover image is a shot of Zevon gazing out its backseat window.

The following year, Zevon's tunes and titles suddenly turned chillingly prescient; the punch lines eerily personal and powerful. It was as if Zevon possessed a sixth sense. In August 2002, at a time when Zevon ironically "had been working out more than Vin Diesel," he was diagnosed with mesothelioma, a

---

1   "My Shit's Fucked Up." Words and music by Warren Zevon. Zevon Music BMI. 2000.

2   For a comprehensive career chronicle on Zevon, see George Plasketes, "Warren Zevon (1947-2003). The Grim and Grin Reaper in the Songwriter's Neighborhood: From A to Zevon" in *Popular Music and Society*, Vol. 28 No 1, February 2005: 95-109.

rare, inoperable form of lung cancer. It was the same disease that killed one of his heroes, actor Steve McQueen. "I think I got a raw deal here, all I wanted was the Steve McQueen haircut," Zevon told Dwight Yoakam (Devenish 2002: 13).

The medical prognosis was three months. Zevon did not flinch in the face of fate and his fleeting future. He envisioned his last stand. "It'll be a drag if I don't make it to the next James Bond movie (*Die Another Day* in November 2002)," he said. "And I want to wear sweaters, a scarf, the overcoat, the whole thing, like a Wynona Rider movie. And I can be this miserable, classic Walter Matthau invalid. Not that I haven't been that before..." (VH-1.com: 2003). When Zevon returned to his cardiologist, he brought copies of *My Ride's Here* and *Life'll Kill Ya.* "This is why I'm not so shocked. Doc, just look at the titles and ask yourself why I have this eerie acceptance" (Gunderson 2002: 12D).

A Black Swan Song

Zevon's ride was late. The initial three month prognosis prolonged past a year. Zevon was three feet deep with six feet under expectations. He said he was "beginning to feel like a fraud" (VH-1 *Inside Out:* 2004). Not only would Zevon survive to see *Die Another Day* in the theater, but he was around for its video release (3 June 2003). Death's reprieve sustained long enough for a unique farewell tour, Zevon's own adaptation of *Die Another Day*, in which he continued to compose and sing a black swan song while headlining his own funeral procession.

Zevon's Dieography is a rock ritual arrangement in three parts: (1) The musical "Prelude" features the records *Life'll Kill Ya'* and *My Ride's Here*; (2) The body, a "Deteriorata," begins with Zevon's terminal diagnosis on 28 August 2002, and is comprised of three primary components: an appearance on *Late Show with David Letterman*, 30 October 2002, which marked Zevon's final live performance; the writing and recording of his final record *The Wind*; and a companion documentary for VH-1's *Inside Out;* (3) The "Coda" bridges the 2004 Grammys with posthumous recording projects and peaks with the oral history *I'll Sleep When I'm Dead: The Dirty Life and Times of Warren Zevon* (2007), compiled by Zevon's former wife.

Dead on Arrival: Cryptic Context

Born in Chicago, Zevon grew up on a cultural and psychological fault line of curious union: a Russian-Jewish immigrant, often-absent gambler-gangster-prizefighter father and a Scots-Welsh Mormon mother. Zevon's ideal as a child was "a dead man—with my name, looks and career intentions. A dead warrior who'd been waylaid by his heroism... I grew up with a painting of an uncle, Warren, who looked just like me. He was a military man, a golden boy, an artist. He'd been killed in action. Uncle Warren was sort of the dead figurehead of the family, and I was brought up to follow in his footsteps. I guess that kind of background gave me the idea that destroying myself was the only way to live up to expectations" (Nelson 1981: 33). "It didn't take a lot of therapy to realize I'd been ingrained with the idea that dying was going to fulfill your parents' ideas of what's good" (Alfonso 1981: 25).

Which may in part explain "Old Velvet Nose," the smirking, cigarette smoking, sometimes bespectacled skull that grins from the covers, corners, and liner notes of Zevon's records like a skeletal Nike swoosh sibling of Edward Munch's painting "The Scream." The "trademark" bears a striking resemblance to Zevon; it is at once a self portrait, mirror image, X-Ray, mask and alter ego. Perhaps a haunting homage to the waylaid warrior Uncle Warren. On *Genius* (2003), one of Zevon's "Best of" compilations, Zevon's reflection is eerily embedded in the skull's eye socket. The record's booklet contains a gallery of "skull-istrations"—Old Velvet Nose in various costumes and poses depicting Zevon's songs.

Zevon expended endless energy writing a reckless rough draft for his own epitaph in lyric and lifestyle. The requisite reference and a touchstone tune in his crypt keeper catalog, "I'll Sleep When I'm Dead," appeared to be his short-term career objective, a self-fulfilling prophecy in progress.[3] His life seemingly on layaway, a *Seventh Seal* sequel, Zevon spent much of the 1970s a somber, soul searching, songwriting self saboteur, inching madly toward paradise and paralysis, vandalizing his gifts via a vodka and valium vortex, accented with a fancy for firearms.[4] It's no coincidence that "up all night" and "the rest of the night" are frequently found phrases in Zevon's songs; his "all night long" is a more shadowy nocturne than Lionel Richie's. "He is among the wildest people I've ever met. For him it was all about trials by fire," said Zevon's longtime friend, singer-songwriter Jackson Browne, who negotiated and produced Zevon's major label deal with David Geffen at Elektra/Asylum in 1976 (Boucher 2002: F1).[5]

Composer, Coroner, Comic: the Grim and Grin Reaper on the Writer's Block

Zevon became one of rock's death defying desperados. Demise and deprivation were his preoccupation, occupation and sneering songwriting signature. Zevon pronounced himself "Dead on arrival" as early as 1969. His independent release, *Wanted: Dead or Alive*, included songs such as "A Bullet for Ramona," which

---

3   Before Crystal Zevon's detailed accounts of her ex-husband's excesses in *I'll Sleep When I'm Dead: The Dirty Life and Times of Warren Zevon* (2007), Paul Nelson provides a stunning account of Zevon's descent and resurrection in the *Rolling Stone* (19 March 1981) cover story, "Warren Zevon: How He Saved Himself from a Coward's Death." Nelson writes, "There were empty bottles everywhere. The room reeked of death" (34).`

4   *Excitable Boy's* inner album sleeve features a photo of a .44 magnum resting atop a plate of vegetables.

5   "Thanks always to Jackson" remained an acknowledgement in the liner notes of most of Zevon's albums.

foreshadowed the twisted tunes that marked his singular songwriting path that was confined to the peripheries during the next three decades. In the span of his 20 records, the hard-living rocker established himself as one of the most distinctive and revered songwriters to emerge from the substantial 1970s Southern California music circle. Within the peaceful easy feeling school, Zevon was a restless insurgent, a full moon rising over Santa Monica's sunsets, casting an odd and ominous shadow over Laurel and Topanga Canyons and Hollywood's boulevards. His striking self-titled debut in 1976 established that Zevon preferred noir to neon, gloom to glimmer and glamour, shadows to shimmer, lowlifes and down-on-their-luck losers to luminaries. Despite being a less accessible entry within the era's California canon, particularly when contrast with the Eagles' classic *Hotel California* from the same year, *Warren Zevon* remains one of the most delightfully demystifying documents of Hollywood desperation and decadence. The record established the peripheral pattern for Zevon's career. With the exception of his Top Ten, platinum *Excitable Boy* (1978), Zevon's music never transcended critical and cult status. An uncompromising artist, Zevon was more methodical than prolific, his discography marked by numerous label changes and a five year creative hiatus between 1995 and 2000.

Beyond his most familiar song—the cavorting novelty hit "Werewolves of London" from *Excitable Boy*, the Zevon songbook is brimming with noir narratives and corrupt, creepy characters. Among his cast are renegades, village idiots, bipolar mamas, burnouts, bandits, bottom feeders, hostages and hustlers, the excitable boy who builds a cage with his prom date's bones, a headless mercenary, "Worrier King," "Mr. Bad Example," and a "Model Citizen" who has a Craftsmen lathe in his basement to show the kids when they misbehave.

Zevon's unique combination of composer, comic and coroner[6] invite scattered whispers of "genius" up and down the Writer's Block. Mastermind or not, "original" is indisputable. Zevon's comic noir is authentic. Defining Zevon's daring, dark drollery is difficult, which may in part be why he is more frequently compared to filmmakers and novelists; the songwriter parallels and reference points are minimal, and often begin with a Randy Newman mention. Literature, philosophy, humor and poetry, like film and popular culture, informed Zevon's work, from Fitzgerald and Hemingway to T.S. Eliot, Robert Lowell, Graham Greene, and Martin Amis to Schopenhauer and Rilke.[7] Zevon's ideal was Ross Macdonald (Ken Millar), author of the Lew Archer detective mysteries: "A nice balance between blood and guts and humanitarianism, with just the right acceptable amount

---

6 Zevon actually held the honorary title of coroner in Pitkin County, Colorado.

7 The film and literary influences are further evident in his record dedications in 1980 to film director Martin Scorsese (the live *Stand in the Fire*) and novelist Ken Millar (*Bad Luck Streak in Dancing School*), who was a saving grace during one of Zevon's drug and alcohol interventions (see Paul Nelson, "Warren Zevon: How He Saved Himself from a Coward's Death." *Rolling Stone* 19 March 1981: 28-34, 70); and to Dr. Hunter S. Thompson (*The Mutineer)* in 1985.

DIE ANOTHER DAY 177

of formal poetry" (Nolan 1999: 375). Part of Zevon's novel nature was that he identified with fictional characters, particularly the kidnapped kid in Macdonald's *Zebra-Striped Hearse* and the rock star protagonist who had the delusion his father was Jesse James in Thomas McGuane's *Panama*.

Zevon's songwriting contains what Jackson Browne refers to as "berserk quality" (Boucher: F1). Calamity and conflict lie at the core of his compositions, madness and mayhem are among the main motifs, with amok and amiss attributes. A "a circus in revolt" (Dees 2003), the approach varyingly borrows stylistic traits from pulp fiction, detective mysteries, novellas, sonnets, tragicomic B-flicks, allegories, ghost stories and cartoons (Fricke 2003: 49). Zevon was also a keen cultural consumer and observer. His array of pop portraits and routine referencing of people and places, familiar and obscure, are reminiscent of Pop Artist Andy Warhol's *Myth Series*. [8]

Enjoy Every Late Night Sandwich

A key juncture, and perhaps the most public, in Zevon's farewell procession took place on 30 October 2002, when David Letterman devoted his entire *Late Show* to Zevon. The date was fitting, beyond the underlying urgency of it being two months into Zevon's three month prognosis. "I notice I have a particularly good gig around Halloween," said Zevon when asked about his sardonic songwriting (Brown 2003: F-01). The unprecedented solo scheduling was not shameless exploitation. Zevon was well established as Letterman's *Late Night/Late Show* favorite son. He had been a recurring character for twenty years, his wit, as much as his music, attuned with the show's comic stylings. In addition to performing as a musical guest, Zevon frequently sat in with the house band, and was Paul Shaffer's substitute leader on numerous occasions.[9] Letterman provided shouting background vocals on the Zevon novelty "Hit Somebody (The Hockey Song)", which he co-wrote with Albom. As Zevon proclaimed during their interview, "Dave's the best friend my music ever had."[10]

The show did not belabor the obvious or wallow in woeful spectacle. The first thirty minutes did not veer from the *Late Show* formula. Letterman's monologue, sketches, and the Top Ten List preceded Zevon's interview and performance. Letterman glorified his guest, promoting Zevon's recently released anthology *Genius*, and marveling at the extensive Zevon song catalog, beginning with the requisite "Werewolves of London" mention. Letterman lingered in admiration of Zevon's "love conquers all" line from "Searching for a Heart"—"you can't start it

---

8   See Plasketes 2005: 101-102 for an expanded discussion of this dimension of Zevon's subject matter.

9   Letterman estimated that Zevon had appeared on his shows "a few dozen times."

10   Following the show, Zevon gave Letterman the electric guitar—"Gray Visitation"— which he always played when a guest on *Late Night*.

like a car/you can't stop it with a gun." Adding levity to the litany, Letterman said that Zevon also wrote "White Christmas."

Shaffer and the band paid tribute by performing Zevon songs as interludes to the show's segments. As Zevon entered in delicate gait, the musicians matched Zevon's morbidity with a rendition of his "I'll Sleep When I'm Dead." Letterman cringed slightly, "I didn't know he (Paul) could play that." Zevon was dressed in a striped suit in his mandatory "lucky color"—gray[11]—with an open collar that revealed a small gold chain and cross around his neck.

As a host, Letterman was in uncharted talk show territory. It was difficult to gauge whether his friendship with Zevon made the task easier or more difficult. Right before the break that preceded Zevon's entrance, Letterman wiped his brow, presumably in anxious anticipation of his guest. The course of conversation was predictable, with exchanges about Zevon's diagnosis, his outlook, consequences, life lessons learned, family, and the irony of his situation. The questions and answers echoed the widespread "death watch" coverage that filtered through primarily print media during the immediate aftermath of Zevon's terminal revelation. Letterman was gracious and reverent, avoiding past tense and looking for an occasional lighter note which Zevon accommodated. Zevon was Zevon; he was courageously quotable and engaging. He responded to his despairing circumstance with usual profundity and droll aplomb (at least on the surface). When Letterman led with a comment about learning how his life had changed radically in a few months, Zevon replied, "You mean you heard about the flu?" Zevon explained that he "might have made a tactical error not going to a physician for 20 years. It was one of those phobias that didn't pan out." He mentioned his misguided reliance on his dentist, Dr. Stan, "If he can't fix it, I'm screwed." And how he only hired enabling crew members who told him his shortness of breath was only due to stress. Zevon answers were laced with wry realism; he masterfully juxtaposed blunt with offhanded humor in the same sentence: "It's tough. You better get your dry cleaning done on special;" and "I don't feel as bad as they say I am...They don't discourage you from doing whatever you want." He was also exacting. When Letterman began to discuss the irony of his writing about death, and held up a copy of *My Ride's Here*, Zevon instantly interjected "Hello!" The lines had become familiar, somewhat rehearsed and recycled; a morbid mantra of terminal talking points he had been delivering in the steady stream of print interviews and press releases since August. Yet the comments resonated more profoundly when seeing Zevon discuss his condition live.

The guest appearance carried greater gravity as it marked Zevon's final live performance. "Everybody who does this should think of themselves as

---

11   Zevon's fascination with the color gray was part of his obsessive compulsive disorder. There are numerous humorous and colorful reflections by his friends and family in Zevon 2007: 222-225. Jimmy Wachtel observed one of Zevon's drawers with "like forty pair of gray socks all balled up" "thought it was one of the greatest art pieces I'd ever seen" (224-225).

DIE ANOTHER DAY 179

an entertainer. I was reading a biography of Sammy Davis Jr., and it said that even when he was diagnosed with cancer, he [still] went out there and danced 'Mr. Bojangles.' I thought, 'Okay, I'm gonna do it. It's not the easiest thing in the world to say goodbye, so it was a little difficult," said Zevon in August (VH-1.com). The *Late Show* scene settled in between post-MTV *Unplugged*, VH-1 *Storytellers* and the more contemporary You Tube, My Space Music or exclusive download domain. Zevon avoided a greatest hits medley with his three song set. Following the commercial break, Zevon led off with what he thought was going to be his closing number, "The Mutineer," the relatively obscure title track from one of his equally remote albums in 1995.[12] The staging framed the solemn piano "born to rock the boat" ballad. Low lighting provided a formal recital hall meets Catholic mass aura, with a standing trio of flute, horn and clarinet accompaniment rising slightly in the background. Zevon's voice strained at times to reach the high notes. Extreme close up shots heightened the emotional impact. Zevon's punctual take to the camera on the phrase, "let's get out of here," was subtly affecting.

His second song, "Genius," from *My Ride's Here* (2001), was an intriguing choice as well. On the shallow surface, it may have appeared to be a never-too-late marketing ploy to promote Zevon's "Best of" compilation of the same title, which had been released by Rhino Records a few weeks earlier. The selection also contained a bound for glory allusion to the "genius" label that had been frequently attached to Zevon in the "Songwriters' Neighborhood," a place he sings about in the noir narrative. Zevon, with guitar, fronted a classical string quartet. While brilliant lines about "ladies' man Albert Einstein making out like Charlie Sheen" stand out, the song's closing 30 seconds are the most revealing. Following the final line, "I'd be a genius," Zevon lowers his guitar, turns to face the string accompanists and strikes a reserved conductor's pose, his arms weakly elevated and slightly swaying. The macabre maestro stance was not a charade, rather a classical climax for Zevon. At age 13, he was inspired by meeting composer Robert Craft and his hero Igor Stravinsky. The classically trained Zevon was a more accomplished pianist than guitarist. Pieces of Zevon's unfinished opus, "Symphony No. 1," are sprinkled throughout his songs, the most evident as "Interludes No. 1" and "No. 2" on *Bad Luck Streak in Dancing School* (1980). Musician Kate Salvidge, who was recruited to play on *My Ride's Here*, was overwhelmed by "Genius" during the session. "It was the most unbelievable arrangement I've ever heard. It's probably my favorite string arrangement of all time. It was musically so advanced, and I could tell he wasn't a rock and roller" (Zevon 2007: 383). Following the orchestral performance, Letterman joked to Zevon, "I think the audition is going very well."

Zevon returned to the piano, with Paul and the band replacing the strings and horns, for the closing song, "Roland the Headless Thompson Gunner," which

---

12   At the end of Zevon's interview, there was a slightly awkward moment as Zevon, Letterman and Shaffer were confused as to the order of Zevon's songs to be played, despite a rehearsal earlier in the day.

180   *B-SIDES, UNDERCURRENTS AND OVERTONES*

Letterman claimed to have "begged" Zevon to perform. The selection from *Excitable Boy* (1978) punctuated the performance as a recognizable souvenir of early era Zevon.

Zevon's three song set was a unique self-elegy, an intimate, authentic, and solemn chorus. Each note, lyric and close up revealed glimpses of Zevon's characters and characteristic arc—a piano fighter, thin ice walker, boat rocker, a thorn looking for a side, rebel, renegade, romantic, genius. The sneering subtext alleged the antithesis of disingenuous pseudo-farewell performances by bands breaking up, only to be reunited, sooner than later, and allegedly retiring entertainers such as Celine Dion that pervade celebrity culture.

Zevon got sick, but he never got stupid. He seldom strayed from the sinister, sensitive steps that marked his strange and singular songwriting path. Zevon did not dumb down, but remained true to his sardonic, smart self. His dark preoccupations did not endear him to the music masses; he seemed content with his loyalists and a permanent residence on the peripheries. Mass appeal, marketing and mindless makeovers meant little. Beyond drug and alcohol rehabilitation, Zevon never reinvented himself, his image, writing or music to fashionably fit in anywhere, at any time. With Zevon, there were no music videos to his songs, no genre crossover, concept album, experimental stage, blatant self promotion or artistic compromise. He toured predominantly on the small club circuit, usually with little or no accompaniment—usually his solo strumming, harmonica, passionate piano pounding—and regularly sought late night refuge with Letterman on his show.

One of the most poignant moments of the night occurred earlier when Letterman asked Zevon what he had learned in his time living and dying. Zevon simply stated: "I know how much you're supposed to enjoy every sandwich." Letterman anointed the phrase, punctuating the unique farewell show with it as he shook Zevon's hand following his final live song. The expression proved pitch perfect for the sound bite era. Within 48 hours, "Enjoy every sandwich" was transported to the Internet and tailored into one-hundred-percent cotton, silkscreen, and memorabilia exploitation ready for beginning bids on eBay. The phrase evolved into a slogan that was employed as a commemorative caption beneath Zevon's memorial photo on his website and as the title of a multi artist tribute recording in 2004.

Tuesdays with Warren: Hasten Down *The Wind*

Days after Zevon's diagnosis, sports columnist and bestselling author Mitch Albom happened to be in Los Angeles and had arranged earlier to meet with Zevon. Albom was one of several literary figures that Zevon shared songwriting credits with.[13]

---

13   The Zevon list of literary collaborators includes Albom, Pulitzer Prize winning poet Paul Muldoon, Thomas McGuane, Carl Hiassen and gonzo journalist Dr. Hunter S. Thompson. Zevon also performed briefly in The Rock Bottom Remainders, a band of bards that included Albom, Stephen King, Amy Tan and Dave Barry.

Having chronicled the dying process of his old professor in *Tuesdays with Morrie*, Albom was a primary resource for dealing with terminal illness. Albom recalls Zevon asking rhetorically, "So am I supposed to die with my boots on? Is that my fate? Is that how I'm supposed to approach this?" (Zevon: 393).

Ironically, Zevon felt that he was in the midst of the most creative period of his life. While he was determined to make as much music as he possibly could in the time he had left, he simultaneously wrestled with the practical, romantic and spiritual perspectives of his looming fate. He met with Deepak Chopra and Catholic priests. He talked about traveling to India and to Florida to fish with novelist friend Carl Hiassen. Finally, Zevon decided that dying with his boots on was the way to go, and music the most appropriate way to say good bye. According to his former wife Crystal, he called one day and said, "My job is music. It's all I leave the kids (daughter Ariel and son Jordan) and the people I love so I'm going to stay in L.A. to make records." Zevon's closest friend and collaborator, Jorge Calderon, was totally supportive, if not relieved. "Warren did the right thing. He went knee-deep into his music" (Zevon: 394-395).

He also contacted his manager, Brigitte Barr, insisting they "go into showbiz mode." Zevon gave her permission to "use his illness in any way she saw fit to further his career right now" (Zevon: 396). Danny Goldberg, Chairman and CEO of Artemis Records, Zevon's label, gave him carte blanche. "I never thought he would have the strength or focus to do a whole album, but I was happy for whatever he wanted to do. I knew it was going to be good and I knew it was going to be the last work. All the way through, I kept being amazed that he was still writing and that he was still doing it. Every time another song would come it was like a miracle" (Zevon: 396). According to Zevon, the songs came quickly and easily. "It's never happened before in my life. Inspiration always came painfully, brutally and rarely," he said (VH-1: 2003),

The subsequent writing and recording of *The Wind* was the climactic centerpiece of Zevon's *Deteriorata*. Along with engineer Noah Snyder, Calderon was the cornerstone of the project. He co-wrote seven of the record's ten original songs with Zevon. Beyond his role as co-producer, Calderon served as a spiritual guide, coach and caretaker who kept the demanding, emotional session grounded and progressing toward completion. The inherently complex and courageous mission grew more complicated as a steadily weakening Zevon grew predictably depressed. He also returned to excessive drinking, often mixing liquid morphine cocktails. Calderon said "it got pretty bad. Just like the old days." Calderon understood, but was uneasy about potentially lethal mixtures. He cautioned Zevon, "It would be a shame for something to happen before you could live out your life as long as you can" (Zevon: 403).

The recording of the album was a musical rite of passage that mingled the components and spirit of an Irish wake with a New Orleans jazz funeral. An inspiring parade of participants, many who had contributed to previous Zevon recordings, gathered to play and pay their requiem riffs and respects to their friend. Among those assembled were Jackson Browne, Bruce Springsteen,

Eagles Don Henley, Joe Walsh and Timothy B. Schmidt, John Waite, Dwight Yoakam, Ry Cooder, David Lindley, drummer Jim Keltner, T-Bone Burnett, Emmylou Harris, Tom Petty, and actor Billy Bob Thornton.

Due to the number of artists involved, eight different studios were utilized during the album's recording and mixing. Only Emmylou Harris's collaboration was done by remote. The personnel pairings were done on a song-by-song basis. "The songs were ironed out before he had [guests] come in. We tried to have it ready to go so it wouldn't be like pulling teeth," said engineer Noah Snyder. "What we wanted to capture on the album was these guys having fun playing with Warren, paying their respects. It was bittersweet, obviously, but it was a wonderful thing to see these legendary rock stars just being totally selfless, good friends to Warren" (*Ice* July 2003: 4).

The bulk of the songs were written and recorded between September 2002 and New Year while Zevon's strength and spirits were optimal. Though the process did not relieve any of Zevon's anxieties, it did provide sustenance. "I think as long as I keep working it's keeping me alive," he said. "So I'm trying to expand the format as much as I can" (VH-1: 2003). A six-week hiatus followed in the first months of 2003 as Zevon's condition steadily worsened. Though not well enough to return to an outside studio, Zevon was able to complete the record's last two songs at his home studio in April 2003.

There is yearning and an undercurrent of urgency in the songs. Inevitable metaphors and transparent allusions to Zevon's past, his current condition and imminent future pervade the lyrics and song titles. Phrases such as "wheels running out of steam," "running out of breath," "shadows are falling," "before I fall asleep," "die too hard," "down in mortal lock in Prison Grove," and "numb as a statue" convey aching without being self-mournful. There is also a part-Spanish-spoken correspondence to the love of a lifetime ("El Amor De Mi Vida"), a fearful plea for companionship ("Please Stay") and a stunning farewell prayer "Keep Me in Your Heart," the first song Zevon wrote following his diagnosis. The rollicking "The Rest of the Night," blues of "Rub Me Raw," the low self esteem of "She's Too Good for Me," and politically tinged, psychological profile of "Disorder in the House" balance the tender tones.

The definitive dirge on the album was not planned—a cover of Bob Dylan's "Knockin' on Heaven's Door." The song originated on the soundtrack to the Western *Pat Garrett and Billy the Kid* (1973), directed by Sam Peckinpah and starring Dylan. The ballad cued one of the early career characterizations of Zevon as "the Sam Peckinpah of rock." Such film, literary and music associations were frequent.[14] The Peckinpah comparison was largely based on Zevon's and the maverick filmmaker's (*Wild Bunch, Straw Dogs*) shared affections for expressing graphic violence and their lifestyle excesses. When Zevon said he wanted to

---

14   Other characterizations include "Warren Fitzzevon," "Jackson Browne's bad conscience," a "Dada-ist Bruce Springsteen," "the John Huston of rock," and separately the "Ernest Hemingway" and "Charles Bronson" "of the twelve string guitar."

record the archetypal "die with your boots on song," Thornton and Calderon both laughed, perhaps nervously. "I thought it was a little too much to do that song, but when I heard him sing it…I thought, oh my God, if anyone will sing it, it's him," said Calderon (Zevon: 406) Recording the song was spontaneous and a spiritual highlight of the sessions. They did not even have the lyrics. Fortunately, Calderon had a copy of Dylan's *Greatest Hits* in his car. He brought it in, they wrote the lyrics down and cut a version at Thornton's studio. "That was the moment that moved me…there's a bunch of his friends, standing there in a circle, singing in one mic," said Thornton. "The spirit in the room was so intense, the reverence that I felt from all the musicians was very soulful," added Calderon (Zevon 407).

While that song may have been a highlight, the entire session was unique in its delightful sorrow. "It's unbelievably sad and unbelievably brave," said Ry Cooder. "You get that kind of intense focus and every word and every note is heartfelt…. There's subtext all over the place. I went around in another mental atmosphere for quite some time after that" (Pareles 2003: 25).

Calderon compared the session to the television show "*This is Your Life*, unplanned and unrehearsed" (Pareles: 25). To him, recording *The Wind* was "like a drug—the creativity, the people that were coming to play, the beauty of this music. But there was also the other side of it for him [Zevon]: This is all happening because I'm dying" (Fricke 2003: 49). Goldberg agreed. "Then suddenly it was done. He [Zevon] was so happy and so sad, it was an amazing time to be around him. He was mostly enjoying all the attention. He was like a little kid…and this one was just a spiritual album for everyone" (Zevon: 413).

Jackson Browne suggested *The Wind* sessions were analogous with "disincorporating," a concept presented in the opening chapter of Robert Heinlein's science fiction novel, *Stranger in a Strange Land,* when an artist dies in the middle of a project on Mars (Brown 2003: F-01). The artist does not notice his own death because he is so involved in his work and there is life after physical death on the planet. His creation is completely unique in that half of it was made when he was alive, and half of it when he was dead.

Zevon was the sole exception to the standard posthumous post production which supplanted "disincorporation" among several other music passings in proximity to his own. The Band's Rick Danko, Mama and Papa John Phillips, Beatle George Harrison, Latin Salsa Queen Celia Cruz and legendary Johnny Cash and his wife June Carter Cash, who died between 1999 and 2003, were not around to complete their final recording projects, let alone witness their releases.[15] *The Wind* was released on 26 August 2003, joining *Life'll Kill Ya'* and *My Ride's Here* to complete Zevon's *Deteriorata* soundtrack trilogy of recordings. Zevon hung on long enough to catch a glimpse of its early sales that eventually garnered Grammy and Gold.

---

15   In keeping with the coroner undercurrent of the chapter, the dates of death are: Danko (10 December 1999), Phillips (18 March 2001), Harrison (29 November 2001), June Carter Cash (15 May 2003), Cruz (16 July 2003), and Johnny Cash (12 September 2003).

184 B-SIDES, UNDERCURRENTS AND OVERTONES

Funereality: Join Me in L.A.

The holiest, most intimate parts of Zevon's procession, from the *Late Show* through *The Wind*, were chronicled in a stirring one-hour VH-1 special (*Inside*)*Out: Warren Zevon: Keep Me in Your Heart.* Everyone involved seemed willing to concede the circling vulture opportunism inherent in the documentary project. The prevailing rationale was that it was a tribute and living funeral, and never too late for the underappreciated songwriter to get his due, fateful irony notwithstanding. Artemis Records CEO Danny Goldberg had approached VH-1 earlier about featuring Zevon in their popular bio-series *Behind the Music*. "I did everything I could to convince them to do one on Warren, and they wouldn't do it, which is ironic given that they ended up having that big special [(*Inside*)*Out*] on him when he was dying," said Goldberg. "I always felt a little irritated that we couldn't have gotten that kind of exposure on *Life'll Kill Ya*, which I think is every bit as good as *The Wind*" (Zevon: 374).

The (*Inside*)*Out* premiere aired on the cable music network without commercial interruption on Sunday evening, 24 August 2003, two days before the release of *The Wind*; and two weeks before Zevon's death. The documentary was a more dignified variation of the often scandalous sensational *Behind the Music*. The presentation blended reality show conventions of MTV's *Real World* with *The Osbournes*, but with the prevailing sensibility of Albom's bestselling *Tuesdays With Morrie*.

The overarching approach is a video diary, With the recording sessions the unifying structural thread, the production deftly adapts traditional bio-documentary conventions into a life affirming musical wake. Billy Bob Thornton leads with a litany—"the crazy bag of labels"—used to describe Zevon. He continues with voice over narration of a career composite that is dotted with observations from Zevon's family, music and literary entourage. From there, the approach shifts to a video diary, from the diagnosis in August 2002 through the recording of *The Wind*'s final song, "Keep Me in Your Heart" on 12 April 2003. Dates and brief Zevon notes appear on the screen in typewriter style font. The entries are preface and transition. Most are inner reflections: "I have good days and bad days—weeks become months until..."[16]

While the sessions are the focal point, the interior locales are not confining or claustrophobic. Intercutting concert footage, highlights from the *Late Night* appearance, from arrival in New York City to rehearsal to the show itself and backstage departing, still photos, music memorabilia and archival home movies shot by Zevon's first wife, Tule Livingston Dillow, enhance the studio story and structure. The dramatic construction is more complementary than cluttered. On the soundtrack, carefully selected and placed lyric and instrumental samples of

---

16   All quotes in this section are extracted from the documentary, *VH-1 (Inside) Out: Warren Zevon.* Nick Read, Producer, Director, Photographer (VH-1/ Artemis Records/MTV Networks, 2004).

the Zevon songbook provide interludes, thematic accents and emotional resonance to the visuals and narrative. Throughout, the prevailing tone is similar to the *Late Show* farewell, celebratory but with sweet sadness a subtext. Hugs and handshakes abound, heartache hovers and hides beneath occasional humor.

The portrayal captures Zevon's complexities, facets and roles. Zevon is thoughtful, engaging and literate, quoting from Mickey Spillane, Steve McQueen in *Tom Horn*, Rilke, and Arthur Schopenhauer. He is a fan, friend and child taking a picture of Springsteen in the studio. A prescription junkie, reaching into his bag of medications by flashlight, routinely popping pills and washing them down with presumably a diet Mountain Dew. A devoted father gently rubbing his pregnant daughter's stomach, and working on a piano arrangement next to son Jordan. A fashion conscious stylist shopping for a suit for the visit with Letterman. The grin reaper, emerging from a limo upon arriving in New York City, proclaiming, "Dead man walking!"

The scenes are rife with poignant moments. Midway through a meeting with his oncologist, Zevon asks the cameras to leave as the discussion of his treatment and side effects becomes more personal. When *The New Yorker* calls his publicist for an interview, the uncompromising Zevon, staring out the limo window, declines, with a blunt, almost resentful "Too late." There are shots of Zevon cuffing cigarettes like Bogart outside the Cherokee Studio in defiant resignation: "What would you do if you had a month to live?" And the curious Zevon, dumbfounded by Internet postings by fans who regard his refusal for chemotherapy treatment "heroic," ruefully rejects such a badge of honor, "I think it's a sin not to want to live."

The December 17 and 18 recording of "Disorder in the House" is a particularly riveting sequence. Zevon's diary entry signals a shifting tone from the preceding scene of light levity and lunch with humorist Dave Barry: "It's nearly Christmas and I still have two songs to complete. I hope I can stay well enough long enough." "Don't Let Us get Sick," bedded under images of holiday lights and neon in L.A., magnify the sombering mood. December 17 marks the "start of a long and grueling day" recording the song which, according to Zevon, "accurately describes my state of mind." Zevon's mental state becomes more of a focal point. Intercut with Jim Keltner drumming his tracks for the song, a series of shots of Zevon taking his medications follows as foreshadowing. Zevon explains that they "mask the symptoms" and that he expected it to be worse." "Life's not over," he says. In contrast to Zevon's pill popping, Calderon is munching snacks behind the audio console, ready to record. Zevon appears unsettled, a presumed result of the meds. He puts on his glasses and slouches in a studio seat, quoting from Schopenhauer about reading. When Noah Snyder's voice intones over the studio microphone, asking if he's ready to give it a shot, Zevon chuckles, "Yeah, why not. The rest of my short life has gone by while I wait for you to ask that question." Zevon continually misses cues. There is a cut to the audio room where Calderon adjusts his glasses and raises an eyebrow. He joins Zevon in the studio, counting, tapping on his knee, trying unsuccessfully to capture a useable take. Cast as patient parent

186   *B-SIDES, UNDERCURRENTS AND OVERTONES*

or teacher working with a child, Caderon maintains a smile, "Maybe we should figure out what we need."

The scene shifts to Zevon and Calderon at the audio console, with Snyder close by. Artist-producer negotiations are underway. A remarkable exchange follows. Calderon cautiously wonders about the energy level and its effect on the takes. Zevon interrupts, saying that he doesn't want to bring some "George C. Scott gloom" to the situation. Calderon continues, suggesting it might be better to return in the morning to record when Zevon is fresh. "I'm dying, Jorge, I don't have no 'fresh'," replies Zevon. "'Fresh' is not in my vocabulary." Calderon displays saintly compassion in the circumstances. "I totally understand, but we're celebrating life everyday—yours, mine and everybody else's." Zevon may be medicated but he is not soothed. "You're taking this too seriously." Calderon disengages, turning his head away. Zevon is clearly feeling the end drawing closer. He slurs, "What do you think boys, am I'm going out in a fiery hole a million miles long." Calderon leans back in his chair, snack in hand, looking straight. He calmly counters, "Where you go after this is way better. I have a special place for you though. Miles (Davis) will come visiting. Blow his horn, jam. There's no fiery hole there."[17]

The studio atmosphere becomes slightly more upbeat the following day, December 18, with the arrival of another heroic figure, Bruce Springsteen. Springsteen's saving grace is reflected in Zevon's December 18 entry: "According to the doctors I should be long gone by now. Every day means the world to me. Especially when my old friend Bruce Springsteen is coming to the studio."

Springsteen's tour had him in Indianapolis the night before. He was due home in New Jersey for Christmas. Instead, as Zevon proudly points out, "he chartered a plane to come see me." The absorbing sequence climaxes on an upbeat note. Following Springsteen's vocal track for the song, he rips a torrid, amp-blowing guitar solo for "Disorder in the House." An awestruck Zevon bows, "You *are* him."[18]

The heart wrenching closing scene of the documentary reveals Zevon, too fragile to record in the studio, teetering on the couch next to Calderon in his home in front of two microphones. His Baritone weak and straining slightly, but rising to complete *The Wind*'s closing song, the hymn-like "Keep Me in Your Heart." The concluding scene may transcend Kurt Cobain in cardigan as the most intimate

---

17   Calderon's saintly presence and qualities are not a camera conscious ploy. His genuine compassion and dedication as Zevon's friend and collaborator are equally striking throughout Crystal Zevon's *I'll Sleep When I'm Dead* (2007). He appeared to grasp Zevon's genius and demons better than anyone in the L.A. scene.

18   Engineer Noah Snyder's said that he and Zevon considered Springsteen's guitar solo a "cosmic event." "There was something magical about the energy that he brought...all he does is turn the amp all the way up. So, after he plays, he kills the amp. The speakers are ripped and torn...It was like Sir Galahad at the moment he finds the Grail. There was nothing left for the amp to do—it had achieved the highest state of amp-dom and went right up to God at that point" (Zevon 2007: 412).

unplugged performance in the music television era, at once a powerful, prayerful parting and shimmering lullaby.

"Paint the Whole Town Gray"[19]

The shadowy packaging and design of *The Wind* CD and the companion (*Inside*)*Out* DVD complement the scope and spirit of the record and documentary. Both disc cases translate as burial vaults that contain the sacred audio and video artifacts of Zevon's *Deteriorata*. Muted tones and shades of gray, the primary palette for the color compulsive Zevon, abound, from Zevon's clothing to backgrounds, letters and graphics to the disc itself and a creased charcoal shroud that drapes the back cover.

The signature skull with sunglasses and dangling cigarette is stamped throughout. By the time Zevon posed for the parting portrait for *Rolling Stone* photographer Matthew Rolston, the "Old Velvet Nose" trademark had morphed into his own ghostly gunslinger guise as portrayed on both covers. The long shot on the DVD cover depicts Zevon in a slight gunslinger stance. He is propped on the edge of a stool, shirt open three buttons down, sleeves rolled up. His right arm hangs, elbow bent, his hand at the hip of his black leather pants, as if ready to draw. The wristwatch on Zevon's opposite arm that rests on his inner thigh is a striking reminder of time. It ticks loudly, a countdown, the last stand. The closeup on the CD is calm yet confronting. There is no smirk, and no cigarette, but there is smoke. A thirty-year habit simmering beneath Zevon's glowering gaze. Ash trays to ash trays, dust to dust. And where there is smoke there is fire, which is where Zevon metaphorically liked to stand, and what he liked to play with. But there was never a smokescreen. The roadmap lines may not be etched in the cold candor of Zevon's face like the Keith Richards, Johnny Cash or Miles Davis close ups which rank among the most revealing in the rock and *Rolling Stone* Rushmore, but "The Look" is there. Point Blank. Point Black. Point Gray. Deadpan.[20]

Bound for Glory, Gold and Grammy

> I better die quick so they'll give me a Grammy nomination. It's a damn hard way to make a living, having to die to get 'em to know you're alive.
>
> Warren Zevon (Zevon: 429-430)

---

19 "Disorder in the House." Warren Zevon and Jorge Calderon, Zevon Music/ Googleplex Music (BMI) 2003.

20 The *Inside Out* documentary reveals Zevon assessing the photos at the shoot, telling "the last girlfriend" Kristen Steffl, that he looks like "a baboon from Newcastle trying to get a job in a toothpaste commercial."

One of the frequently circulated Zevon quotes that framed his Dieography was resurrected from a 1993 interview in *Entertainment Weekly*, "If you're lucky, people like something you do early and something you do just before you drop dead. That's as many pats on the back as you should expect" (Fretts 1993: 88). Zevon's chronology contains such parenthesis of praise. Early on, Linda Ronstadt (un)covered his songwriting brilliance by baptizing "Carmelita," "Poor Poor Pitiful Me," "Hasten Down the Wind," and "Mohammed's Radio" into hits during the 1970s. Toward the end, Bob Dylan paid homage by including covering Zevon songs during his Fall 2002 tour. "Boom Boom Mancini," "Accidentally Like A Martyr," "Mutineer," and "Lawyers Guns and Money" were a regular part of Dylan's set list.

The Wind sold 48,000 copies its first week, debuting at number 16 on the *Billboard* Top 200 chart. It marked Zevon's first Top Twenty appearance since *Bad Luck Streak in Dancing School* in 1980. The album also received five Grammy nominations, eventually winning in two categories.[21] According to Calderon, as the end neared, Zevon did not read many of *The Wind*'s rave reviews "because they all talked about him dying. I remember him telling me, 'Just tell me the good news'" (Fricke 2003: 49).

Shadows are Falling: Knockin' on Heaven's Door

At 56, Zevon was, as he co-wrote with producer extraordinaire T-Bone Burnett, "too old to die young, too young to die now."[22] But Zevon was lucky and he knew it. He lived the familiar, full force, fatally flawed fable much longer than his perished predecessors. Zevon was mystified by and perversely proud that he was not "deader than a Door." "I chose a certain path and lived like Jim Morrison, but lived 30 more years, who knows why?" he told Letterman. Morrison appeared to be the benchmark, his name and fate frequently invoked during Zevon's interviews. Zevon was routinely reminded of his emblematic "Wild Age" narratives and corresponding "running straight in their graves" lifestyle.[23] Looking back in 2003, he observed of his route from recklessness to redemption, "I lucked out big time because I got to be the most fucked up rock star on the block, at least my block, and then I got to be a sober dad for 18 years. I've had two very full lives" (Gunderson: 12D).

Familiar lines of questioning persisted during the *Deteriorata* as journalists probed Zevon about his continual deciphering of death in songwriting. In 1981,

---

21 The nominations were for "Song of the Year" ("Keep Me in Your Heart"), Best Male Pop Vocal ("Keep Me in Your Heart"), Best Rock Song ("Disorder in the House"), Best Contemporary Folk Album and Best Rock Performance by a Group or Duo ("Disorder in the House" with Springsteen).

22 "Bed Of Coals." Words and music by Warren Zevon and T-Bone Burnett. Zevon Music 1980.

23 "Wild Age." Words and music by Warren Zevon, Zevon Music 1980.

he explained in a *Songwriter* interview, "I consider that what we're essentially dealing with is an existence that we don't understand. That's why a lot of my work is about death. I have news for everyone, including myself—don't make long range plans, 'cause there is an inevitable adieu for everyone. I don't consider it a subject to be avoided" (Alfonso: 24). In 2002, as the mystery unraveled within the context of his own history, Zevon's view was slightly more comprehensible: "I've often infuriated sincere interviewers who asked why I write all these 'death songs.' I'd tell them 'I don't know.' I guess I have the answer now. Maybe we as writers carry some kind of physical knowledge of our fates, and work through them. To me the message of my songs, of all songs, is 'enjoy life.'... It's the only message I ever thought art had any business having" (Gunderson: 12D).

Zevon got to go out on his own terms, dying like the anti-hero in F. Scott Fitzgerald's *Tender is the Night*, exiting in the shadows he so often sang about, the shadows that lurked and those he chased; the shadows he cast and those that cast him. And the late shadows cast by the glare of media coverage. Rather than dying what he called "a coward's death" as a drunk, by a drug overdose or gunshot in a garage—all three well within Zevon's realm of reckless roulette at one time— Zevon died with dignity. He had played the doomed protagonist of noir for so long; this was his apotheosis.[24] On 7 September 2003, more than thirty years after he blazoned, "I'll Sleep When I'm Dead," Zevon fulfilled his lifelong piano pounding pledge; the desperado died with his boots on.[25]

Coda: Posthumous Profusion and the Great Beyond

Zevon's ashes were scattered in the Pacific Ocean during a private ceremony of family and friends. True to death's ripple effect on an artist's mythic ascension and marketability, Zevon particles proliferated posthumously. The groundwork for commemorative momentum that was established during the course of his *Deteriorta* sustained for the next three years in honors, ceremony, song, video and print. At the 46th Grammy Awards (8 February 2004), Zevon won two Grammys for *The Wind* in somewhat contrasting categories—Best Contemporary Folk Album and Best Rock Performance by a Group or Duo ("Disorder in the House" with Springsteen).[26]

---

24 This view, received 10 October 2002, was among many insightful Zevon perspectives shared with me by Greg Metcalf during regular e-mail correspondence following Zevon's terminal diagnosis.

25 Following Carl Hiaasen's Foreward in *I'll Sleep When I'm Dead*, the book begins with an extraordinarily intimate account of Zevon's final moments with perspectives from Crystal, Jordan, and Ariel Zevon, friend and confidant Ryan Rayson, and Jorge Calderon at his home in Los Angeles (Zevon 2007: 1-5).

26 Placing *The Wind* in the Contemporary Folk category may have been a sympathetic stretch, a genre designation that may have been further contradicted by removing "Disorder in the House" to place it in the Rock duo list. Whether it was industry exploitation, or a

190   *B-SIDES, UNDERCURRENTS AND OVERTONES*

"This record has one soul but it has many hearts," reiterated Jordan Zevon when accepting the awards on his Father's behalf. The ceremony further celebrated Zevon with a lovely live choral tribute with Ariel and Jordan Zevon, Jorge Calderon, Emmylou Harris, Billy Bob Thornton, Timothy B. Schmit, Jackson Browne, and Dwight Yoakam singing "Keep Me in Your Heart." The song was instantaneously enshrined into the canon of pop eulogistic hymns, joining standards such as Sarah Mclachlan's "Arms of an Angel" and "I Will Remember You."

The same month, the VH-1 *Inside:Out: Warren Zevon* DVD became available in the marketplace, followed by a steady stream of record releases. There were three tribute records—a string quartet (2003), and two multi-artist collections, one an alternative independent label (*Hurry Home Early*, 2005) and another a pop/rock set (*Enjoy Every Sandwich*, 2004) featuring Springsteen, Browne, Henley, Bonnie Raitt, Jill Sobule, and Steve Earle among the contributors. Jordan Zevon performed a family heirloom, "Studebaker," one of his father's unrecorded songs. Jordan carried on the Zevon lineage with his recording debut in 2005. The family affair was further evident in Zevon's daughter Ariel's touching liner notes for a compilation of thirteen love songs culled from her father's songbook (2006). There was also the characteristic afterlife archival activity with a profusion of remastered, reissued editions of Zevon recordings featuring requisite rare and unreleased materials (see Dieography).

Before he died, Zevon commissioned his former wife and lifelong friend, Crystal, to conduct and compile exhaustive interviews with friends, family, lovers, cavorters and cohorts. The result was an unflinching oral history, *I'll Sleep When I'm Dead: The Dirty Life and Times of Warren Zevon*, that surpasses Barney Hoskins' *Hotel California* (2006) with its unsettling, penetrating antihero account of the heart, soul and excesses of the 1960s-1970s Los Angeles music scene. Published in May 2007, the 452-page chronicle is an intimate portrait of tortured brilliance, obsessive compulsive behavior, recklessness and redemption that marks Zevon's posthumous peak and perpetuates his legacy.

Procession and Passage: Reconfiguring Rock Ritual

Warren Zevon's desperado *Deteriorata* within his over arching Dieography was a captivating small scale spectacle of compassion, curiosity and chronicle. The rich rite of passage embodied qualities of the human condition and meanings which transcended the rock and roll sphere. With death an anticlimactic inevitability, preface and process proved more compelling than pinnacle or postscript. In addition to Zevon having the opportunity to say goodbye, the death watch circumstances afforded journalists, fans and cultural observers a unique opportunity to ponder

---

current or career parting gift—a Lifetime Achievement for the dying—was a mortal moot point. The recognition may not have been about Zevon's "best for last," rather affirmation that Zevon's best will last.

and prepare preemptive eulogistic career retrospectives. The grim nature of the narrative was enriched by the looming shadow of irony cast by Zevon's dark songwriting preoccupations, his wry humor and excessive lifestyle.

The portrayal, permission and participation in Zevon's dying days reflected the "reality show" realm of media and celebrity culture where an endless cycle of compulsive coverage is a carnival attraction that matches a boundless consumer curiosity. The value shift from private to public was deeply entrenched, with the most intimate details of lives and lifestyles such as sex and death a vital part of the all access pass and audience expectations.

As a narrative ritual form, the dieography reconfigured the conventional rock and roll mortal methodology and martyrdom from plane crashes, gunshot wounds, murder, suicide and accidental overdoses to a more honorable sacrament. Mingling ceremonial elements of tour, recording session and living funeral, the *Deteriorata*'s devices and arrangement reflected a more reverent staging and tone than the sensationalism that tends to characterize the media saturation and audience fascination in the immediate wake of a sudden or expected death of a public figure. In Zevon's case, the shock came with the public disclosure of his terminal diagnosis rather than the death itself. The cumulative anticipatory media treatment during the next year held its own with the shorter term concentration of coverage of Johnny Cash and popular comic actor John Ritter who died the week following Zevon's death.

From the announcement of his terminal condition in September 2002, through the posthumous Grammy tribute in February 2004 and the continued flurry of afterlife activity, Zevon received more press coverage than he had his entire career. Perhaps that was part of the plan, both personally and professionally. Grudgingly pondering posterity, Zevon said his hope was to be remembered better than the "bad watercolor" of Humphrey Bogart on the DVD case of *Maltese Falcon* (Pareles 2003: 25). Jordan Zevon likely had the best vantage point for providing insight and context to his father's final year:

> People look at the album and what Dad did in the last months of his life and just think, like, how could he do it? The strength and the courage. But the part that people will never really understand is that beyond the strength and the courage, which is undeniable, there was this incredible, intuitive savvy of marketing. He just like…"Okay, I'm going to die but I'm not going to go out John Prine-style with the record that sells ten thousand copies." He knew what he was doing. He'd been in the business for his entire life, and he hit it right on the head. I mean, there are gold records, the things keep selling, people talking about him. It really proves that even though he made music that wasn't geared toward instant commercial success or trying to conform to something…and though he may have had times when he was frustrated by the sales or poor attendance at concerts, when it all came down to it, he knew what he was doing more than anybody at any of these labels did. (Zevon: 399)

B-SIDES, UNDERCURRENTS AND OVERTONES

While Zevon's permanent status as a B-Sider may have not only been a motivating factor for the exposure inherent within the *Deteriorata*, it also contributed to the process being more manageable. Arguably, a similar preface procession for Beatle George Harrison, who, at 58, was in Zevon's age range when he died, or the elder legend Johnny Cash during their prolonged illnesses may have proved overwhelming due to the magnitude of their careers. It may have taken death's career enhancing cliché and a little help from his musical friends and family, particularly an amp-melting Springsteen guitar solo, but Warren Zevon, a dweller on music's peripheries, crossed over. He passed from life and from the B-side, his preparation for passage to the afterlife and the A-side documented in a distinctive and dignified desperado *Deteriorata* of words, images and music.

Warren Zevon Dieography (2000-2007)

This Dieography adapts the standard Biographical chronology into a (running out of) time line. The three part structure—Prelude, Deteriorata, Coda—highlights Warren Zevon's final three years and early afterlife activities, spanning 2000 and 2007.

Prelude

2000

25 January   *Life'll Kill'Ya* (Artemis) magnifies Zevon's career long preoccupation with death as a songwriting motif. The theme is pervasive, from the title track to the closing "Don't Let Us get Sick" and the doctor phobic "My Shit's Fucked Up" in between.

2001

7 May   *My Ride's Here* (Artemis) continues with death preoccupations. The "ride" is an an allusion to a hearse, which Zevon gazes out from on the record's cover shot.

Deteriorata

2002

August   Zevon is diagnosed with mesolthelioma, an inoperable form of lung cancer. The medical prognosis is three months.

September   Zevon begins writing as many songs as he can with longtime friend Jorge Calderon with the hopes of recording them in the time he has remaining. VH-1 begins filming Zevon's activities for an *Inside Out* documentary special.

15 October   *Genius* (Elektra/Rhino), Zevon's third "Best of" anthology, is released. The anthology contains 22 songs.

DIE ANOTHER DAY 193

30 October   David Letterman devotes the entire *Late Show* to Zevon. Following an interview, Zevon sings "The Mutineer," "Genius," and "Roland the Headless Thompson Gunner" in what is his final live performance.

November– December   Many of Zevon's musical friends gather in L.A. to collaborate on the recording of his final record. The studio sessions are the primary focus of the VH-1 documentary special.

2003

24 January   Zevon turns 56 years old.

18 March   *The First Sessions* (Varese Sarabande) compiles early recordings and demos, including Zevon's folk duo (with Violet Santangelo), lyme and cybelle, whose songs "Outside Chance" and "Like the Seasons" were B-sides for their White Whale labelmates The Turtles. Also of note are the duo's Follow Me" which reached #65 in 1966, and Beatles, Dylan and Jimmy Reed covers.

April   Zevon records the final two songs for *The Wind*.

6 May   *Sentimental Hygiene* (1987) and *Tranverse City* (1989) are reissued.

11 June   Zevon becomes a grandfather as his daughter, Ariel, gives birth to twin sons, Maximus Patrick and Augustus Warren Zevon Powell.

15 June   A movement is underway via Internet petitions to induct Zevon into the Rock and Roll Hall of Fame.

26 August   *The Wind* (Artemis) is released. Benefiting from Zevon's "terminal exposure," the record sells 48,000 copies its first week and opens at #46 on *Billboard's* Top 200. The chart position is the highest for Zevon since 1980 with *Bad Luck Streak in Dancing School.*

7 September   Zevon dies in his home in Los Angeles at age 56.

Coda

25 November   *String Quartet Tribute to Warren Zevon* (Vitamin) is an interesting classical interpretation of ten of Zevon's songs.

11 December   The Recording Industry Association of America (RIAA) certifies *The Wind* a Gold record as its sales surpass 100,000 copies.

2004

8 February   Jordan Zevon appears on cable network A & E's *Breakfast with the Arts* to discuss his father's life, music and final recording.

8 February   At the 46th Grammy Awards, Zevon wins two Grammys for Contemporary Folk Album and Best Rock Performance by a Duo or Group. The ceremony features a live choral performance of "Keep Me in Your Heart" as a tribute to artists who died in 2003.

10 February   The VH-1 documentary *Inside Out: Warren Zevon, Keep Me in Your Heart* is released. The DVD features two music videos and expanded interviews with Zevon.

3 March   Tule Livingston, Zevon's first wife and mother of their son, Jordan, dies of breastcancer at age 57. She was the subject of Zevon's "Tule's Blues" (*Wanted Dead or Alive* and reissued on *Preludes*) and "Hasten Down the Wind."

12 October   Jordan Zevon and Wallflowers perform "Lawyers Guns and Money" on *Late* Night with David Letterman to promote a forthcoming Zevon tribute album (see this chapter)

19 October   *Enjoy Every Sandwich* (Artemis), the most mainstream Zevon tribute record, features many artists from *The Wind* sessions, among them Springsteen, Browne, Lindley, Cooder, Calderon, Henley and Thornton. The star studded cast also includes Bob Dylan, Bonnie Raitt, Jill Sobule, Jennifer Warnes, Pete Yorn, Adam Sandler, the Pixies, Steve Earle, Reckless Kelly, and Wallflowers. Jordan Zevon performance of his father's previously unrecorded song "Studebaker" is an eerie echo of the 1970s California sound.

15 December   Adam Sandler performs "Werewolves of London" on *Late Show.*

2005

8 July   *Hurry Home Early: The Songs of Warren Zevon* (Wampum Mutlimedia) is tribute featuring independent label artists.

13 July   Jordan Zevon launches his recording career with a five song self-titled EP. A full length album, *Insides Out*, follows in 2008.

2006

31 January   *Reconsider Me: The Love Songs* (New West) features 13 romantic ballads culled from the Zevon songbook. Ariel Zevon contributes a touching introduction in the liner notes, that begins "In a sense, a father is a daughter's true love…"

2007

27 March   Rhino/WEA releases remastered versions of *Excitable Boy* (1978), *The Envoy* (1980), and the long out of print fan favorite live set, *Stand in the Fire* (1981). All contain previously unissued versions of songs.

May   Zevon's former wife Crystal publishes a 452-page biography *I'll Sleep When I'm Dead: The Dirty Life and Times of Warren Zevon.* The absorbing oral history, commissioned by Zevon, is constructed from extensive interviews with his friends, family, lovers and accomplices in the music industry.

1 May   *Warren Zevon Preludes: Rare and Unreleased Recordings* (New West) is a two-disc set of stripped down songs and extensive interviews with Zevon. The package also includes an attractive booklet containing photographs and ruminations from Zevon's family, friends and fellow artists. The passages are excerpts from Crystal Zevon's book.

16 May   On the season finale of the ABC situation comedy, *According to Jim*, "Keep Me in Your Heart" is the soundtrack for the bio-montage Jim's wife has assembled to commemorate her husband's 50th birthday.

Bibliography

Alexander, Kavichandran. (Liner notes). Ry Cooder and V.M. Bhatt. *A Meeting by the River* (Water Lily Acoustics, 1993).

Alfonso, Barry. "Warren Zevon: Rock"s Stout-Hearted Man," *Songwriter Magazine* (April 1981): 23-25, 48-49.

Applestein, Mike. "We Are Your Friends: The Langley Schools Music Project," *Scram Magazine: The Journal of Unpopular Culture*, No. 15 (Spring 2002): 26-31.

Becker, H.S. "Art Worlds and Social Types," in R.A. Peterson (ed.) *The Production of Culture* (Beverly Hills, CA: Sage, 1976): 41-57.

Berger, John. *The Success and Failure of Picasso* (Baltimore: Penguin, 1965).

Besch, Clark. (Liner notes). *Cryan'Shames Sugar & Spice, A Collection.* Columbia Legacy/Sony Music Entertainment. 1992: 7.

Bianco, Robert. "BBC America Gambles on Quirky Musical," *USA Today* (July 22 2005): 4A.

Binelli, Mark. "The Children of Rock," *Rolling Stone* (April 7, 2005): 50-60.

Boucher, Geoff. "Facing Mortality with Mischief Rather than Tears," *L.A. Times* (September 13, 2002): F1.

Bradley, Tim. "David Lindley: Eclectic, Electric, Eccentric," *Guitar World* (May 1983): 26-31.

Breskin, David. *Rolling Stone: The Twentieth Anniversary* (5 November-10 December 1987): 284.

"Bridge: Jotting Down Notes." (1999). Retrieved 25 February 2008 from http://www.two-riders.co.uk/jotting5.html.

Broughton, Simon. Mark Ellingham, David Muddyman, Richard Trillo (eds), *World Music: The Rough Guide* (London: The Rough Guides, 1994).

Brown, G. "Rock Talk: Zevon Presents Role Model for Living in Face of Death" *The Denver Post* (March 23, 2003): F-01.

Brown, Scott. "Kokomo: The Strange History of Summer"s Most Annoying," *Entertainment Weekly* (May 28, 2004): 51-52.

Buium, Greg. "Kid Stuff: Art Projects Empower Children and Make Adults Think." CBCNews (February 4, 2008). Retrieved February 26, 2008 from http.//www.cbc.ca/arts/artdesign./haircuts.html.

Byrds (Untitled). (Liner notes). (Columbia Records, 1970).

Callahan, Mike, David Edwards, and Patrice Eyries. "Dunwich Singles Discography" October 27, 2005. Retrieved December 17, 2007 from http://www.bsnpubs.com/chicago/dunwich45.html.

Cantor, Muriel. *The Hollywood Producer, His Work and His Audience* (New York: Basic, 1971).

——. *Prime-Time Television: Content and Control* (Beverly Hills, CA: Sage, 1981).

Cardinal, Roger. *Outsider Art* (Westport, CT: Praeger, 1972).

Carter, Bill. "Why Bochco's Cops Say it with Music," *New York Times* (September 23, 1990): 34-36.

Carter, Chelsea J. "Performers Still Flock to Music-Happy 'Ally'," *Atlanta Journal—Constitution* (February 1, 2002): E2.

Cash, Roseanne. "Songs My Daddy Sang Me," *Joe Magazine*. Number 3. (1999). Reprinted as "The Ties That Bind," in Peter Guralnick and Douglas Wolk (eds), *Best Music Writing 2000* (Cambridge, MA: Da Capo Press 2000): 7-13.

Christensen, Mark. "Bochco's Law," *Rolling Stone* (April 21, 1988): 75-82.

Chusid, Irwin. "The Langley Schools Music Project." (Liner notes). *Innocence and Despair: The Langley Schools Music Project* (Hoboken, N.J.: Bar None Records, 2001).

——. *Songs in the Key of Z: The Curious Universe of Outsider Music.* Chicago: A Capella Books/Chicago Review Press, 2000.

——. http://www.keyofz.com Retrieved 28 February 2006.

Coleman, Cy. "November 26, 2004 Terry Melcher," Retrieved 14 February 2005 from http://www.blogofdeath.com/archives/001235.html.

Connelly, Christopher. "Warner Drops Morrison, Thirty Others," *Rolling Stone* (July 5, 1984): 41.

Cooder, Ry. (Liner notes, introduction), *Buena Vista Social Club* (World Circuit/Nonesuch, 1997).

——. (Liner notes), *Chicken Skin Music* (Reprise 1976).

Cosh, Colby. "The Miracle Worker," *Up Front* (December 3, 2001). Retrieved February 23, 2008 from http:www.colbycosh.com/print/uf9.htm.

Crow, Cameron. "Neil Young: The Last American Hero," *Rolling Stone* (February 1979): 42.

Diamond, Neil. (Liner notes). *Tap Root Manuscript* (Uni Records, 1970).

Dawson, and Steve Propes. *45 RPM: The History, Heroes & Villains of a Pop Music Revolution* (San Francisco: Backbeat Books, 2003).

Dees, Jim. "Intruder in the Dust: The Savage Wit of an American Original," draft of a column for *The Oxford Eagle* (Oxford, Mississippi) via e-mail correspondence, September 23, 2003.

Devenish, Colin. "Zevon"s Fight," *Rolling Stone* (October 17, 2002): 13.

Drate, Spencer (ed.) *45 RPM: A Visual History of the Seven-Inch Record* (New York: Princeton Architectural Press, 2002).

Dylan, Bob. *Chronicles Volume 1* (New York: Simon and Schuster, 2004).

Ettema, James S. and D. Charles Whitney (eds), *Individuals in Mass Media Organizations: Creativity and Constraint* (Beverly Hills, CA: Sage 1982).

"Feature Story: New Frontier: Dave Matthews Band teams up with super-producer Glen Ballard," *Ice,* Number 166 (January 2001): 6-7.

Fenger, Hans. "Reminisces" (Liner notes) *Innocence and Despair: The Langley Schools Music Project* (Bar None Records, 2001).

Flanagan, Bill. *Written in My Soul* (New York: Contemporary Books, 1987).

——. "The Real Neil Young Stands Up," *Musician* (November 1985): 34.

Forte, Dan. "David Lindley: Silvertone Sideman Steps Out Front," *Guitar Player* (April 1982): 50-60, 65-69.

Fortenberry, John. (Videotape editor, Technical Director), *Graceland: The African Concert* (1987), Personal interviews: formal and informal; in person, phone, and e-mail. (1980-present).

Fretts, Bruce. "He Put His Licks in Route 66," *Entertainment Weekly* (June 4, 1993): 88.

Fricke, David. "Browne Remembers Zevon: Warren's Earliest Champion Pays Tribute" (September 7, 2003). Retrieved June 28, 2004 from http://www.rollingstone.com/news/story?id+5940091&pageid=rs.Artistcageandpageregion=triple3.

——. "Warren Zevon's Last Words" (November 2002). Retrieved February 18, 2008 from http://www.rollingstone.com/artists/warrenzevon/articles/story/5940086/warren_zevons_last_words.

——. "The Confessions of Jakob Dylan: A Wallflower's Coming Out," *Rolling Stone* (October 26, 2000): 45, 48, 126.

——. "Sean Lennon: The *Rolling Stone* Interview," *Rolling Stone* (June 11, 1998): 38-42, 128.

——. "An Historical Essay," *The Byrds Box Set* (Columbia/CBS Records, 1990).

——. "Paul Simon"s Amazing *Graceland* Tour," *Rolling Stone* (July 2, 1987): 43-48, 59.

Gablik, Suzie. *Has Modernism Failed?* (New York; Thames and Hudson, 1984).

Gans, Herbert. *Deciding What's News* (New York: Pantheon, 1979).

Gehr, Richard. "Henry Kaiser" in Ira. A. Robbins (ed.) *Trouser Press Record Guide: The Ultimate Guide to Alternative Music*, 4th ed. (1989): 360.

Getzels, J. W., and M. Csikszentmihalyi. "From Problem Solving to Problem Finding," in R. A. Taylor and J. W. Getzels (eds.), *Perspectives in Creativity* (Chicago: Aldino, 1975).

Gold, Nick and Nigel Williamson (Liner notes). *Buena Vista Social Club* (World Circuit/Nonesuch 1997).

Goldberg, Michael. "The Insider: Tentative Accord Reached on DAT," *Rolling Stone* (August 22, 1991): 28.

Goodman, Fred. "MTV Nixes Neil Young's Acerbic 'This Note's for You' Video," *Rolling Stone* (August 11, 1988): 25.

Grula, Richard. "David Lindley: Guitar Vaudevillian," *Guitar World* (December 1988): 42-48.

Gunderson, Edna. "Sad Fate for an Excitable Boy," *USA Today* (September 13, 2002) p. 12D.

Hagan, Joe. "The Untamed Sounds from Well Beyond the Margins," *New York Times*. 10 June 10, 2001.

Hamilton, Doug. "With Famous Roots, Wainwright Finds Own Wings," *Atlanta Journal Constitution* (August 7, 1998): P3.

Harrington, Richard. "Ry Cooder's Sound Judgment," *The Washington Post.* January 26, 2003): G1, 4-5.

Henke, James. "The *Rolling Stone* Interview: Neil Young," *Rolling Stone* (June 2, 1984): 43-49, 74.

Hill, Walter. (Liner notes). *Music by Ry Cooder* (Warner Bros 1995).

Hoblyn, Ian (Producer), Michael Lindsay-Hogg (Director). *Graceland: The African Concert.* Showtime Entertainment/Peregrine, Inc./Zenith Productions Ltd. (1987).

Hoskyns, Barney. *Hotel California: The True-Life Adventures of Crosby, Stills, Nash, Young, Mitchell, Taylor, Browne, Ronstadt, Geffen, the Eagles, and their Many Friends* (Hoboken, NJ: Wiley and Sons, 2006).

——. "Ry Cooder: Man of the World," *Uncut* (August 2005): 66-70.

——. *Waiting for the Sun: Strange Days, Weird Scenes and the Sound of Los Angeles* (New York: St. Martin's, 1996).

Hughes, Rob. "45 Revolutions Per Minute: The Stories Behind the Singles that Rocked the World, The Byrds' 'Mr Tambourine Man,'" *Uncut* (August 2005): 28.

Jennings, Nicholas. "Chips Off the Old Rock," *Maclean's* (June 8, 1998): 54-55.

Jerome, Jim. "Blues Guitarist Ry Cooder Turns Into Rock "N" Reel Star as a Hot Hollywood Composer," *People Weekly* (June 2, 1986): 127-130.

Kaufman, Jason. "In the Studio with Sean Lennon," *US Magazine* (June 1998): 31.

Kirkeby, Marc. (Liner notes). *Rising Sons featuring Taj Mahal and Ry Cooder* (Columbia Legacy, 1992).

Kotapish. Paul. "Big Little Music: The Weird and Wonderful World of String Wizard David Lindley," *Acoustic Guitar* (June 2000): 48-53, 56-63.

Landau, Jon. *It's Too Late to Stop Now* (San Francisco: Straight Arrow Press, 1972).

Lindsay, Arto. (Liner notes), *Brazil Classics 1: Belza Tropical* (Fly/Sire Records, 1989).

Lindsay, Deb. "Terry Melcher...the Whole Picture," reprinted from 1998 issue of Mark Lindsay's *Steppin' Out!* Retrieved February 14, 2005 from http://www.marklindsay.com/terrymelcher.htm.

Lowry, Brian. "*Two and a Half Men*" (Review) (September 17, 2004). Retrieved February 25, 2008 from http://variety.com/review/VE111792124918.html.

Mansfield, Brian. "A Little Traveling Music, Please! Good for the Long Haul, or a Traffic Backup," *USA Today* (August 12, 2005):1D.

Marchese, David. "Audiofile: Conversations: Ry Cooder" (March 20, 2008). Retrieved 20 March 2007 from http://www.salon.com/ent/audiofile/2007/03/14/conversations_cooder/index.html?source=rss.

Marcus, Greil. *Like a Rolling Stone: Bob Dylan at the Crossroads* (New York: Public Affairs, 2006).

Marsh, Dave and John Swenson (eds) *The New Rolling Stone Record Guide* (New York: Random House, 1983): 39.

BIBLIOGRAPHY

——. "Rock and Roll 1980: Hold On Hold Out," *Rolling Stone* (25 December 1990-January 1981): 1.

McDonough, Jimmy. *Shakey: Neil Young's Biography* (New York: Anchor Books, 2002).

McLaughlin, Lisa. "Music Goes Global: Making Tracks," *Time Magazine* (special issue) Vol. 158, No. 14. (Fall 2001).

McParland, Stephen J. *Sound Waves and Traction: Surf and Hot Rod Groups of the '60s, Volume 1* (Stratfield, Australia: CMusic Books 2002).

——. *Bull Sessions with Big Daddy: Interviews with Those Who Helped Shape the California Sound* (Startfield, Australia: CMusic Books 2001).

McWilliams, R.C. "R.C. McWilliams Recalls Art Roberts' 'Swingin Majority.'" Retrieved December 18, 2007 from http://www.60sgaragebands.com/scenesthings/swinginmajority.html.

Metcalf, Greg. Personal correspondence via e-mail (October 10, 2002).

Metting, Fred. *The Unbroken Circle: Tradition and Innovation in the Music of Ry Cooder and Taj Mahal* (Metuchen, NJ: Scarecrow Press, 2001).

Mitchell, Elvis. "Soundtrack: Cooder Been a Contender," *Film Comment* (March 1986) 76-77.

Mr. Bonzai. "David Lindley Tuggin' at the Artstrings," *Mix* (May 1990): 104-111, 194.

Nelson, Paul. "Warren Zevon: How He Saved Himself from a Coward's Death," *Rolling Stone* (March 19, 1981): 28-34, 70.

Newcomb, Horace, and Robert Alley. *The Producer's Medium* (New York: Oxford University Press, 1983).

Nolan, Tom, *Ross MacDonald: A Biography* (New York: Scribner, 1999).

——. "Surf's Up! Terry Melcher's Nightmare is Over," *Rolling Stone* (May 9, 1974): 77.

"Offspring: *Rolling Stone* Spring Style" (Fashion by Patti O'Brien; Photographs by Robert Maxwell), *Rolling Stone* (April 16, 1998): 58-66.

Pareles, Jon. "In His Time of Dying: Warren Zevon's Last Waltz," *The New York Times Magazine* (January 26, 2003): 22-25.

——. "Work Hard, Play Hard," *Rolling Stone* (20 December 1984-4 January 1985):137.

Peterson, R.A. (ed.), *The Production of Culture* (Beverly Hills: Sage, 1976).

Peterson, R.A. and D.G. Berger. "Entrepreneurship in Organizations: Evidence from the Popular Music Industry," *Administrative Service Quarterly*, 16 (1971): 97-107.

Plasketes, George. "Pimp My Records: The Deluxe Dilemma and Edition Condition: Bonus, Betrayal or Download Backlash?" *Popular Music and Society* Vol. 31, No. 3 (July 2008): 389-393.

Price, Simon. "They Can Be Heroes—But Just for One Day," *The Independent* (June 16, 2002). Retrieved 28 February 2008 from http://www.independent.co.uk/arts-entertainment/music/features/they-can-be-heroes--but-juts-for-one-day-645624.html.

Prince, Dan. *Passing in the Outsider Lane: Art from the Heart of Twenty One Self-Taught Artists* (Boston: Journey Editions, 1995).

"Prod. By Terry Melcher Arr. & Cond. Jack Nitzsche" (eight part series). Retrieved December 13, 2007 from http://spectropop.com/TerryMelcher/index.htm.

Quaglieri, Al. (Liner notes), *Bruce and Terry* (Sundazed Records,1993).

Ravage, John. *Television: The Director's Viewpoint* (Boulder, CO: Westwood, 1978).

Read, Nick. (Producer, Director, Photographer), *VH-1: Inside-Out: Warren Zevon* (documentary) (VH 1/Artemis Records/MTV Networks, 2004).

Roush, Matt. "Should Programs Court the Cutting Edge? Bold Moves Are Rewarding," *USA.Today* (October 30, 1990): 3D.

Ryan, John and R.A. Peterson. "The Product Image: The Fate of Creativity in Country Music Songwriting," in James Ettema and Charles Whitney (eds), *Individuals in Mass Media Organizations* (Beverly Hills, CA: Sage 1982).

Santoro, Gene. "Ry Cooder: Blues and Roots," *Down Beat* (August 1986): 26-28.

Scherman, Tony. "Ry Cooder"s Crossroads Blues," *Rolling Stone* (October 10, 1985): 55-56, 75-77.

Schreuers, Fred. "Van Morrison Won't Play the Industry's Game," *Rolling Stone* (November 22, 1984): 61-62.

Scott, William and David Hart. *Organizational America* (Boston: Houghton-Mifflin, 1980).

Shebar, Bill. (Producer), "Steven Bochco and Denis Potter." *Edge* (Thirteen WNET/BBC-TV, PBS, 1992).

Smith, R.J. "Drama King," *Spin* (March 1998): 39.

Soocher, Stan. *They Fought the Law: Rock Music Goes to Court* (New York: Schirmer Books, 1998).

Steinberg, Susan (director) and Susan Lacy (producer). *Paul Simon: Born at the Right Time* (documentary), (Thirteen/WNET and MTM Enterprises, 1992).

The Rock Video 60's Project: Rock Artist TV Cameos" (January 27, 2003). Retrieved June 2, 2005 from http://members.aol.comRockvideo2/TVCcameo.html.

Thigpen, David. "Hidden Havana," *Time Magazine* (special issue) (Fall 2001): 19-21.

Tucker, Ken. "A Blue Streak," *Entertainment Weekly* (October 11, 1996): 62-65.

Unterberger, Richie. "Shadows of Knight," in Michael Erlewine, Vladimir Bogdanov and Cris Woodstra (eds). *All Music Guide to Rock* (San Francisco: Miller Freeman Books 1995): 684.

VH-1.com. "Interviews: Warren Zevon: Dirty Life and Times" (August 11, 2003). Retrieved August 11, 2003 from http://www.vh1.com/shows/dyn/inside_out/68383/episode_interviews_int.jhtml?start=1.

Walker, Michael. *Laurel Canyon: The Inside Story of Rock and Roll's Legendary Neighborhood* (New York: Fraser and Fraser, 2006).

Ward, Ed, Geoffrey Stokes, Ken Tucker. *Rock of Ages: The Rolling Stone History of Rock and Roll* (New York: Summit/Rolling Stone Press, 1986).

BIBLIOGRAPHY

We All Go Home: Crosby Loggins and the Light. Retrieved 11 August 2008 from http://www.amazon.com/All-Home-Crosby-Loggins-Light/dp/B000ULGW88/ref=sr_1_?...

Weekend Edition Saturday. Scott Simon, host. "Interview: Hans Fenger Discusses His Music Students' Renditions Of Popular Songs From 1976 to 1977" (October 27, 2001), National Public Radio.

Wiener, Jonah. "*Cold Case*, Hot Tunes: Springsteen's Soundtrack" (January 7, 2006). Retrieved March 16, 2006 from http://www.nytimes.com/2006/01/07/arts/television/07cold.html.

Wildfeuer, Mara. "Words," *Pulse!* (July 1993): 92.

Wilkinson, Alec. "Who Put the Honky Tonk in 'Honky Tonk Woman'?," *Esquire*, (June 1999): 101-105, 144.

Woodard, Josef. "*A Meeting by the River*" (Record review), *Rolling Stone* (May 13 1993): 110-111.

Zevon, Crystal. *I'll Sleep When I'm Dead: The Dirty Life and Times of Warren Zevon*, New York: (Ecco/Harper Collins Publishers, 2007).

"Zevon Hastens Down the Wind," *Ice Magazine* (July 2003): 4-5.

Zimmer David. *Crosby, Stills and Nash: The Biography* (Cambridge, MA: DaCapo, 2000).

Index

18 Tracks 5
45 r.p.m. records (also 45s, singles) 1-3, 6, 8, 13-14, 28, 30

A Hard Day's Night 16, 141
A Knight's Tale 120
A Meeting by the River 70*n*, 72, 92-3
Across the Great Divide 5
Adventures of Pete and Pete, The 10, 146, 148
Albom, Mitch 177, 180-81, 184
Alexander, Kavichandran 71, 92
Allman Brothers 154
Allman, Elijah Blue 155, 160, 167
Allman, Greg 160, 167
Ally McBeal 120, 128, 130-31, 133, 141, 148
    music from 131
American Bandstand 29, 106, 136
American Breed 8, 25, 33
American Idol 30, 148, 157, 165, 167
Animals 21-2, 27-8
Artemis Records 45, 181, 184
Asylum Records (also Elektra/Asylum) 18, 58-9, 62, 175
Association 17, 26-7

BAFTA (British Academy of Film and Television Awards) 93
Bachman, Tal 159
Bachman Turner Overdrive 155, 157
Bad Luck Streak in Dancing School 176, 179, 188, 193
Band 5, 11, 155, 183
Bangles 3, 87
Barry, Dave 180*n*, 185
Basta Audio-Visuals 44-5
BBC 10, 112, 117, 121, 123, 133
Beach Boys 2, 8, 13-14, 16, 18-20, 27, 37-9, 45
Beatles 2-3, 8, 15-16, 21-2, 26-8, 37-8, 85, 96, 136-7, 140-41, 145, 161, 193

Beau Brummels 26, 137
Behman, Sheila 37-8, 45, 47
Behind the Music 184
"Bend Me, Shape Me" 26, 30
Bergen, Candace 19
Berry, Chuck 28, 72
Bhatt, V.M. 69, 70*n*-71
Bickerton, Pat 36, 44
Biondi, Dick 25, 29
Billboard Magazine 3, 15, 26, 31, 159, 188, 193
Blaine, Hal 15, 20
Black Cadillac 169
Black, Jack 36, 47
Bochco, Steven 10, 119-33 *see also Cop Rock*; *Hill Street Blues*; *L.A. Law*
Bolger, Sarah 35, 47
Bonham, Jason 155, 164
Boone, Pat 14, 19
Bop Till You Drop 72-3*n*, 78, 81
Boule, Michele 42
Bowie, David 8, 37-8, 42, 46-7
box set 3, 5-6, 96
"Boy in the Bubble" 107-12
Brady Bunch, The 138
Braff, Zach 143-4
Brazil Classics 87, 95
Brickell, Edie 168-9
Briggs, David 58, 61, 64, 66
Brill Building 14, 21-2, 28, 103
British Invasion 8, 13, 15-16, 26
Broadway Video 10, 91*n*, 93, 115, 117*n*
Browne, Jackson 58, 78, 83, 89, 106*n*, 145, 175, 177, 181-3, 190, 194
B-side 1-6, 20, 28, 30, 42, 60-61, 65, 193
    as a critical concept 6-11
    as a metaphor 13, 18, 21, 23, 30, 42, 48-9, 65, 67, 76, 87-8, 98-9, 102-3, 116, 118, 120, 133, 136-7, 158, 166-8, 180, 192
"B-Side of Life" 11
Buckingham, Lindsey 126

Buckinghams 8, 25-7, 29-31
Buena Vista Social Club 9, 69, 98-9
Buena Vista Social Club (record) 70n, 94,
    96-8
documenrtary film 168
Buenos Hermanos 70n
Buffalo Springfield 21, 60, 88, 137
Buffy the Vampire Slayer 120, 127
Burnett, T-Bone 54, 143, 182, 188
Byrds 2, 5, 8, 13-18, 20-22, 26-8, 165
Byrne, David 9, 87, 94-8

Calderon, Jorge 80, 181-3, 185-90, 192,
    194
"Calling Occupants of Interplanetary
    Craft" (The Recognized Anthem of
    World Contact Day) 44-6
Campbell, Glenn 14, 19
Cardinal, Roger 43
Cash, Johnny 11, 145, 154, 183, 187, 191-2
Cash, Roseanne 164, 169
Chase, David 126
Cher 17, 141, 155, 160
Chess Studios (Chicago) 27
Chicago Hope 120, 128-30, 133
Chicken Skin Music 70n, 73, 81
Christgau, Robert 39, 46, 73, 159
Chusid, Irwin 35n, 42, 46, 48
Clark, Dick 22, 29
Cobain, Kurt 145-6, 186
Cohen, Leonard 155, 159
Cold Case 132
Concert in Central Park, The 106, 109
Connick, Harry Jr. 141
Cole, Natalie 30, 83, 164
Cole, Nat King 154, 169
Coltrane, John 36, 90, 156
Cooder, Joachim 82-3, 92, 95, 156-7,
    162-3, 168-9
Cooder, Ry 9, 194
    Bhatt and 92-3, 97
    Buena Vista Social Club sessions
        93-9
    "Califorrnia Trilogy" 69
    Cuban music 93-5
    ethnographic approach 94
    Lindley and 89, 91, 169
    mutuality 70-71

Rising Sons and 20-22
Rolling Stones and 72
score and soundtracks 70, 73-84
session and solo career 72-3
The Wind sessions *see* Zevon 182-3
World Music 88
see also Hill, Walter; Little Village;
    Mahal, Taj; Toure
Cop Rock 10
critical response to 124-5
inspiration for 119-22
legacy 131-3
as musical production 122-4
see also Bochco, Steven
Copeland, Stewart 70
Costello, Elvis 4, 10, 135, 142-3, 145
CPR 155, 159, 165
Creedence Clearwater Revival 2
Crosby, David 15, 155, 159 165, 173
Crosby, Stills, Nash and Young (CSNY)
    160, 165
Crossroads 75-6, 165
Cruz, Celia 183
Cryan' Shames 8, 25-9, 31-4
Cyrus, Billy Ray 153, 165
Cyrus, Miley 153, 165

Dancer in the Dark 120
Danko, Rick 11, 183
Davis, Miles 36, 85, 90, 154, 186-7
Day, Doris 8, 13-14, 19-20, 22-3, 154
Deadsy 155, 160
Demme, Jonathan 10, 91
DeShannon, Jackie 14n, 21, 72
"Desperado" 35, 38-9n, 44-7
Dharma and Greg 139-43
Diamond, Neil 8-9, 26, 37, 86, 97-8
Dickson, Jim 15-16, 22
Dickinson, Jim 78-80, 98
Dillow, Tule Livingston 184, 194
Dino, Desi and Billy 154
"Disorder in the House" 182, 185-9
Dixon, Willie 21, 28, 72
Doobie Brothers 138, 146, 167
Drew Carey Show, The 120, 127, 140-41
Dual Disc 5
Due South 126
Dunwich Records 29-30

INDEX

Dylan, Bob 3, 10, 15-18, 21-2, 72, 96*n*, 101, 135, 141-3, 155, 161-2, 165, 182-3, 188, 193-4
Dylan, Jakob 11, 157, 160-61, 165, 167, 169 *see also* Wallflowers

Eagles 8, 35, 37, 47, 176, 182
Earle, Steve 4, 135, 155, 190, 194
Ed Sullivan Show, The 29, 136
Enjoy Every Sandwich 169, 180, 190, 194
Esquivel, Juan 43, 45
Everybody's Rockin' 58, 60-61, 65
Everly Brothers 72, 91
Every Picture Tells A Story 3
Excitable Boy 175*n*-6, 180, 194

Family Guy 145-6
Fenger, Hans 8, 35-48 *see also* Chusid, Irwin; *Innocence and Despair*; *Langley Schools Music Project*
Ferrer, Ibrahim 70*n*, 93, 95, 97-8
Finseth, Greg 41
Finster, Reverend Howard 137
Fitzgerald, F. Scott 176, 189
Fleetwood Mac 37, 53, 126, 155
Flintstones, The 137
Fortenberry, John 10, 101-18 *see also* Broadway Video; Graceland, *The African Concert*
Fortis, Cheri 103-4, 108
Foster, Ruth 93-4*n*
Frah, Rakota 90-91
Fricke, David 15, 18, 103*n*, 166
Friends 140, 148

Gabriel, Peter 9, 86-7, 94, 97-8
Gablik, Suzi 55-7
Galban, Manuel 70*n*, 93, 95
Garfunkel, Art 106, 109, 155
Geffen, David 8-9, 18, 51, 56-67
Geffen Records 51, 56-8, 60, 65-6, 67
   see also Asylum Records; Young, Neil
Genius 175, 177, 179, 192-3
Gentle Soul 13, 19
George, Lowell 137-8*n*
Giammarese, Carl 25, 27, 30
Gilmore Girls 127, 169

"Gloria" 31-2
Goffin, Gerry 21, 28, 155, 167
Goffin, Louise 155, 167, 178
Goldberg, Danny 78, 181, 183-4
Gonzalez, Ruben 93, 97
"Good Vibrations" 20, 38, 45
Graceland
   album (*Graceland*) 9, 19, 66, 87-8, 95, 97, 98, 103, 106, 108, 111, 115
   song ("Graceland") 112
   The African Concert (documentary) 10, 95, 101-5, 107-10, 115-17
   tour 103-4, 112
   see also Fortenberry, John; Simon, Paul
Grammy Awards 9, 22, 62, 66, 70, 73, 80*n*-82, 93, 95, 97, 124, 154, 168, 189, 193
Grass Roots 13, 26, 137
Guess Who 26, 155, 157
Guthrie, Arlo 54, 72, 85, 155
Guthrie, Woody 71-2, 155

Halee, Roy 108-9
Harris, Emmylou 182, 190
Harrison, George 11, 22, 28, 169, 183, 192
"Hasten Down the Wind" 188, 193
Hazan, Al 14
Harvest 58, 62-3, 67
Hiassen, Carl 180-81
Heavy Circles 169
Helm, Levon 5, 155
"Help Me Rhonda" 38, 45, 48
Hendrix, Jimi 28, 128
Henley, Don 47, 66, 182, 190, 194
Herman's Hermits 17, 26
"Hey Little Cobra" 14, 20
Hiatt, John 10, 73, 79, 80, 93, 135, 141, 144, 153, 169
Hill, Walter 74, 77-83
Hill Street Blues 10, 119, 121-4, 130-32
   see also Bochco, Steven
Hillman, Chris 15, 20
Hoblyn, Ian 104, 108
Hodges, Eddie 14
"Hold On" 26, 28, 30
Hollies 15, 26-8

206   *B-SIDES, UNDERCURRENTS AND OVERTONES*

Hoskyns, Barney 18*n*, 22
Hynde, Chrissie 140

Ides of March 1, 8, 25, 25-34
Iger, Robert 124-5
"I'll Sleep When I'm Dead" 178, 189
*I'll Sleep When I'm Dead: The Dirty Life
    and Times of Warren Zevon* 174-5,
    186*n*, 189*n*-90, 194
"I'm a Believer" 26, 86
Incorrect Music Hour 42
"In My Room" 37-8, 45
*Innocence and Despair: The Langley
    Schools Music Project* 8, 35*n*, 45-6,
    49
It's Garry Shandling's Show 139

Jackson, Michael 51, 53, 145, 161, 168
Jan and Dean 14
Jagger, Mick 74, 77, 98, 135, 144-5
Jimenez, Flaco 71
Joel, Billy 123, 166, 168
John, Elton 38, 59-60, 66, 130, 141, 145
John From Cincinnati 35
Johnston, Bruce 14-15, 20
Jolly Boys 9, 87
Jones, Norah 84, 156

Kaiser, Henry 88, 90-91, 94-9
"Keep Me in Your Heart" 182, 184, 188,
    190, 193-4
Kelley, David 128, 130-31
Keltner, Jim 73, 78, 80, 93, 95, 182, 185
King, Carole 21, 28, 38, 155, 168
King of the Hill 135, 145-6
King, Stephen 173, 180*n*
Kincaid, Jesse Lee 20-21
"Kind of a Drag" 26-7, 32
Kinks 17
Klaatu 41, 44
Knechtal, Larry 15, 20
"Knockin' on Heaven's Door" 182
"Kokomo" 8, 13, 20-21

Ladysmith Black Mambazo 95-6, 103, 109
"L.A. Goodbye" 25, 29-30
Laine, Frankie 14
L.A. Law 10, 121, 128*n*, 130

lang, k.d. 139, 141
Langley Schools (District) (Vancouver,
    B.C.) (also Glenwood, Lochiel,
    South Carvoth, Wix-Brown) 35-6,
    40-42, 44-5
Langley Schools Music Project 8, 45, 47-9
    see also Chusid, Irwin; Fenger,
    Hans; *Innocence and Despair*
Last Man Standing 74, 77
Last Temptation of Christ, The 86-7, 94,
    97
Late Show with David Letterman 11, 169,
    177, 179, 184-5, 193-4
Lauper, Cyndi 87, 140, 145
Laurel Canyon (California) 31, 59, 176
"Lawyers, Guns and Money" 169, 188,
    194
Lennon, John 2, 141-2, 154-5, 158, 161,
    164-5, 168-9
Lennon, Julian 161, 154, 160
Lennon, Sean 11, 161, 164, 166
Leonard, John 119, 131
Letterman, David 177-80, 185, 188,
    193-4
Lewis, Gary, and the Playboys 13, 17, 26,
    154
Life'll Kill Ya' 173-4, 183-4, 192
Lindley, David 9, 73*n*, 78-9, 81-2, 88-91,
    94-100, 169, 182, 194
Lindsay, Mark 16-18
Linds, Brian 42-3
Lindsey-Hogg, Michael 94-9, 114-17
Little Steven's Underground Garage 7,
    48*n*
Little Village 20, 73, 93
Loggins, Crosby 155-6
Loggins, Kenny 141, 143, 145, 155, 167
"Long and Winding Road, The" 2, 38, 45
Long Riders, The 70, 74, 78, 89
Los Lobos 10, 80, 83, 141
Lovett, Lyle 140, 143
Lovin' Spoonful 17, 26, 136
Lowe, Nick 73, 93
Lucky Thirteen 65
Luhrman, Baz 119

McCartney, Linda 135, 145, 156*n*
McCartney, Paul 2, 38, 145, 156*n*

INDEX

MacDonald, Pat 11
MacDonald, Ross 80, 175
McGarrigle, Kate 155, 159-60, 164-5
McGuinn, Roger (also Jim) 15-16, 18, 22
McGuane, Tom 177, 180*n*
McLachlan, Sarah 4, 190
McQueen, Steve 174, 185
Mad About You 140
Madonna 3, 141
"Maggie May" 3
Mahal, Taj 20-22, 72
Majumadar, Ronu 93
Makeba, Miriam 95, 103-4, 107-8, 112
Mambo Sinuendo 70n, 146
"Mandy" 38, 45
Mangione, Chuck 146
Manilow, Barry 38, 170-71, 141
Mann, Barry 21, 28
Mann, Michael 119, 121-2, 133
Marcus, Greil 17, 53
Marley, Bob 87, 169
Marley, Rita 154
Marley, Ziggy 154, 169
Marsh, Dave 52, 86, 167
Martin, Dean 128, 154
Masakela, Hugh 108, 111-12
Mauds 8, 25-9, 31, 33-4
Maysles brothers (David, Albert) 10, 101
Melcher, Terry 8, 13-23, 154 *see*
    also Byrds; Day, Doris; "Mr.
    Tambourine Man;" Nitzsche, Jack;
    Revere, Paul and the Raiders;
    Rising Sons; surf music
Mellencamp, John 3,
mento 9, 87
"Mercy, Mercy, Mercy" 26, 28
Miami Vice 10, 119, 121-2, 126, 132-3
Michaels, Lorne 93, 117*n*
Midler, Bette 103*n*, 107*n*, 145
Milch, David 121
Mitchell, Joni 18, 58-9, 66, 130, 165
Monkees 17-18, 21, 26, 86, 136
Monterey Pop 101
Monterey Pop Festival 17
Morissette, Alanis 141, 151, 168*n*
Morrison, Jim 188
Morrison, Van 28, 31, 54-5, 155, 164
Moulin Rouge 119-20, 131

"Mr. Tambourine Man" 8, 15-17, 20-21,
    138
MTV 53, 61, 119, 125-6, 136, 139-40, 148,
    155
    "MTV Cops" 119, 122
    Music Video Awards 160
    Rock the Cradle 167
    The Real World 148, 184
    Unplugged 87, 179
Mutineer, The 176
"Mutineer, The" 179, 188, 193
My Ride's Here 173-4, 178-9, 183, 198

N'Dour, Youssou 86, 96
Nelson, Paul 63, 175*n*, 176*n*
Nelson, Ricky 10, 136, 154
Newman, Randy 14, 70, 72, 77, 103, 115,
    123, 176
New Colony Six 8, 25-9, 31-4
Newton, Wayne 14, 19
Nickelodeon (cable network) 10, 93*n*, 140,
    146, 165
Nitzsche, Jack 14, 19, 74, 77
Northern Exposure 126-7, 135

"Old Velvet Nose" 175, 187
Old Ways 61, 65-6
Ono, Yoko 10, 35, 140-41, 155, 161
Orff, Carl 8, 39-41, 48
Osbournes, The 10, 125, 136, 168, 184
Ostin, Mo 58, 60, 65
"outsider art" 8, 42-3
Ozzie and Harriet 10, 136

Pahinui, Gabby 71
Pareles, Jon 54, 95
Paris, Texas 74, 77, 79, 83, 92
Parks, Van Dyke 72, 81, 159
Parsons, Gram 18, 22
Partridge Family, The 135-6
Patinkin, Mandy 129
Pecos Bill 70*n*, 74*n*, 81
Pennebaker, D.A. 10, 101
Pennies From Heaven 119, 133
Perkins, Carl 15, 72
Petty, Tom 10, 135, 139, 144-6
Peterik, Jim 1, 25, 30
Phillips, John 11, 20, 22, 154-5, 183

Phiri, Ray 107, 113
Polanski, Roman 19
Portuondo, Omara 93, 97
Post, Mike 122
Potter, Dennis 10, 119-20, 122, 129, 132
Presley, Elvis 1, 72, 125, 133
Presley, Lisa Marie 11, 168, 171

Raitt, Bonnie 54, 78, 190, 194
Raymond, James 155, 159, 165
reality shows/series (television) 10-11, 123, 125-6, 148, 167-8, 184, 191
R.E.M. 3, 66, 145, 147
"Reason to Believe" 3
Reprise (also Warner-Reprise) 58-60, 62, 65, 66n, 72
Revere, Paul and the Raiders 13-18, 21-22, 27, 72, 137
"Rhiannon" 43, 45
Rhino Records 4, 6, 179
Richards, Keith 9, 55, 72n, 87-8, 97, 144-5, 187
Rip Chords 13-14
Rising Sons 13, 20-22, 72
Ritter, John 121, 191
Robertson, Robbie 5, 155
Roche, Suzzy 147, 155
Rogues 14
"Roland the Headless Thompson Gunner" 179, 193
Rolling Stone (magazine) 21, 46, 63, 159, 163-4, 166, 187
Rolling Stones 19, 22, 27, 72, 77, 87, 101, 115, 135, 144-5, 157, 167
Ronstadt, Linda 188
Rossy 90, 95
Rust Never Sleeps 51, 58, 63

Sampedro, Frank "Pancho" 58
Saturday Night Live 103, 115n, 136, 138
Schmidt, Timothy B. 182
School of Rock 35-6, 47
Schulwerk 39-41 *see also* Orff, Carl
Scorsese, Martin 10, 86, 94, 97, 101, 143, 176n
Scrubs 127, 133, 143-4
Shadows of Knight 8, 25-34
Shaffer, Paul 177-9

Shanachie Records 90, 95-6
Singing Detective, The 119-20, 122, 129, 132-3
Sgt Pepper's Lonely Hearts Club Band 13, 18
Shandling, Garry 139
Shear, Jules 9, 87, 97
Shepard, Vonda 130-31, 133
Shocking Pinks 60-61
Simon and Garfunkel 106
Simon, Carly 78, 106, 155, 166-7, 169
Simon, Harper 169
Simon, Paul 9, 10, 66, 85-6, 88, 90, 95-9, 102n, 103-4, 106-12, 114-17, 123, 155, 165, 168-9
Simpsons, The 10, 135, 139n, 144-6, 148
Sinatra, Frank 129, 153
situation comedy (television) 101, 132, 135, 139-40, 147-8, 194
Six Feet Under 127, 133, 140
slack key (guitar) 71, 89
Sloan, P.F. 13, 137
Smile 4, 14, 39
Snyder, Noah 181-2, 185-6
Sohns, Jim 25, 30
Songs in the Key of Z: The Curious Universe of Outsider Music 42
Sonny and Cher 17, 155
Soumar, Chuck 25n, 27
Southern Comfort 74-5, 78, 82
South Park 145-6
Spears, Britney 141, 144, 147n
"Space Oddity" 38, 40-43, 45-6
Spector, Phil 3, 8, 13, 14n, 15, 39, 44, 136
Spence, Joseph 71
Spin (magazine) 46
Springsteen, Bruce 3, 5, 53, 78, 132, 160, 181-2n, 185-6, 188-90, 192, 194, 8, 191
Standells 137
Stanton, Harry Dean 75, 79, 142
Starr, Ringo 45, 137, 140, 155, 159
Stewart, Rod 3, 168
Stills, Chris 160, 163
Stills, Steven 155, 160, 165
Stranger in a Strange Land 11, 183
Stravinsky, Igor 179
Strawberry Alarm Clock 2, 136-8

INDEX

Strummer, Joe and the Mescalinos 35
surf music 8, 13-15, 18-20, 23, 28, 136
sweeps (television ratings) 127, 142, 144, 148
Sweet Sunny North, The 91, 96
Swingin' Majority 29

Talking Heads 4, 43, 53*n*, 87, 101
Talking Timbuktu 70*n*, 93
Tap Root Manuscript 9, 86, 98
Tate, Sharon 19
There is a Season 5
Timbuk 3, 11
Taylor, Ben 155, 166, 169
Taylor, James 78, 113, 155, 166, 168*n*-9
Taylor, Sally 155, 167
That 70s Show 127, 141, 143
This Note's For You 51, 65
Thompson, Dr. Hunter S. 176*n*, 180*n*
Thompson, Richard and Linda 155
Thompson, Teddy 155
Thornton, Billy Bob 182-4, 190, 194
Topanga Canyon (California) 31, 176
Townshend, Emma 155, 160
Townshend, Pete 155
"Township Jive" 88, 111
Toure, Ali Farka 69, 70*n*, 93, 98
Tracks 3, 5
Trans 59-9*n*, 60-61, 65, 67
Tuesdays With Morrie 181, 184
Tufano, Dennis 27, 30
Turtles 17, 26, 193
Two and a Half Men 135, 142
Tyson, Clay 155, 159
Tyson, Ian and Sylvia 155, 159

Ullman, Tracey 130, 139
Untitled 18
Usher, Gary 13-14, 18

Van Zandt, Little Steven 7, 48
Vega, Suzanne 6
"Vehicle" 26, 28-30, 33-4
VH-1 31, 157, 167
   (Inside) Out 11, 174, 184, 190, 192-3
   Langley School reunion 47
   Save the Music Foundation 48
   Storytellers 179

The Greatest series 135
videotape editor 101-2, 105
Viva Blackpool 10
Viva Laughlin 10, 120, 133
Von Trier, Lars 120

Wadleigh, Michael 10, 101
Wainwright, Loudon 155, 164
Wainwright, Lucy 155, 165
Wainwright, Rufus 11, 155, 157, 159-60, 163-5
Wallflowers 155, 161-2, 169, 194
Walsh, Joe 127, 140-41, 167, 172
Warhol, Andy 177
Warner Brothers 3, 54, 66, 73, 159
Waronker, Lenny 22, 54*n*, 159
Weill, Cynthia 21, 28
Wenders, Wim 79, 83, 96-7, 168
"Werewolves of London" 176-7, 194
Weschler, Lawrence 7
WGN-TV (Chicago) 25, 27
White, Barry 141, 145
Who, The 3, 63, 127, 135, 145
Wind, The 11, 174, 181-4, 186-9, 193
Will and Grace 141, 148
Williams, Hank 81, 163
Williams, Hank Jr. 153, 155
Williams, Lucinda 4, 156*n*
Williams, Robin 70*n*, 81
Wilson, Brian 4, 8, 14, 23, 37, 39, 46
Wilson, Dennis 19, 126
Wilson-Phillips 154, 167
Wingless Angels 9, 87-8
WLS Radio (Chicago) 2, 28-9
Wonder Years 25, 121, 127, 146
World Out of Time 90-91, 94, 96

Yardbirds 17, 27
Yes, Dear 141, 144
Yoakam, Dwight 174, 182, 190
Young, Neil 8-9, 18-19, 51-67, 101, 165

Zappa, Frank 80, 155, 160
Zevon, Ariel 189*n*, 194
Zevon, Crystal 175, 186, 194
Zevon, Jordan 169, 190-91, 193-4
Zevon, Warren 11, 135, 140, 155, 169, 173-94

CPSIA information can be obtained
at www.ICGtesting.com
Printed in the USA
BVHW040738041220
594196BV00027B/25